THE
OUTSTANDING
NEGOTIATOR

**Other books by Christian Godefroy
published by Piatkus**

The Complete Time Management System
(with John Clark)

The Power Talk System: How to Communicate Effectively
(with Stephanie Barrat)

Super Health

Mind Power
(with D R Steevens)

THE
OUTSTANDING NEGOTIATOR

CHRISTIAN H. GODEFROY
& LUIS ROBERT

PIATKUS

© 1991 Christian H. Godefroy and Edi Inter S.A.,
Geneva, Switzerland

First published in Great Britain in 1993
by Judy Piatkus (Publishers) Ltd of
5 Windmill Street, London W1P 1HF

Reprinted 1993
First paperback edition 1994

The moral right of the author has been asserted

A catalogue record for this book is available
from the British Library

ISBN 0–7499–1108–5
ISBN 0–7499–1366–5 (Pbk)

Edited by Carol Franklin
Designed by Paul Saunders

Typeset in 11/13½pt Linotron Plantin Light by
Wyvern Typesetting, Bristol
Printed and bound in Great Britain at
The Bath Press, Bath, Avon

Contents

Foreword

A successful negotiator is often portrayed as a sly person, living in the lap of luxury, who spends his time extorting the maximum gains from his poor adversaries who are completely disarmed by his infallible strategies and trickery.

In fact, this picture is completely untrue.

A good negotiator is an ordinary person who has learned how to turn a seemingly futile situation into a profitable one, or who is able to facilitate discussion between two parties who cannot arrive at an agreement on their own.

Nor is negotiation necessarily a selfish act. When the head of a family gets the best possible price when selling the family house, everyone in that family benefits.

When a community succeeds in convincing an industrial polluter to treat its waste properly, the whole environment benefits.

So when Luis Robert talked to us for the first time about his method for becoming a successful negotiator, we were all enthusiastic. Not only is he an excellent communicator, he is also an incomparable negotiator. And he has a unique talent for popularising difficult material. His method is easy to read, practical and very interactive. He is used to training executives and corporate directors, and has transcribed the experiences gained from his training seminars into written form. More than a simple method of negotiation, this work is the result of a lifetime of experience, study and research, and provides a complete guide to the art of communicating effectively.

As far as we know, this is the most complete and practical method of its kind. It represents a constant source of reference material for all managers and business people. It will help you to prepare your meetings and your interviews and teach you how to delegate work more effectively.

I participated in two alternative seminars on negotiation before reading this book. They each lasted four days, and were very expensive. The book provided me with more information, helpful hints and proven strategies than the other two seminars combined.

I'm sure the method will work for you too, so that in a short time you may consider yourself to be an effective negotiator.

Stephanie Barrat
Communication consultant and author of
The Power Talk System

'A book isn't something sacred or intangible. Books are not written to ornament someone's bookshelf. They are, first and foremost, meant to ornament the mind.

'You should think of them as tools of your trade. Intellectual work is no different from manual work. A tool which has become worn from use is more beautiful than one which lies discarded and forgotten in some corner.

'The same goes for books. There is nothing sacrilegious about putting a book through some rough treatment, if it helps you accomplish your work. A book full of personal notes and marked pages loses none of its value. On the contrary, its value increases as its owner attains ever greater measures of success.'

François Richaudeau, psychologist and author

Introduction: What Will This Book Do for You?

Do you find the following situations familiar?

- You have to convince someone to give you something you want or need.

- You want to convince someone to undertake, or not to undertake, a project.

- You have to confront someone.

- You want to persuade someone you're right.

- You're about to buy or sell a house, and you want to get the best possible price.

- You find yourself in confrontational situations at work, and you would like to come out a winner.

These situations all have one thing in common: you will always have the upper hand if you know how to negotiate effectively. The better you know how to negotiate, the better the position you will be in to profit from the situation – and not necessarily at the expense of others.

Like most people, you probably learned to negotiate on the job. You may get adequate results, but somehow you feel you could do better.

Well, you're absolutely right.

If you are one of these individuals, then this method was made for you. In short, it will allow you to *develop your innate negotiating talents.*

Negotiation: an Everyday Activity

Take a moment to think about other situations where you have to negotiate. How many can you list? Here are some everyday examples which show that we are constantly negotiating in all areas of our lives.

1. **When you are shopping:** It is probably not worth trying to bargain in large department stores, but in smaller shops and boutiques there is usually a margin of between 10 and 20 per cent to play with.

2. **In every contract you sign:** Many people sign on the dotted line without questioning anything. You will discover how to overcome this tendency later on.

3. **At work:** You are constantly negotiating with your superiors, your colleagues and your subordinates – for a better salary, better production facilities, more work space, more time or simply for a little peace!

4. **At home with your family:** You may have to negotiate here even more than at work. Almost every action can be interpreted as forming part of some strategy to get something – some concession or bonus. There are very few who never play any games and never try to manipulate those close to them!

   Children and spouses alike have their own personal, seemingly irreconcilable, objectives – Do we go on holiday to the beach or the mountains? How can we learn to resolve these differences peaceably? Through the great art of negotiation!

5. **In your social life:** With friends, neighbours (especially those who play their stereo late at night!), at the club or association, at informal gatherings – in short, in one way or another, almost all social activity resembles a negotiable situation, and those in the know are at a great advantage.

Negotiation Means Considerable Gain

The gains you can make from the art of negotiation are considerable. And for the moment we're talking about cash gains only. What is your gross annual income? Calculate 2.5 per cent of that amount, and think about whether you would prefer to find that money in your own pocket, or in some government or supplier's coffer? Even small negotiating successes can make a large difference if spread across all your financial dealings.

We have calculated that by applying the techniques given in this book you can save a *minimum* of 10 per cent of your annual expenditure – and that's a conservative estimate. It could be as high as 25 per cent.

Negotiate to defend yourself

For a business person, knowing how to negotiate can make the difference between a weak enterprise, constantly on the verge of bankruptcy, and one that is prosperous and continually in the process of healthy expansion.

Take a small business that's just starting out. Experienced business people will tell you that it is precisely at this moment that it becomes crucial to know how to discuss things in order to obtain the most advantageous terms possible: if not, your suppliers, distributors and clients will take as much from you as they can, until they suffocate your budding enterprise.

There is no secret: you have to know how to defend yourself. An entrepreneur must go after the best possible prices, and also create a network of people and corporate partners who are willing to support him or her at the outset. That too is the result of effective negotiations.

The World is a Huge Negotiating Table

In fact, every time you want something, every time you are in conflict with someone, every time you compete or co-operate with someone, you are negotiating!

Learning to negotiate means equipping yourself with the means to simplify your life.

Learn to Identify Negotiable Situations

Do you know when you're most likely to be 'taken for a ride'? Well, it isn't necessarily *during* negotiations. No, *it usually happens when you are not aware that you are in a negotiable situation.* By learning to identify these situations, you will automatically improve your chances for coming out on top.

Every time you want an article or a service that someone else is in a position to provide, you are in a negotiating situation. Examples are infinite.

- When your teenage son decides that he absolutely must have a Walkman just like the other kids at school (the most expensive model, of course!) you have to negotiate.

- When your cleaning lady says she's leaving because she thinks she's found a better client who lives much closer than you do, you have to negotiate in order to retain her services.

- When your spouse decides to buy a couch that is much too expensive or unsuitable in your opinion, you'd like to convince him or her that you're right without placing the stability of your household in danger.

- A garage does some repair work on your car, and a short time later the same problem reappears, even though all the defective parts were supposedly replaced with new ones. Would you prefer to pay the towing and repair costs all over again, or would you like the garage to pay?

Of course, not all these situations represent turning points in your existence (although your teenage child may think it does!). But imagine for a moment that you've learned to handle these minor obstacles with ease, that you are satisfied with the results *and so are the people with whom you've conducted your negotiations*. This leaves you unburdened of a host of minor problems.

There is No School of Negotiation

A lawyer friend heard about this book when it was still only an idea. Here's what he had to say:

> 'I think that this kind of a book is indispensable, and I look forward to reading it when it's finished. In my field, I'm constantly negotiating. The vast majority of cases are settled out of court. If not, the judicial system would get completely bogged down. But what's curious is that during all our years of study, we are never taught any of the basic techniques of effective negotiation!
>
> 'We study for years, but as far as negotiating is concerned, we're left to develop our own little formulas, in an empirical way, through trial and error. We learn an essential part of our work in a haphazard fashion, as we go along.'

A Method You Can Apply in Under 21 Days!

This book has been designed to be clear and accessible, and as interactive as possible. Reading alone is not sufficient for a person to assimilate a subject fully.

That's why we've conceived tests and exercises to simulate actual situations you will find yourself in.

What would you do if . . .? In this way, you ask yourself the question, and respond in a much more concrete manner than if you simply read: 'In such and such a situation, proceed in the following manner . . .'.

This book has been designed to facilitate the learning process so that you can become the best negotiator possible, as quickly as possible.

Negotiating is a daily activity which most people learn about as they go along; this method will help you develop your innate talents of negotiation in everyday situations. It will result in considerable gains in your professional, social and financial life.

In less than 21 days, if you follow this book, you will become an Outstanding Negotiator.

PART I

TEST YOUR ATTITUDES

CHAPTER 1

What Is Your Potential as a Negotiator?

As a child, when did you feel the most motivation to answer questions in class? Was it when another student was called to the blackboard, or when the teacher asked the entire class, or when you were asked directly?

The following tests are composed of questions designed to simulate actual situations, in which you have to ask yourself questions and then find the answers.

In this way you get to know your own negotiator's 'portrait', and start thinking about the important aspects of successful negotiation. The aim is not to guess what an experienced negotiator might do, but to *get to know yourself better*. A number of the questions covered in the tests will be developed further later on in the book. They refer to formal kinds of negotiations which you have probably already experienced. If you haven't been through exactly the same situation, you can relate it to another, similar one that you do know about. Answer as spontaneously as possible, without too much reflection, and without making corrections: once you've responded, then let your answer stand!

Test Your Potential

1. I do my utmost to prepare for a negotiation, even a minor one.

Always ☐   Often ☐   Sometimes ☐   Rarely ☐   Never ☐

2. When I feel that the person I'm talking to is getting impatient, or is in more of a hurry than I am, I try to speed things up.

Always ☐   Often ☐   Sometimes ☐   Rarely ☐   Never ☐

3. I carefully plan the location where a negotiation will take place.

Always ☐   Often ☐   Sometimes ☐   Rarely ☐   Never ☐

4. I try to get help when preparing for a negotiation.

Always ☐   Often ☐   Sometimes ☐   Rarely ☐   Never ☐

5. If there's a secondary point which I don't fully understand during a negotiating session, I let it pass and wait for things to clear up later.

Always ☐   Often ☐   Sometimes ☐   Rarely ☐   Never ☐

6. If there's something I'm not sure I understand during the course of a negotiation, I wait to clear it up later because I don't want the person I'm dealing with to gain an advantage by seeming less intelligent than he (or she) is.

Always ☐   Often ☐   Sometimes ☐   Rarely ☐   Never ☐

7. When necessary I allow for minor deviations from my standard code of ethics.

Always ☐   Often ☐   Sometimes ☐   Rarely ☐   Never ☐

8. I have no special technique for negotiating: I adapt according to the circumstances and the people I'm dealing with.

Always ☐   Often ☐   Sometimes ☐   Rarely ☐   Never ☐

Test continues ▶

9. I try to get on the same wavelength as the person I'm dealing with: if he or she treats things in a positive way, I do the same. If, on the contrary, his or her attitude towards the situation is negative, I react in a similar manner.

Always ☐   Often ☐   Sometimes ☐   Rarely ☐   Never ☐

10. When dealing with an important issue, I behave as if my career depended on the outcome.

Always ☐   Often ☐   Sometimes ☐   Rarely ☐   Never ☐

11. When I consent to negotiate at work, I feel I'm laying my entire career on the line.

Always ☐   Often ☐   Sometimes ☐   Rarely ☐   Never ☐

12. When I enter into a negotiation, I form a global idea of what I want, and then adapt to the specific circumstances.

Always ☐   Often ☐   Sometimes ☐   Rarely ☐   Never ☐

13. I evaluate all the possible repercussions of my objectives.

Always ☐   Often ☐   Sometimes ☐   Rarely ☐   Never ☐

14. I am ready to justify my position and my demands.

Always ☐   Often ☐   Sometimes ☐   Rarely ☐   Never ☐

15. If I'm asked to justify my position and I don't feel like elaborating, I respond by saying, 'That's just the way it is' or 'That's the way I want it' or 'Take it or leave it'.

Always ☐   Often ☐   Sometimes ☐   Rarely ☐   Never ☐

16. I enter a negotiation with documents to support my position.

Always ☐   Often ☐   Sometimes ☐   Rarely ☐   Never ☐

17. Concerning my documentation: If I can't get hold of the facts, I try to put together some expert opinions.

Always ☐   Often ☐   Sometimes ☐   Rarely ☐   Never ☐

Test continues ▶

18. Once I've established my position I do everything I can not to change it.

Always ☐　　Often ☐　　Sometimes ☐　　Rarely ☐　　Never ☐

19. The best indicator of success is money.

Always ☐　　Often ☐　　Sometimes ☐　　Rarely ☐　　Never ☐

20. I assume that the only thing that interests the person I'm dealing with is money.

Always ☐　　Often ☐　　Sometimes ☐　　Rarely ☐　　Never ☐

21. When I enter into a negotiation, I have a good idea of what the person I'm dealing with wants.

Always ☐　　Often ☐　　Sometimes ☐　　Rarely ☐　　Never ☐

22. When the other person is speaking, I respond to his or her arguments in my head.

Always ☐　　Often ☐　　Sometimes ☐　　Rarely ☐　　Never ☐

23. When I see that I'm in a favourable position, I re-evaluate my objectives and raise my stakes in order to get as much as possible out of the situation.

Always ☐　　Often ☐　　Sometimes ☐　　Rarely ☐　　Never ☐

24. When I see that things aren't going as I'd like, I show my exasperation, and sometimes even get angry.

Always ☐　　Often ☐　　Sometimes ☐　　Rarely ☐　　Never ☐

25. I quickly form an opinion of the person(s) I'm dealing with.

Always ☐　　Often ☐　　Sometimes ☐　　Rarely ☐　　Never ☐

26. I am modest in victory.

Always ☐　　Often ☐　　Sometimes ☐　　Rarely ☐　　Never ☐

Test continues ▶

27. I make friends while negotiating.

Always ☐ Often ☐ Sometimes ☐ Rarely ☐ Never ☐

28. I make enemies during a negotiation.

Always ☐ Often ☐ Sometimes ☐ Rarely ☐ Never ☐

29. When I feel close to an agreement, I suggest drawing up a first draft in writing.

Always ☐ Often ☐ Sometimes ☐ Rarely ☐ Never ☐

30. I study the personality of the person(s) I'm dealing with carefully before entering into negotiations.

Always ☐ Often ☐ Sometimes ☐ Rarely ☐ Never ☐

31. A correct negotiating position should be firm and solidly established.

Always ☐ Often ☐ Sometimes ☐ Rarely ☐ Never ☐

Great! You've persevered to the end!

Now, let's take a look at your answers. They will give you some clues as to your instincts as a negotiator.

Evaluate your answers

Compare your answers to the comments that follow. To evaluate your instincts as a negotiator, consider your answers according to the following numbering system from 4 down to 0.

- Each time you chose the 'right' answer, give yourself 4 points. For each degree of difference from our answer, take away 1 point. For example, we recommend always being well prepared for a negotiation, whatever its importance. So if (up to now) you've never prepared for a negotiation, give yourself 0 for this question. If, on the other hand, you replied 'sometimes', you would only take off 2 points from the maximum score of 4, and give yourself 2 points.

Answer 1. Always, of course. The more up to date you are about the issues, the less probable it is that you will be taken by surprise (not impossible, but much less probable!).

Answer 2. Never. Not everyone works at the same pace, and you must make sure you've fully assimilated all the information you've been able to gather as it becomes available. If a session is too long, suggest taking a break. Remember that pretending to be in a hurry is a common tactic of intimidation which should not overly impress you.

Answer 3. Always. Our environment has a profound effect on us, and the location of a negotiation should be chosen with extreme care.

Answer 4. You've heard the expression 'two heads are better than one'. Brainstorming can help you clarify your objectives and discover possible objections and problems.

Answer 5. Never. This is a variation of Question 2. Don't let anything go by that you don't understand. Excuse yourself for being slow, and demand a clarification.

Answer 6. Never. Once again, if the discussion gets too technical, ask that it be put into comprehensible terms.

Answer 7. Rarely. It takes much longer to establish a good reputation than a bad one. You should consider carefully before embarking on a doubtful path. But an excess of ethical rigidity does not always produce the best results either. It's up to you to judge!

Answer 8. Rarely. Obviously you sometimes have to adapt. But you should have your own negotiating style, one which conforms to your personality. It is not a good idea to adopt a role which doesn't suit you, even if that same role might have worked for others.

Answer 9. Rarely. Try to work from a positive point of view as much as possible. Emphasize the things you want rather than the things you don't want.

Answer 10. Rarely. Your career rarely depends on the outcome of a single issue. It's useless to expend too much effort: there aren't many situations where you have to agree at any price. This is the reason we sometimes negotiate better on someone else's behalf than for ourselves.

Answer 11. Don't let the previous question mislead you. Your career doesn't depend on the outcome of each negotiation, but each time you conclude an agreement, you place your name and reputation on the line.

Answer 12. Never. Define your objectives and needs precisely. There is some room for variation, of course, but you should have a clear idea of your needs and desires.

Answer 13. Always. Knowing what you want also means knowing what will happen when you get it. Obviously, 'always' is somewhat extreme in this case. It's impossible, you say, to predict everything. But you should at least explore the main avenues. What we want doesn't always correspond to what we really need . . .

Answer 14. Always. Your position becomes much weaker when you can't explain it to the person you're dealing with. Therefore, the fewer arguments you have, the less convincing you will be.

Answer 15. Never. This is the kind of answer you're forced to give if you can't justify your demands. These are extremely weak arguments, even coming from the best of negotiators.

Answer 16. Always. It's always a good idea to have documents, photocopies, summaries, etc., at your disposal. They show that you're well prepared.

Answer 17. Always. Objective facts are always preferable to opinions, and they help the parties reach an agreement. As a last resort, expert opinions will suffice.

Answer 18. Never. Have you forgotten? A negotiation is an exchange, which implies that you remain flexible. To succeed, steer the discussion towards an area of agreement rather than trying to dwell only on what you want.

Answer 19. Often. Not always. There are a host of other advantages you may obtain through negotiation, and they sometimes don't cost anything.

Answer 20. Never. This is sometimes the case. But never take it for granted. Don't underestimate the motives of the person you're dealing with – there's no better way of arousing his or her antagonism, and getting yourself off to a bad start.

Answer 21. Always. But even if you think you know, act as if you didn't. This will help your concentration and get rid of preconceived notions that may dull your perception.

Answer 22. Never. Do one thing at a time. If not, you end up hearing (a) only what you're afraid to hear; or (b) only what you want to hear. If the person you're dealing with merits your presence, he or she also merits your attention. When absolutely necessary ask for a few minutes to think things over.

Answer 23. Sometimes. It's not always a good idea to squeeze too much.

Answer 24. Never. The other person shouldn't suspect anything. There's no better way to destroy your image as a serious negotiator. You should do everything possible not to show your exasperation.

Answer 25. Sometimes. It seems we form opinions about people very rapidly. But do not jump to conclusions. Make careful observations before settling on an opinion. Watch out! You may actually be dealing with a wolf when you think you're dealing with a lamb!

Answer 26. Always. Never give the impression that you take pleasure in destroying someone. This will only be detrimental to your reputation. The best attitude is never to allow anyone to leave a negotiating session completely empty-handed.

Answer 27. Often. Why not!

Answer 28. Rarely. An effective negotiator rarely makes enemies. An excellent negotiator *never* makes enemies.

Answer 29. Always. It's a very good way to clarify things and make them more concrete.

Answer 30. Always. This is similar to Question 26: it's another way of getting rid of prejudices. No two individuals are identical. The more you study the person you're dealing with, the more you can anticipate events and manœuvre yourself into a favourable position.

Answer 31. Never. This is a variation of Question 18. Instead of establishing a fixed position, try to define your *field of interests and needs*. Here you can – and should – be specific. But don't become the prisoner of a rigid, inflexible position. Flexibility is indispensable.

Results

Now count up your points to work out your aptitude for negotiation.

0–39 points: Don't get involved in any negotiations without the help of a seasoned negotiator (which is still one of the best ways of learning). If no one is available to help you, run through the contents of this book before undertaking any negotiations!

40–69 points: Nobody's perfect. Don't imagine that skilful negotiators were born skilled and didn't learn anything from others. This book contains everything you need in order to improve!

70–94 points: Your talent for negotiating, which is no doubt intuitive, is above average. All you have to do is study the book in order to become an excellent negotiator.

95–124 points: You are a superior negotiator! Your instinct is excellent. But don't forget that a test is not a real negotiation.

The important thing here is not to accumulate a maximum number of points. What counts is how much *you develop your talents as a negotiator* over the next few weeks.

Now that we've covered your *aptitude* for negotiation, let's evaluate your *attitude* towards negotiation.

**ALWAYS prepare yourself for a negotiation session.
Preparation is the key to success.**

CHAPTER 2

Do You Like to Negotiate?

The answer may surprise you. Be honest with yourself. You should give this question some serious thought, since it may prove a determining factor in your performance as a negotiator.

To begin with, think about what you like (or don't like) about negotiating, even if you've had only limited experience. Does it offer a challenge and keep you on your toes? Does it give you a buzz, or a sense of satisfaction when the negotiation is completed satisfactorily? Does it make you feel responsible and fully involved in your work?

Think about the positive feelings negotiating can give you.

To make your task easier, we have devised the following test which is based on a questionnaire exploring the reasons why executives like, or sometimes hesitate, to negotiate. The more honestly you answer, the more accurate the results will be, enabling you to identify your strong points and your weak points and plan your course of study accordingly. Remember that this is an attitude test. Don't be too cerebral, thinking, 'Let's see . . . what would the right answer be?' Base your answers on how you *feel* ('What does this mean to me?').

Test Your Attitude

1. Would you say that the talent to negotiate is an indispensable attribute of a good leader?

   Yes ☐   No ☐   Sometimes ☐

2. Are you afraid of not being able to measure up during a negotiation session?

   Yes ☐   No ☐   Sometimes ☐

3. Do you enjoy working as part of a team?

   Yes ☐   No ☐   Sometimes ☐

4. Do you find that negotiating is a burden in terms of time and energy invested?

   Yes ☐   No ☐   Sometimes ☐

5. Does negotiating represent a way of breaking your routine?

   Yes ☐   No ☐   Sometimes ☐

6. Do you think of negotiating as a useful way to get what you want?

   Yes ☐   No ☐   Sometimes ☐

7. Are you afraid that negotiating will bring undesirable aspects of your personality or embarrassing facts about your past to the surface?

   Yes ☐   No ☐   Sometimes ☐

8. Would you say that negotiating is an important aspect of modern business?

   Yes ☐   No ☐   Sometimes ☐

Test continues ▶

9. Somewhere deep down, to you regard negotiating as an unsavoury set of bargaining tricks?

Yes ☐   No ☐   Sometimes ☐

10. Does the prospect of successfully concluding a difficult negotiation excite you?

Yes ☐   No ☐   Sometimes ☐

11. Does the possibility of failure cause you to hesitate before entering into a negotiation?

Yes ☐   No ☐   Sometimes ☐

12. Are you able to say *No!* and mean it?

Yes ☐   No ☐   Sometimes ☐

13. Would you say that negotiating is a fascinating game and a challenge with risks and rewards?

Yes ☐   No ☐   Sometimes ☐

14. Would you agree that an honourable defeat in a negotiation is a kind of victory?

Yes ☐   No ☐   Sometimes ☐

15. Do you resent the preparations you have to make for a negotiating session, finding the work less than satisfying?

Yes ☐   No ☐   Sometimes ☐

16. Do you dread the extra physical and emotional stress you may undergo during the course of a negotiating session, where you have to confront persons with opposing opinions, who may even seem to hold you in low esteem?

Yes ☐   No ☐   Sometimes ☐

Test continues ▶

17. Would you say that negotiating forces you to develop qualities which you are proud to possess?

Yes ☐   No ☐   Sometimes ☐

18. Would you say that negotiating represents an important aspect of your personal development?

Yes ☐   No ☐   Sometimes ☐

19. Do you find that you anticipate a successful conclusion to a negotiating session with pleasure?

Yes ☐   No ☐   Sometimes ☐

20. Are you apprehensive about the unknown factors which may arise during the course of a negotiating session?

Yes ☐   No ☐   Sometimes ☐

21. Do you have confidence in your talents as a negotiator?

Yes ☐   No ☐   Sometimes ☐

22. In the eventuality that a negotiation fails, do you dread the consequences of defeat?

Yes ☐   No ☐   Sometimes ☐

23. If you run a business, do you prefer to issue orders and directives, or to negotiate a *modus operandi* with your employees?

Yes ☐   No ☐   Sometimes ☐

Evaluate your answers

Now compare your answers with those listed overleaf. *Each time your response differs from the sample, give yourself one point. Also give yourself one point for each time you answer 'sometimes'.*

Don't forget that there are no right or wrong answers. The 'yes' answers we give represent those of a person who enjoys all aspects of negotiation – which, in reality, is highly improbable, while the 'no' answers indicate reasons for hesitating to negotiate.

Answer 1. Yes **Answer 2.** No **Answer 3.** Yes **Answer 4.** No
Answer 5. Yes **Answer 6.** Yes **Answer 7.** No **Answer 8.** Yes
Answer 9. No **Answer 10.** Yes **Answer 11.** No **Answer 12.** Yes
Answer 13. Yes **Answer 14.** Yes **Answer 15.** No **Answer 16.** No
Answer 17. Yes **Answer 18.** Yes **Answer 19.** Yes **Answer 20.** No
Answer 21. Yes **Answer 22.** No **Answer 23.** No

Results

0–5 points: It seems that, if you responded honestly and spontaneously, negotiating is second nature to you. All you have to do is approach the subject systematically, and you will soon reap the fruits of your efforts.

6–10 points: You have identified your soft spots, which are probably in the areas where your responses differed from the sample. All you have to do is work to correct them.

11–23 points: According to the specific nature of the points you accumulated, there are a number of possibilities:

a. Most of your points were due to a 'Sometimes' response. Either you are not admitting your real feelings, or you haven't had enough experience as a negotiator to know what they are.

   However, this indecision may be a problem in itself: negotiating is a situation which requires knowing how to say 'Yes' or 'No'. That's why 'Sometimes' responses are given the same points as 'wrong' answers.

b. You collected points in questions where the sample answer was 'Yes', while you responded with a 'No'. In this this situation negotiation does not necessarily repel you, but you haven't yet learned to like it. Start practising immediately, for reasonable stakes.

c. You collected points mainly by giving a 'Yes' response to questions where the sample response was 'No'. This indicates that deep down you are repelled by negotiations.

   Don't give up hope, but if the stakes involved in your next negotiating session are too high, it might be better to send someone in your place, since you presently lack the positive motivation which is essential to success.

Continue to study the subject. For the time being, stay away from highly stressful situations, and negotiate only when the stakes aren't too high. Once you have won a few victories, your perception of negotiations may be very different. Do the test again: who knows – you may be pleasantly surprised!

In the next chapter, we'll see just what you think of your own talents as a negotiator.

Negotiating must become a familiar situation. Practise as often as possible, starting with reasonable stakes.

CHAPTER 3

What Do You Think Makes a Good Negotiator?

What do you think are the qualities that make someone a good negotiator?

In this test you can compare your opinions to those of 32 top-level loan officers working for a large American bank. Professor John Hammond of the Harvard Business School proposed 34 qualities to them, which they were asked to evaluate according to importance. You will see how your answers correspond to those of the executives, remembering that this questionnaire was based on personal opinions, and not on any scientific data.

First rate your answers according to the importance you give to each quality. Then answer 'Yes' or 'No', according to whether you feel you possess each quality or not.

Test What You Think of Your Talents as a Negotiator

Do you think you possess the quality or attitude described? Do you almost always act in the described manner (taking into account the special needs of your particular organization and those of the organization with which you are negotiating)? Which qualities do you think are the most important?

The Qualities of an Effective Negotiator

1. Being aware of the underlying needs and trends in one's own organization, as well as those of the organization one is dealing with.

Useless ☐   Slightly useful ☐   Useful ☐   Very useful ☐   Extremely useful ☐

I possess this quality: Yes ☐   No ☐

2. Knowing how to lead and control the members of one's team.

Useless ☐   Slightly useful ☐   Useful ☐   Very useful ☐   Extremely useful ☐

I possess this quality: Yes ☐   No ☐

3. The ability to identify power levers and use them to attain objectives.

Useless ☐   Slightly useful ☐   Useful ☐   Very useful ☐   Extremely useful ☐

I possess this quality: Yes ☐   No ☐

4. Past experience in negotiation.

Useless ☐   Slightly useful ☐   Useful ☐   Very useful ☐   Extremely useful ☐

I possess this quality: Yes ☐   No ☐

5. Perseverance and determination.

Useless ☐   Slightly useful ☐   Useful ☐   Very useful ☐   Extremely useful ☐

I possess this quality: Yes ☐   No ☐

Test continues ▶

6. A sense of personal security.

Useless ☐ Slightly useful ☐ Useful ☐ Very useful ☐ Extremely useful ☐

I possess this quality: Yes ☐ No ☐

7. An intuitive understanding of the feelings of others.

Useless ☐ Slightly useful ☐ Useful ☐ Very useful ☐ Extremely useful ☐

I possess this quality: Yes ☐ No ☐

8. A tolerance of others' points of view.

Useless ☐ Slightly useful ☐ Useful ☐ Very useful ☐ Extremely useful ☐

I possess this quality: Yes ☐ No ☐

9. Good self-control, especially when it comes to emotion.

Useless ☐ Slightly useful ☐ Useful ☐ Very useful ☐ Extremely useful ☐

I possess this quality: Yes ☐ No ☐

10. A competitive spirit (a desire to compete and to win).

Useless ☐ Slightly useful ☐ Useful ☐ Very useful ☐ Extremely useful ☐

I possess this quality: Yes ☐ No ☐

11. An analytical mind and the ability to solve problems.

Useless ☐ Slightly useful ☐ Useful ☐ Very useful ☐ Extremely useful ☐

I possess this quality: Yes ☐ No ☐

Test continues ▶

12. The ability to communicate and co-ordinate different objectives within one's own organization.

Useless ☐ Slightly useful ☐ Useful ☐ Very useful ☐ Extremely useful ☐

I possess this quality: Yes ☐ No ☐

13. The ability to gain the respect and confidence of people one is dealing with.

Useless ☐ Slightly useful ☐ Useful ☐ Very useful ☐ Extremely useful ☐

I possess this quality: Yes ☐ No ☐

14. Being a good speaker (skilled at answering questions).

Useless ☐ Slightly useful ☐ Useful ☐ Very useful ☐ Extremely useful ☐

I possess this quality: Yes ☐ No ☐

15. Being decisive.

Useless ☐ Slightly useful ☐ Useful ☐ Very useful ☐ Extremely useful ☐

I possess this quality: Yes ☐ No ☐

16. Accepting the risk of not being liked.

Useless ☐ Slightly useful ☐ Useful ☐ Very useful ☐ Extremely useful ☐

I possess this quality: Yes ☐ No ☐

17. Patience.

Useless ☐ Slightly useful ☐ Useful ☐ Very useful ☐ Extremely useful ☐

I possess this quality: Yes ☐ No ☐

Test continues ▶

18. The ability to negotiate well in different roles and situations.

Useless ☐　Slightly useful ☐　Useful ☐　Very useful ☐　Extremely useful ☐

I possess this quality: Yes ☐　No ☐

19. The ability to persuade others.

Useless ☐　Slightly useful ☐　Useful ☐　Very useful ☐　Extremely useful ☐

I possess this quality: Yes ☐　No ☐

20. Good standing or a high-ranking position in one's organization.

Useless ☐　Slightly useful ☐　Useful ☐　Very useful ☐　Extremely useful ☐

I possess this quality: Yes ☐　No ☐

21. Integrity.

Useless ☐　Slightly useful ☐　Useful ☐　Very useful ☐　Extremely useful ☐

I possess this quality: Yes ☐　No ☐

22. Tolerance in the face of ambiguity and uncertainty.

Useless ☐　Slightly useful ☐　Useful ☐　Very useful ☐　Extremely useful ☐

I possess this quality: Yes ☐　No ☐

23. Good judgement and common sense.

Useless ☐　Slightly useful ☐　Useful ☐　Very useful ☐　Extremely useful ☐

I possess this quality: Yes ☐　No ☐

Test continues ▶

24. A mastery of non-verbal language (signs, gestures, silence, etc.).

Useless ☐   Slightly useful ☐   Useful ☐   Very useful ☐   Extremely useful ☐

I possess this quality: Yes ☐   No ☐

25. The ability to listen.

Useless ☐   Slightly useful ☐   Useful ☐   Very useful ☐   Extremely useful ☐

I possess this quality: Yes ☐   No ☐

26. An accommodating nature.

Useless ☐   Slightly useful ☐   Useful ☐   Very useful ☐   Extremely useful ☐

I possess this quality: Yes ☐   No ☐

27. The ability to express thoughts verbally.

Useless ☐   Slightly useful ☐   Useful ☐   Very useful ☐   Extremely useful ☐

I possess this quality: Yes ☐   No ☐

28. An endearing personality and a sense of humour.

Useless ☐   Slightly useful ☐   Useful ☐   Very useful ☐   Extremely useful ☐

I possess these qualities: Yes ☐   No ☐

29. The ability to think clearly and rapidly under pressure, and in unfamiliar situations.

Useless ☐   Slightly useful ☐   Useful ☐   Very useful ☐   Extremely useful ☐

I possess this quality: Yes ☐   No ☐

Test continues ▶

30. Natural self-confidence.

Useless ☐   Slightly useful ☐   Useful ☐   Very useful ☐   Extremely useful ☐

I possess this quality: Yes ☐   No ☐

31. Knowledge of the subject under negotiation.

Useless ☐   Slightly useful ☐   Useful ☐   Very useful ☐   Extremely useful ☐

I possess this quality: Yes ☐   No ☐

32. Being ready to take risks that are unusual in business.

Useless ☐   Slightly useful ☐   Useful ☐   Very useful ☐   Extremely useful ☐

I possess this quality: Yes ☐   No ☐

33. The ability to prepare and plan.

Useless ☐   Slightly useful ☐   Useful ☐   Very useful ☐   Extremely useful ☐

I possess this quality: Yes ☐   No ☐

34. Being ready to use force, threats and bluff in order to avoid being exploited.

Useless ☐   Slightly useful ☐   Useful ☐   Very useful ☐   Extremely useful ☐

I possess this quality: Yes ☐   No ☐

Results

Now that you've filled in your responses, here, in descending order of importance, are the qualities which the 32 executives considered most valuable to a good negotiator. Don't just consider the first few: it's just as useful to know what they considered to be unimportant.

Comparing their responses with yours will give you food for thought, especially if, for example, you consider aggressiveness an important quality for a negotiator.

The number of each question from the list above is indicated in parentheses, so that you can compare their responses to your own.

1. The ability to prepare and plan (**33**)

2. Knowledge of the subject under negotiation (**31**)

3. The ability to think clearly and rapidly under pressure, and in unfamiliar situations (**29**)

4. The ability to express thoughts verbally (**27**)

5. The ability to listen (**25**)

6. Good judgement and common sense (**23**)

7. Integrity (**21**)

8. The ability to persuade others (**19**)

9. Patience (**17**)

10. Being decisive (**15**)

11. The ability to gain the respect and confidence of people one is dealing with (**13**)

12. An analytical mind and the ability to solve problems (**11**)

13. Good self-control, especially when it comes to emotion (**9**)

14. An intuitive understanding of the feelings of others (**7**)

15. Perseverance and determination (**5**)

16. The ability to identify power levers and use them to attain one's objectives (**3**)

17. Being aware of the underlying needs and trends in one's own organization, as well as those of the organization one is dealing with (**1**)

18. Knowing how to lead and control the members of one's team (**2**)

19. Past experience in negotiation (**4**)

20. A sense of personal security (**6**)

21. Tolerance of others' points of view (**8**)

22. A competitive spirit (a desire to compete and to win) (**10**)

23. The ability to communicate and co-ordinate different objectives within one's own organization (**12**)

24. Being a good speaker (skilled at answering questions) (**14**)

25. Accepting the risk of not being liked (**16**)

26. The ability to negotiate well in different roles and situations (**18**)

27. Good standing or a high-ranking position in one's organization (**20**)

28. Tolerance in the face of ambiguity and uncertainty (**22**)

29. A mastery of non-verbal language (signs, gestures, silence, etc.) (**24**)

30. An accommodating nature (**26**)

31. An endearing personality and a sense of humour (**28**)

32. Natural self-confidence (**30**)

33. Being ready to take risks that are unusual in business (**32**)

34. Being ready to use force, threats and bluff in order to avoid being exploited (**34**)

Take a good look at those qualities which were deemed most desirable, and those which are least desirable. Notice that *preparation* comes at the head of the list, while the use of force or threats comes last. Also, a confident nature is not judged to be an essential quality of a good negotiator.

Remember that these are subjective evaluations – the loan officers were asked what *they judged* to be the most important qualities. If, for example, you have an endearing personality and a great sense of humour, you don't have to become sarcastic and serious in order to be a good negotiator. Not at all. But neither should you rely only on your likeability.

It is worth listing those qualities which you think you already possess, and those which you do not. The qualities you have are a gift – take advantage of them.

Yes, but what about the others, you may ask?

Read over the qualities which were judged to be most important for a good negotiator again. Do they have anything in common? No? Well, there is at least one thing which will encourage you:

**Nearly anyone can acquire the qualities needed
to be an Effective Negotiator.**

We will provide you with the tools you need to acquire these qualities, one by one. In fact, the only qualities that *cannot* be acquired are good judgement and common sense.

Summary

The 10 most important qualities for a successful negotiator in descending order of importance are:

1. **knowing how to prepare and plan**

2. **knowing your subject**

3. **the ability to think clearly and rapidly**

4. **the ability to express your thoughts**

5. **knowing how to listen**

6. **good judgement**

7. **integrity**

8. **the ability to persuade people**

9. **patience**

10. **a decisive mind.**

PART II

PREPARING TO NEGOTIATE

CHAPTER 4

To Negotiate or Not to Negotiate?

This is the first question you should ask yourself when a possible negotiating situation arises. You may think that you have no choice, but you are under no obligation to enter negotiations just because someone else suggests it.

We have already said how important it is to recognize a negotiating situation when it occurs, but it's just as important to weigh up the pros and cons, and refrain from negotiating at all when the circumstances are not favourable.

Here are some situations where it would be preferable not to negotiate.

- **When the party you're dealing with has overwhelming power – and plans to use it.**
  If you sit down at a negotiating table under these circumstances you would be offering yourself up as a sacrifice!

- **When your own alternatives are better than the ones being proposed.**
  It's pointless to get into a discussion when you already know you can do better elsewhere. That's why it's important always to study all other angles and possibilities.

- **When the time is not right.**
  If you are already working to full capacity, it would be useless to sign a contract for a large order. Or, if the company you are approaching is undergoing a management shuffle, better wait until things settle down.

- **When you have no experience in the area under negotiation.**
  The reasons for this are obvious!

- **When the act of negotiating weakens your position.**
  If you need something, and there's no possibility of a compromise, it's

useless to negotiate. For example, governments often refuse to accede to the demands of terrorists, figuring that doing so would only result in more demands from them.

Before your next negotiation take the time to complete the following test.

Pre-Negotiation Test

	Yes	No
1. Do I have some experience of this precise type of negotiation?	☐	☐
2. If so, does my experience tell me that I have a good chance of succeeding?	☐	☐
3. If not, are there any competent experts or advisers I can consult?	☐	☐
4. Are the stakes not so high that to lose would put me in the red?	☐	☐
5. Do I have a fairly precise idea of the possible reactions of the other party?	☐	☐
6. Does the other party seem to be dependable and worth dealing with?	☐	☐
7. Does the negotiation in question have the potential to be advantageous to both parties?	☐	☐
8. Is the time right for negotiating?	☐	☐
9. Is the issue negotiable?	☐	☐

Now total up your answers: ☐ Yes ☐ No

- If you answered *No* to more than four questions, there is no doubt that you'd be better off postponing any upcoming negotiations, or at least not negotiating on your own. It is usually less costly in the long run to hire someone to help you negotiate than to sit down at the table when you are not equipped to discuss the issue properly.

- If you answered *Yes* to at least six questions, then the conditions seem right for proceeding. The next step is to prepare yourself and we will look at this in the following chapter.

CHAPTER 5

Early Preparations

So where do negotiations really begin? Is it when the following situations occur?

1. When both parties sit down at the negotiating table? ☐

2. When the parties begin their preparations? ☐

3. At the first contact, when the parties don't even know that they will be negotiating with each other? OR ☐

4. When the parties decide to do business with each other? ☐

It isn't easy to say. But it *is* true that negotiations begin well before the actual discussions start.

To illustrate this, let's say you want to open a small shop, and you know of premises for sale which look ideal. You meet the current owner and tell him that you're interested.

Making Contact

From this point on, negotiations have, to all intents and purposes, started. In general, the other party will be very prudent, and won't want to say too much about their business. They may boast about the merits of its location, but will avoid divulging anything more than the strict minimum of information. This is the first stage; that of establishing contact.

This is the moment when both parties learn that they are (perhaps) going to negotiate with each other. At this stage, it's in your interests to be courteous, amiable and discreet. This is the time to *observe*, *listen* and *learn*, when the parties evaluate and start getting to know each other. You have to form a very rapid opinion of the person you're dealing with. And obviously, the process works both ways. So your first meeting is of great importance.

Some people tend to be less cautious at this point, simply because formal negotiations have not yet been established, but, in fact, this is not the time to reveal all your plans. The important thing is to solicit the confidence of the other person while taking care not to discuss the important issues before the appropriate time.

Getting Informed

You might go into the shop in question, pretending to be an ordinary customer. After making a few minor purchases, you ask the person behind the counter, 'How's business?'.

From your point of view, negotiations have now already started. Why? Because you're in the process of doing something very useful, something that is too often ignored: you are out on location, researching issues. By informing yourself in this way, you are actually beginning negotiations – and you're already acting in an efficient (and therefore effective) manner.

Perhaps the employee you're talking to says, for example, that sales have decreased a lot since a big supermarket opened in the area. You now possess a piece of information which could prove to be decisive during your eventual negotiations.

Preparation is an essential aspect of negotiation, an aspect which is entirely invisible to the outside observer. If the other party arrives fully prepared and you don't, you may assume that he's started without you, and that he already has a sizeable advantage.

The chess champion

It cannot be emphasized enough just how important this aspect of negotiating is. Look at chess champions – what do they do during a game? They calculate the greatest number of manœuvres possible, move by move. And before the game, what do you think they do?

They study their opponent's previous games, one by one. They also study their adversary's psychology: mentality, general attitude, resistance to stress, etc.

This is a theoretical stage of the game, true enough. It may not be as stimulating as the actual discussions. The action hasn't started yet. But you must study all the angles, discover as much as you can and try to anticipate the reactions of the other party. You must formulate proposals and arguments which will result in you obtaining what you want. Indeed, the negotiation game can be just as fascinating as chess.

Find the facts

What is the first thing you should do once you've decided to negotiate and want to begin preparing?

The first thing to do is get informed and study the issue in question. You need to develop an overall view of the situation. To do this, ask yourself the following kinds of questions.

- What is it about?
- Who does it involve?
- What are the different versions of the facts?
- What information do we have at our disposal?
- What problems can we foresee?

Say your negotiation will involve the purchase of a business. You will need to draw up a list of the information you need to acquire, as in the example overleaf.

So, just how healthy is the business in question? Knowing the annual turnover and seeing the last three years' sets of company accounts will give you an indication, but trading results are often masked by tax planning. A serious buyer will need to have sight of a current set of accounting records in order to get a true picture.

You should take the trouble to visit the location yourself. Employees often enjoy talking about their work, so you can gain information by catching them off their guard. You should also explore the neighbour-hood, walk through it, observe it. And if you find that a competitor has set up shop not far away, you might want to modify your plans.

Finally, ask yourself why the owner would want to sell if the place was such a gold-mine. Having a fairly accurate idea of the true extent of his problems could make a big difference during your negotiations.

We'll discuss techniques for gathering information and advice and the kind of information you should try to accumulate in Chapter 7. But at this stage you have to decide what you want to get out of the negotiations, by formulating your interests and objectives clearly!

Prospective Purchase of X Ltd

1. current profitability _____

   _____

2. the choice of items sold _____

   _____

3. annual growth rate of revenues _____

   _____

4. stock turn in relation to turnover _____

   _____

5. cost of the lease _____

   _____

6. annual rent increases _____

   _____

7. length of the lease _____

   _____

8. insurance costs _____

   _____

9. salaries _____

   _____

10. annual taxes _____

    _____

11. suppliers' fees _____

    _____

12. seasonal cycles _____

CHAPTER 6

Working Out Your Interests and Objectives

Interests Versus Objectives

Interests and objectives are two sides of the same coin. They are closely related, yet being able to differentiate one from the other can often make all the difference during negotiations.

- Your interests are your long-term priorities. You establish what they are, and re-examine them periodically, whatever the prevailing circumstances.

- Your objectives are the specific goals which are likely to serve your interests. So it's essential to determine your interests, because it is on them that you base your objectives.

For example:

1. You want to move because you're tired of the house you live in. So making money is not your only objective in selling.
2. You're a speculator: you don't care about the quality of the house. All you want to do is sell it.

In both cases the objective is the same (selling), but the interests (domestic and speculation) are different.

In every undertaking you should always keep your interests in mind. This allows you to:

1. define your objectives better; *and*
2. modify these objectives if they don't correspond to your real interests.

Also, when you study the interests as well as the objectives of the other party, you are apt to come up with much more appealing solutions.

How to Define Your Objectives

Think about the last important negotiation in which you participated.

- Did you write down your objectives?
- If not, *would* you have been able to write them down in a few simple, clear sentences?

If so, the chances are that you came close to attaining those objectives. If not, do not be surprised if you weren't satisfied with the results.

Surprising as this may seem, many people sit down at a negotiating table with only a very foggy idea of their objectives. They start out very enthusiastically, determined to achieve 'as much as possible' – without knowing what 'as much as possible' really means. They have such high hopes! That's why so many negotiations are centred around the question of money. Money is an easily definable objective – you want as much as possible! But, in fact, it is only one aspect of negotiation.

There is a direct relation between defining your objectives properly and succeeding in negotiations. You must take the time to establish objectives and also to outline some alternatives. Because another rule of negotiation is that **things rarely happen as planned**.

First, you must ask yourself some questions in order to set your objectives, remembering that there are usually at least two types of objectives in every negotiation.

1. Ideally, what would I like to get from these negotiations?

2. What do I absolutely need to get from these negotiations?

3. What are my alternatives if no agreement can be reached?

4. What is the worst that can happen if no agreement is reached?

Now, let's look at these questions in detail.

1. What Would I Like to Get from These Negotiations?

This first question is rather like wishing on a star, hoping to make your dreams come true. Dreams and desires are things you wish for, but could do without if necessary. They are the bonus factor – the extra reward. If you attain them, all the better. If not, you'll get along anyhow. They figure in your demands as a wish rather than a requirement. In other words, you are ready to sacrifice these objectives, which means that you will not allow the negotiations to break down if you don't attain them. However, you may exact a price for such a sacrifice – you may demand that the other party agrees to drop certain objectives too. On the other hand, once the other party knows what your 'ideal objectives' are, he will also know what to propose to make his offer irresistible, if by any chance you are debating whether or not to conclude the deal.

By establishing these kinds of ideal objectives you create a margin of space for manœuvring in areas where you can make concessions without really giving up anything important.

So, you have to formulate objectives that ask a lot, yet remain reasonable. You have to decide just how far you can go, without overstepping the limits of reality, since unreasonable demands can destroy the entire negotiation. For example, the other party, when confronted with your demands, may also make demands that are entirely unreasonable and unacceptable, which obviously leads to a dead end.

Be realistic – but be sure to aim high!

There is a direct relation between the level of your aspirations and your chances of success. Role-playing studies have shown that the higher the objectives, the better the results that can be obtained. And inversely, the lower your expectations, the worse will be your results.

2. What Do I Absolutely Need to Get Out of These Negotiations?

This is called the *bottom line*, tolerance level or breaking point – your absolute minimum requirement. Without achieving this objective, the negotiations will do nothing, or almost nothing for you, and you might as well break the discussions off.

Many people are happy enough to set their ideal objectives, but neglect to specify their bottom line because they think that doing so is a sign of weakness or an acceptance of failure before the fact. However, this is a mistake because there is always some margin of difference between your ideal objectives and your bottom line, thus providing an area in which you can manœuvre. When you know what your bottom line is, you also know that as long as you're still above it, the negotiations are worth continuing.

Suppose someone makes an offer that doesn't meet your ideal objectives. You are a little disappointed, but you're a realist and you decide to negotiate anyway. What if you haven't established your bottom line?

This means you're going to be negotiating in an area where you're not fully prepared. For one thing you haven't identified the maximum number of concessions you are ready to make.

In such an instance you'd probably be better off stopping the negotiations – unless you can resume them at a later date, when the offer is more in line with your aspirations – rather than make a deal which doesn't meet your bottom line. But your minimum requirements aren't always easy to establish.

Remember that:

● setting a bottom line is a subjective evaluation, which varies from one person to another;

● it is not always simply a question of money or profit;

● the situation in which you find yourself at the moment you decide to negotiate also plays an important role.

Be sure to establish your bottom line with care, by evaluating all the advantages and disadvantages. As for money, be judicious in setting your base figure. You should take market trends into account, including market value, market research on the demand of a product, its predicted availability, etc. Write all these figures down, and examine all the issues from as many different angles as possible.

3. What Are My Alternatives if No Agreement Can Be Reached?

Think about the following.

● What do I do if negotiations break down?
● Can I make a deal with someone else?
● Am I sure I can't get a better deal elsewhere?
● Have I looked at the competition?

Try to visualize all the alternatives and evaluate each one. Compare these alternatives to your bottom line. Is each of the alternatives likely to be:

– Lower than my bottom line?
– Equal to my bottom line?
– Better than my bottom line?

Obviously, if you find an alternative that's better than your bottom line, you should re-evaluate your position. In general, this gives you *much more power during the course of negotiations.*

Say you're negotiating your terms and conditions at work. You decide that one of your minimum requirements is a secretary. You'd also like one week more holiday a year. But your bottom line is getting a secretary. An alternative is presented to you.

Someone you know is starting his own business and offers you a job. He has already hired most of his personnel. His business promises to offer the same advantages as the company you're with now, and he's willing to give you a secretary to do the same amount of work. Your friend means well, but you realize that it may take some time before he can live up to his offer. On the other hand, the prospect of being involved in a new enterprise excites you, even though you realize objectively that the job is more risky than the one you already have.

Having this alternative changes the strength of your position in negotiating for better working conditions. You now have the choice. Either you raise your bottom line (to include both a secretary and an extra week's holiday) or you set conditions which make the negotiated agreement as advantageous to you as possible.

The more numerous, varied and attractive your alternatives are, the greater will be your bargaining power, however strong the other party may be.

4. What Is the Worst That Can Happen if No Agreement Is Reached?

This is nothing more or less than another way to develop alternatives, which are powerful levers to use during negotiations. Think about what you would do if the negotiations were a disaster and you couldn't reach a conclusion. You will sometimes have to face this possibility in order to find really creative solutions. It's a fact that once we find ourselves with our backs to the wall, we are often able to find the energy to climb over it.

If there is anything else you can do, don't forget it during the course of your negotiations and remember, **it's better not to negotiate at all than to come to a badly negotiated agreement.**

We sometimes hesitate to consider the worst, imagining that it might lead to a defeatist attitude. Some people even consider it negative thinking. But it is important always to evaluate all the possible alternatives, including the worst of them. In so doing, you avoid unpleasant surprises. Positive thinking does not exclude being realistic!

Setting Out Your Objectives

A hierarchy of objectives

Place your objectives on a scale, as below:

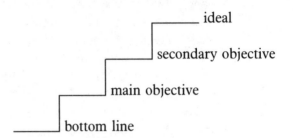

ideal

secondary objective

main objective

bottom line

The higher you go on the scale, the more your objectives become exchangeable. In real negotiations certain objectives will have to be sacrificed by both parties. If you are well prepared you will have determined in advance which objectives you're willing to sacrifice, and in exchange for what. In other words, you know how much each objective is worth to you, not forgetting that the other party will also have a scale of objectives.

Your post-negotiating report ought to read something like this:

Ideal: Next time

Main objective: Achieved

Secondary objective: Sacrificed for main objective

Bottom line: Achieved

Evaluating Your Objectives

How do you determine the value of each of your objectives? Here's a method you can use. Ask yourself the following questions in order to justify each of your objectives:

- Why is this objective important?
- How much do I think it's worth?
- Can I give it a pound value?

- Are there any other objectives which are just as useful? (What are my alternatives?)

During negotiations you will manœuvre between the boundaries of your ideal objectives and your bottom line – and between the boundaries of your opposition's ideal objectives and bottom line.

Get your objectives down on paper

For important negotiations write your objectives down, being sure to include your ideal objectives. In this way, you automatically set your standards high, giving you the psychological advantage of appearing to be confident of your position, especially if you've managed accurately to anticipate the other party's desires, and have come up with creative proposals whereby you can *both* get what you want.

For example, evaluating the objectives in a divorce situation could result in written notes like these.

Objective 1: I want to negotiate a satisfactory settlement out of court, both for my ex-wife's benefit and for my own.

Objective 2: We will part on good terms and avoid destroying what we've built up over the last 20 years.

Objective 3: We will not involve the children in our disputes. We will act like responsible adults.

**Arrange your objectives in order of importance.
But remember, your objectives may be of equal importance.**

Keep Your Objectives Flexible

It is important to keep your objectives flexible for the following reasons.

- As we've seen, your objectives and interests are not always the same. So it's important to be able to 'let go', if what is being proposed is in fact more advantageous than the objectives you've set for yourself.

- Some options or alternatives put forward could be equally as attractive as the objectives you have established for yourself.

- If you stick rigidly to your objectives, you risk limiting yourself to a sterile, unproductive position, especially if the other party does the same. When both parties remain stuck to their respective positions, the negotiations are usually very painful and ultimately fruitless.

You should *establish* your objectives without *attaching* yourself to them.

Instead of saying, 'I want this and that and that . . .', you should say something along the lines of 'I'd like to come to some agreement whereby I'd obtain this and that in some substantial quantity . . .'.

A good way to avoid getting stuck in one position is to determine in advance the different options that could interest you, and the options you could propose to the other party as compensation.

For important negotiations, write your objectives down.
Arrange them in order of importance.
Keep your objectives flexible:
don't get stuck in an overly rigid position.

How to Find Alternatives

Alternatives or options are the different ways you can attain your objectives and the different methods you can use.

The advantage of always keeping alternatives in mind is that you have a better chance of seizing the initiative and bringing the ball into the negotiating court. It is important to have evaluated how much each option you add to your 'package' (i.e. the groups of options which could prove viable) is worth to you, and how much each option over and above those offered by the other party, will cost you.

For example, a car salesman may offer you an option such as a rear windscreen wiper in order to make the sale. He will get the piece at cost price and will have to pay his mechanic for a few minutes' installation time. But he knows that this detail might be what tips the scale in favour of you buying his car in preference to someone else's. The key phrase to remember concerning options is: 'What would you say if . . .'.

Reorganize your interests and those of the other party

The secret of success in a large number of negotiations consists of redefining and reorganizing your interests and those of the other party. To do this you have to come up with one, or better still a number of, proposals which take into account your own interests and those of the other party. Experience shows that agreements like these are the most likely to be ratified and to prove viable.

During the preparation stage, it is sensible to work out several different 'packages'. Then when you are face to face with your opponent at the negotiating table you can:

- offer a number of options which are likely to interest the other party;
- define the options you are interested in obtaining in exchange for each of your packages.

This supposes that:

- you have identified the interests of the other party;
- you have done the groundwork of evaluating the different possible options; and
- you've done your preparation work with care!

Evaluate your options

Follow the example of Chinese restaurants who offer complete ready-made menus, and do the same yourself by putting together ready-made packages, so that you know what to ask in exchange.

When you are concerned with buying or selling only, where each of the opposing parties is looking to make the most money, this evaluation of all the options is not very difficult to calculate, but as soon as you start dealing with slightly more complex situations, like business or industrial relations, it becomes more difficult to assess.

For example, what value would you place on:

- an extra week's holiday?
- an assistant to help you with your work?
- the opportunity to negotiate with seasoned experts?
- peace of mind, or the feeling that you've done your duty?

Obviously such values are subjective, and depend on the individual concerned and on the situation to which they are related. Here is a method which you can use to evaluate any given set of options.

1. List the options open to you, noting the pros and cons of each one.

2. Now you have to compare apples with oranges. In other words, you have to assign a numerical value to each of your listed advantages and disadvantages. Work with a scale of -5 to $+5$ representing the following:

$$
\begin{array}{ll}
-5 & \text{very bad, to be avoided at all costs} \\
-4 & \text{very inconvenient} \\
-3 & \text{inconvenient}
\end{array}
$$

−2	slightly inconvenient
−1	very slightly inconvenient
0	neutral, neither positive nor negative
+1	very slightly advantageous
+2	slightly advantageous
+3	advantageous
+4	very advantageous
+5	extremely advantageous

Option A

Advantages   **Scores**

1. _____   + _____

2. _____   + _____

3. _____   + _____

4. _____   + _____

5. _____   + _____

Disadvantages

1. _____   − _____

2. _____   − _____

3. _____   − _____

4. _____   − _____

5. _____   − _____

                                                           Total   _____

Option B

Advantages   **Scores**

1. _____   + _____

2. _____   + _____

3. _____   + _____

4. _____   + _____

5. _____   + _____

Disadvantages

1. _____   − _____

2. _____   − _____

3. _____   − _____

4. _____   − _____

5. _____   − _____

                                                        Total _____

The procedure of isolating the different components and giving each of them a numerical evaluation should allow you to reach an overall positive or negative figure for each option, but there are two rules you must follow for this method to work:

- you must correctly identify the respective advantages and disadvantages;
- the values you assign to them must correspond to your real feelings.

When you work out your final tally, stop and take a few minutes to consider: does it correspond to what you *really* feel? It should do, since this method is designed to provide you with a methodical way of arriving at a decision. But you must remember that there can be no infallible scientific or mathematical method to guarantee the validity of your choice.

The two-column system

A simpler way of evaluating the merits of one option against another consists of setting up two columns for each option, one for advantages and the other for disadvantages.

Option A

Advantages	Disadvantages
+ _____	− _____
+ _____	− _____
+ _____	− _____
+ _____	− _____
+ _____	− _____

Option B

Advantages	Disadvantages
+ _____	− _____
+ _____	− _____
+ _____	− _____
+ _____	− _____
+ _____	− _____

Using this system you get a clear view of the pros and cons of each option and you can not only focus on the simple objectives, but also on your interests as well. In this way you have to study all the aspects of a question separately.

But there's more to it than this, of course. After all, you don't negotiate with yourself. It is very important to take the other party into consideration during the course of your preparations and look at each option from the other party's point of view as well as from your own.

CHAPTER **7**

Finding Out About the Other Party

Playing Detective

Any detective looking for a murderer or seeking to solve a crime always starts by looking for the *motive*. Who stood to gain the most from killing the wealthy heir? And it's just as important to the art of effective negotiation. You need to understand the motivation of your opponent – in other words, what makes the person you're dealing with want something? This is what you use to help you predict and plan your strategy.

If you are not aware of their motives, how are you going to predict the strategy and tactics of the persons you're negotiating with?

Identifying their interests

In order to identify the interests of the other party, ask yourself the following questions:

1. What would I want to obtain from this situation if I were in the other party's shoes?

2. Why would I want to obtain this?

3. How would I want to obtain it?

4. When?

5. In which manner?

These questions allow you to begin determining the interests of the other party. It's not always easy to put yourself in someone else's shoes, but you do have some clues to work with.

Discovering the other party's interests and not confining yourself to their objectives only, presents you with the following advantages:

1. You will often be able to identify interests which are common to both parties, even where they seem to hold positions diametrically opposed to yours. This means that negotiations could take an entirely different course than if you simply confronted each other with your respective positions; then

2. you can find solutions which correspond to the interests of both parties; and further,

3. during discussions, you can refer to these common interests and add more weight to your own arguments.

Interests and motives are not always easily identifiable, so, during negotiations, it is most important always to keep your eyes – and mind – open for clues which can help you evaluate whether or not you're on the right track.

Identifying their objectives

When you think you've identified the interests of the other party, move on to the objectives. They may sometimes be obvious, but when they're not you can get some idea of these objectives by proceeding in a methodical manner.

A good way of discerning the objectives of the people you're dealing with is to ask yourself the following question: 'Why don't they want to give me what I'm asking for?' Of course, they do not want to give you what you're asking for because whatever it is runs counter to one or a number of their objectives. In this way you can more easily identify what they are.

What you should be doing is to follow the example of police investigators looking for a criminal and build up a composite portrait of your opponent. The best way to do this is to put yourself in the other party's place. Imagine that your demands are being asked of you, by answering the following questions as if you were in the other person's shoes.

Questions to ask yourself
Imagine first that you would accept the demands that are being made (your own) and ask yourself these questions:

1. Would it mean a gain or loss in prestige for me?

2. Would it be financially advantageous?

3. Would it result in praise or blame from my colleagues?

4. Does accepting the demand run counter to my principles?

5. What would the short-term consequences be?

6. What would the long-term consequences be?

7. Are there are precedents which indicate that I should not agree to the demand?

8. Could I take some more time before making a final decision without harming my position?

We deliberately go beyond the simple question of money because we are trying to find the other motives that the people you're dealing with might have, and other ways you may find of fulfilling them.

Why? Because if you identify them correctly, it will cost you a lot less to convince them! Remember the 2.5 per cent we mentioned on page 12? Imagine if you managed to increase the margin of profit in your negotiations by that much over the coming year...

As for negotiations which centre on things other than money, responding properly to these sensitive questions will be worth as much, if not more than 2.5 per cent to you. The set of answers – hypothetical though they may be – you apply to these questions will help you form a composite portrait of the interests of the person(s) you're dealing with. You will then be able to identify their needs more accurately.

What is the other party's bottom line?

Some negotiators expend a lot of energy on trying to sound out the other party in order to establish their bottom line. Why is this?

Because if you know the other party's minimum requirements you obviously have the advantage of being aware of the field in which they have to manœuvre, and just what they are prepared to give up. You also know in advance whether or not the offer you're making more or less corresponds to their bottom line. In other words, how far can you push them before they will break off negotiations altogether?

Once you have identified the other party's objectives and bottom line, organize them into a list as follows:

---

1. Other party's main objective:

2. Secondary objective:

3. Subsidiary objectives:

4. Bottom line:

The bottom line is of prime importance: when the other party formulates their demands, will you know which ones are only included as small change?

For example, conditions such as a maximum 30-day delivery for 80 per cent of the merchandise, and a three-month extension on payment might be proposed by your buyer. But really the other party might be willing to accept 60 per cent of the delivery within 30 days, if a slightly longer time were allowed for payment. In other words, do they really need the merchandise to supply their clients, and so be likely to agree to pay more quickly, or could they afford to wait for delivery and maintain a better cash flow?

You can answer this and similar questions by taking the time to get as well informed as you can about the situation. In so doing, you may discover that, by some unexpected set of circumstances, you are the only one who can supply a certain essential commodity and their most important client has given them 30 days to deliver the product or he'll look elsewhere.

This places you in a position to negotiate for much more advantageous conditions, or to refuse an offer where the price you're asking is not met.

Make an in-depth study of the other party's position

There are a number of other questions you can ask that will help you to clarify the other party's position.

1. *If I were in the other party's place, what would I do to attain my objectives?* What are their needs and basic problems, and how can I help solve them? In other words, what strategies are they likely to use? Are they known to resort to certain particular methods? Some people use the same strategy over and over again, and you have to know about it to be able to counter it with ease!

2. *What are their alternatives in the event that we cannot reach an agreement?* The same question applies to you: it is essential to evaluate all the possible responses to this question, as this is as much of a powerful bargaining point for the other party as it is for you.

   An accurate response may depend on your knowledge of the market: what other similar products are available, at what price and under what conditions?

3. *What is the worst that can happen to the other party if no agreement is reached?*

This is another question which can help you to determine the other party's bottom line and could put you into a strong position.

4. *What's the best thing that can happen to the other party if we cannot reach an agreement?*
Yet another alternative – with luck on their side, does the other party have any other possibilities?

5. *In the other party's place, what arguments would convince me to change my mind?*
By once again putting yourself in the other party's shoes, you try to discover the options that are open to them.

The composite portrait you are building up is only concerned with the other party's interests, and not at all with the kind of person they really are. However, if you do this preparatory work with care, you will be able to obtain an overall picture of the needs, interests and objectives of the person with whom you have to deal. But remember that your portrait is composed of points of reference rather than scientific data.

The aim of these questions will not only help you see things from the other party's point of view, but also serve to direct your thinking towards finding fruitful solutions.

So much for the motives, interests and objectives of the other party. You now need to examine the organization your other party represents.

Confidential Information About Their Organization

Do you know what kind of enterprise the person you're preparing to negotiate with works for? Are you aware of its preferences, its 'personality' and its characteristics?

No? Well, you should be, because this information can be very useful. Your preparations should be based not only on the interests and objectives of the person with whom you will be negotiating, but also of the organization for which he or she works or which he or she represents. It is extremely useful to have some idea of the working environment in which your opponent's ideas have evolved.

1. What style of negotiation is favoured by the company?

Most large companies generally promote a style of negotiation which they deem effective. They base their policies on their past experience, and devise strategies appropriate to their specific sector and their unique set of conditions. In many cases, professional negotiators are hired by these companies as advisers.

The American multi-national Pepsi, for example, prefers to work from a positive viewpoint, favouring amenable agreements acceptable to both negotiating partners: this results in long-term business relations, which they consider to be more profitable.

If you were going to negotiate with a company with this kind of reputation, what kind of negotiating strategy would you tend to apply? Naturally, you'd do better to adopt a co-operative approach to the negotiations, rather than assuming a position which is highly competitive and aggressive.

Small and medium-sized businesses usually have their own favoured approach to negotiations as well. The difference is that the methods they use are usually formed directly by the president of the company him- or herself, or by his or her vice-president. Generally those persons delegated to negotiate tend to stick to the negotiating style adopted by their bosses.

2. What are the working conditions like?

One way to get some idea of the general negotiating strategies of a company is to gather information about its prevailing working conditions. These can furnish you with clues about the company's outlook and mentality. The same attitudes that are brought to bear when dealing with employees can often be detached in negotiations with other businesses.

Competitive or co-operative negotiations?
A company whose relations with its employees are dictated in the form of decrees and where the employees themselves have little say in the decision-making process, in other words a company that operates from an authoritarian standpoint, will be more likely to favour a competitive negotiating atmosphere.

On the other hand, a company that favours consultation and delegating tasks, where communication between management and employees is encouraged, and which emphasizes team-spirit and friendship, would, in principle, be more likely to prefer co-operative negotiations.

But always remember that these are just indicators and not infallible rules. The company could, of course, operate with double standards, and approach their internal negotiations in a completely different way than when negotiating with someone from outside the organization.

But generally a company that encourages consultation and employee autonomy, that negotiates instead of decreeing its policies, can almost always be assumed to favour a co-operative approach to negotiation.

If you're negotiating with another department in your own company, you can adapt this procedure by asking yourself how the head of the department would react.

3. How have negotiations been settled in the past?

Knowing how negotiations have been concluded in the past allows you to anticipate the kind of reactions you may get during the course of the current negotiations.

Say you work for a company manufacturing beauty products. You contact a new distributor with the aim of tapping into a new market. But you find out that this distributor systematically refuses to give his partners more than 43 per cent of his revenues and it is impossible to get him to budge on this point. His reputation is firmly established around it, and he will stick to it tenaciously, since breaking it would mean setting a precedent whereby he would be flooded with similar demands from his other partners. It would be a waste of time to argue this point.

Forewarned with this information, how, then, could you reach an agreement which is advantageous to you?

Obviously, you'd be better off looking for concessions in other areas (payment arrangements, delivery deadlines, etc.).

4. What style of negotiation does the person I'm dealing with prefer?

As we've seen, each company has its own general preferences. But what about the actual person you'll be dealing with? One negotiator may play it safe and stick to a basic strategy, while another will adjust to the circumstances. Yet another person may be very creative, and change his or her approach for each new negotiation. Some people are highly competitive, while others prefer an atmosphere which is more open to exchange. Some stick to rigid policies, while others favour business partnerships which are advantageous to both parties.

You should therefore try to determine the personality of the person you'll be facing: is he or she ambitious, enthusiastic, highly partisan, uncompromising? Is he or she likely to co-operate when presented with a reasonable offer which is beneficial to both parties?

Suppose you're dealing with two persons, one of whom has a reputation for being intractable, while the other has more of an open, conciliatory attitude: the chances are you could apply the 'good and evil' tactic with success (see Chapter 8).

Find Out About Their Professional Standing

What standing does the person you're dealing with have in his or her own company? Ask yourself this question *before* negotiating – afterwards may be too late.

1. What powers does he or she have?

You should ask yourself the following questions about the person you'll be dealing with before negotiations start.

---

1. Can he/she make a final decision?

2. Is he/she skilled at taking the initiative?

3. What is the scope of his/her responsibilities?

4. If he/she has limited powers, what are the limits?

It is vital to get precise answers to these questions. Imagine spending a lot of time negotiating with someone, and finally getting to the point of concluding a formal agreement. You feel you are on the verge of an understanding, when the other person says, 'I'll have to get permission from my superiors.' There's nothing more frustrating!

Referring to a person who is absent may be a tactic used to gain time. The time gained could be used to look for a more competitive offer, for example, or to bring the deadline closer and thus weaken your position. Here the person who can actually make the decision is allegedly absent, and so the delicate question must be put off. In cases where you are negotiating with a person (or persons) delegated by a small or medium-sized business, this information is all the more important: be sure to verify that the position of the person you'll be talking to actually covers the area of negotiation.

Do everything you can to ensure that you deal directly with the person who can actually make the final decision. Often responsibilities are clearly defined: one person can make decisions on questions where the sum involved is less than £20,000, while another may have jurisdiction up to £100,000.

Just suppose you are dealing with someone, and everything points to the fact that it's not that person who is authorized to make a decision, but it is in fact his immediate superior. What do you do?

You could try broaching the subject like this: 'If we do manage to agree on my proposals, are there any other persons who would have to participate in making the final decision?'

The important thing is to find a way to state the question without arousing anyone's anger or hurting their pride.

Suppose he answers in the affirmative: yes, his boss has to take part in the final decision-making process. From this you understand that it's the signature of the boss that you need. Now what do you do?

You should ask politely to meet the boss. You could phrase it something like this: *'Well, in that case, do you think he'd have any objection to meeting me after I've outlined my proposals to you?'*

By doing this you get some notion of the person who has the final say in the matter, and vice versa. You're not just a name attached to a written proposal, you have a face, and you are associated with whatever impression you make.

You should always be tactful because most people have a horror of someone going over their head and talking directly to their superior. And, if you phrase the suggestion to show that you just want a simple, informal meeting, simply a handshake and a few polite words, then you can act openly and inspire confidence. Most people, unless they are extremely insecure, will have no objection to your meeting the person who is to make the final decision.

2. Who else has to be consulted?

In negotiations there are often other persons whose views have to be taken into account, and who may have some word on the final decision or on the various conditions proposed during the course of the negotiations. Think about and name those persons who were likely to have had something to say in the last negotiations in which you were involved, or in those you are preparing to undertake.

Here is a list of persons with whom you may eventually have to consult, or who the person you're negotiating with will have to consult before making a final decision. Obviously, we can't hope to cover all the circumstances you may encounter. The most important thing is to become aware of the probability that the person you're dealing with will have to consult someone else.

1. The president of the company ☐

2. The director of the department in question ☐

3. The treasurer, or head of accounting ☐

4. An important shareholder, or a body of shareholders ☐

5. A business partner ☐

6. The head of a specific project ☐

7. The foreman ☐

8. The personnel director ☐

9. The tax accountant ☐

10. Employees who will be directly affected by an eventual decision ☐

11. The secretary, especially an executive secretary ☐

12. The spouse (or even the children, in some cases) of a buyer ☐

13. A close friend or relative ☐

It is not always the case that these people will make the final decision, but they can, in some cases, tip the scales one way or another.

And if the person you're dealing with asks for someone else's advice, that outside opinion may make the difference between your proposal being accepted or rejected. Take the case of the secretary, for example. It's important to do everything you can to be tactful and polite towards the secretaries of the persons you are dealing with. An executive secretary can be an important source of information, not that you'd ask her to disclose anything confidential. But after all, there's nothing to prevent her from making a few suggestions, is there? And she is in an excellent position to provide information of a personal nature about the person or persons with whom you'll be negotiating.

However, you must keep in mind that such information can only act as a guide. Remember, too, that the more important the negotiations in which you're involved, the more it is in your interest to know about the parties involved.

3. What are the other party's sensitive points?

We all have them: personal complexes, physical defects, conflicting personalities, etc. If you can, obtain clues about such idiosyncrasies, about who the person facing you really is, what makes him or her tick, how he or she is likely to react. Then you'll know better how to deal with them.

It's up to you to build a file on the individual characteristics of the persons with whom you negotiate. Its accuracy and comprehensiveness will depend largely on your own intuition, and on the indiscretions of the other party's colleagues.

4. Weak points?

Weak points to look for include a chronic deficiency or recurring fault in the organization, an inability to meet deadlines, for example. Or it may be a lack of preparation in negotiations!

The other party may have a reputation for being very competitive, so you could decide to delegate a woman to negotiate with him, since she might manage to negotiate a more advantageous agreement. Another person may be more open to the influence of a grey-haired father figure.

Obviously you can't always delegate someone to take your place, or disguise yourself to please the other party. But this kind of information can be useful, especially if you're negotiating as part of a team, and you know that the other party has a preference for dealing with a certain type of person. You would then assign the roles accordingly.

You should also consider the standing of the person in his or her organization: perhaps they have failed to reach an important agreement recently because they were too demanding or said something inappropriate. Knowing this, you can assume that they won't want to mess things up a second time. Don't think that this is the right moment to abuse the situation; many people will not hesitate to cancel 10 deals in a row if they think the offers are not advantageous. On the other hand, if you offer a package which isn't especially attractive, the other party may accept it just to give the impression that he or she is not continuously wasting his or her and the company's time, and in order to rebuild his or her image within the company hierarchy.

5. What about the company itself?

Companies have their own weak points. They possess a personality, just like people, with a particular way of thinking and set of faults.

So, how can you identify these weak points? Once again the answer lies in obtaining as much information as possible. Seek out the people most likely to be able to provide you with information and get them to talk, about anything, the weather, their personal lives and so on. Inevitably they will let something slip that could be useful to you. But always be discreet, and don't let on that you're trying to extract information and turn someone into an informer.

6. Did the other party succeed last time?

We can learn a lot from other people's failures. It is in your interests to know what happened when the other party failed, why the person in question met with failure, what strategies he or she used, what proposals and counter-proposals were made, the degree of flexibility he or she showed, etc.

Of course, this information is often kept secret. However, by keeping your eyes and ears open, you can learn a lot.

Some negotiators have no qualms about explaining either why a deal they were involved with fell through or was concluded successfully. Such people are generally confident of their talents, and do not fear outside scrutiny or judgement. In some cases, they may even use this openness as a strategy to influence the course of current negotiations.

7. Past litigation

Find out about past ligitation in which the company, or the person representing the company, has been involved, and the outcome. Litigation is a very particular kind of negotiation and can sometimes be very revealing.

8. The habits of the other party

What restaurants does the other party frequent? Does he or she belong to a club? Does he or she take part in any special activities (environmental protection groups, sports, charities, etc)? All this information can be very useful.

Political preferences can also, to some degree, help you to predict the negotiating style the other party is likely to adopt, but as a general rule this is a subject that should be avoided during negotiations. There are enough points on which to disagree without getting into politics...

9. General profile

To form a more precise picture of the person you'll be dealing with you should try to discover as much as possible about their background and personality. Try to answer the questions posed on page 80.

Profile of the Other Party

1. How long has the other party had his or her job?

2. What kind of education has he or she had?

3. What is his or her tax bracket?

4. What is his or her professional record? Note successes, failures, companies worked for.

5. Which part of town does he or she live in?

6. Does he or she own or rent his or her house?

7. What is his or her family status?

8. What are his or her habits and tastes? Include hobbies, car, food/restaurant preferences, holidays.

9. What are his or her needs according to the Maslow scale? See page 83.

10. What sort of relationship does he or she enjoy with others? Is he competitive, co-operative, dominating, etc?

11. Does he or she enjoy negotiating, or would he or she be happier doing something else?

12. Is he or she the sort of person who is likely to go for a quick, easy solution or would they be happier arguing every point in great detail?

When you've tackled as many of these questions as you can, use the information you've gathered to form a portrait, to get some idea of the flesh-and-blood person you'll be dealing with. Doing this can help you to avoid unpleasant surprises.

And remember that the more important the negotiations, the more in-depth your preparations and information gathering should be.

Learn to seduce

A seductive offer is by definition an attractive one. This means that if you are aware of what the desires of the other party are, and you are in a position to at least partially fulfil them, then you have a considerable amount of bargaining power.

Think about why Americans pay two or three times the price of a Japanese car to buy a Mercedes or a BMW, even though the difference in quality is not justified by the difference in price.

It's because they don't just want to get from one place to another (need), they want to be seen in a particular car and not in another (desire). If you are able to come up with a proposal that, for one reason or another, stimulates the desires of the other party, then you will often be able to achieve important concessions in other areas. In other words you'll be able to draw up made-to-measure negotiations.

Made-to-Measure Negotiations

Think about the person you'll be negotiating with: can you say what makes this person different from anyone else? Also ask yourself this question: How can I satisfy this person better than anyone else?

By proceeding in this way, you should do everything possible to adjust your proposals so that they meet the specific needs of the person across the table.

This doesn't mean that you can best satisfy all the other party's desires. But at least you'll know what *you* can deliver that someone else can't. And you'll be in a position to emphasize those aspects which have an extra attraction for the person in question. This can be very useful, since in many situations all it takes is one little supplementary factor to tip the scales in your favour.

Perhaps the same arguments would leave the next person cold. It doesn't matter. What counts is to hit on something that sparks that person's interest at that moment. And to do this, you need to know what that person's needs are.

Satisfy the other party's hidden needs

A highly regarded executive with a company in the process of expanding asks for a pay rise. Since cash flow is critical and the company does not wish to set a precedent by giving in to the demand for more money, the request is refused. A conflict is imminent. It turns out that the executive needs the rise to buy a new car. When the head of accounting discovers this, the executive is offered a company car instead of a rise. It works out cheaper for the company, and the executive is perfectly satisfied with the arrangement.

When negotiating, many people make the mistake of concentrating only or mainly on themselves. This is what's going on in their minds:

- 'What do *I* want?'
- 'How am *I* going to get what I want?'
- 'What will *I* have to give up in exchange?'

Many people ask themselves these questions when they negotiate. Maybe you're one of them! If so, that's fine, because you have to ask these questions.

But don't stop there!

It should be added that to think this way – 'What can I do so that I won't have to give up anything?' – can lead only to deception, because this ignores one of the fundamental rules of negotiation:

You get nothing for nothing.

Expect to make an exchange!

Assuming that in all probability you will have to give up something in exchange for obtaining something you want, what is the most advantageous thing to do? The answer is to define what you are going to give up yourself, and what you will exchange it for.

As we've already seen, once you've established your objectives, the second step consists of determining what the other party wants, and this must be worked out just as assiduously. When you are aware of the ambitions and objectives of the person you're dealing with:

- you avoid unpleasant surprises like, 'I never would have believed he'd want something like that!';

- you can much more easily predict what type of negotiating strategies the other party will use;

- you can develop attractive options and packages tailored for the other party, emphasizing those aspects which are likely to arouse their interest just that extra little bit that counts;

- you will be more adept at reacting to their perception of the situation, and getting them to appreciate the advantages of your proposals.

If you are able to detach yourself from your own point of view for a moment, and put yourself in the other person's shoes, this is a very useful exercise. Someone who can think for both sides has a decided advantage in a negotiating situation: he or she is not concerned only with his or her own perspective, but also explores things from the other party's point of view, and sees twice as far, so to speak.

So, what does the other party want? Money? Happiness?

Of course they do, just like everyone else! But more precisely, what is it that would satisfy them in this negotiation? If you know that, you possess much greater power.

A scale of universal needs

Aside from knowing about the other party's financial needs, there are other factors to be aware of that can work to your advantage. Let's take a look at the scale of human needs developed by the American psychologist Abraham Maslow.

As you will see when you examine the scale, the so-called 'basic needs' are by no means the only human needs, although they do occupy an important place on it. It begins with the basics and builds to include needs which are more psychological in nature.

Ideally, you should be able to identify which needs provide the strongest source of motivation to the person you're dealing with, apart from the financial ones, and this may give you an advantage over one of your competitors.

Now put the person you're negotiating with on Maslow's scale, below.

And put yourself on the scale (by comparing yourself with the people you know and asking yourself which of the four non-essential needs is most important to you.

Maslow's Scale

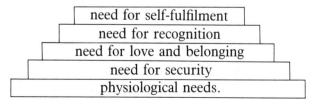

need for self-fulfilment
need for recognition
need for love and belonging
need for security
physiological needs.

Circle the relevant position on the scale for each category of needs.

My needs

1. Physical survival	Weak	Strong
2. Security	Weak	Strong
3. Belonging	Weak	Strong
4. Esteem and recognition	Weak	Strong
5. Self-fulfilment	Weak	Strong

Needs of the person I'm negotiating with

1. Physical survival	Weak	Strong
2. Security	Weak	Strong
3. Belonging	Weak	Strong
4. Esteem and recognition	Weak	Strong
5. Self-fulfilment	Weak	Strong

When you have worked out where the person you're negotiating with is situated on the scale of needs, you can then adapt your proposals and the way you formulate them to suit those needs and make them attractive.

How to adapt your proposals

In order to adjust your proposals and arguments differently, to suit the type of person you're dealing with, take a closer look at the characteristics of each category of Maslow's scale and the kinds of arguments that are likely to influence them.

1. Physical survival

Persons you meet in the context of everyday negotiations are not motivated by this need!

2. Security

Such a person is mainly preoccupied with attaining his objectives.
Arguments: A negotiator who has identified this as the predominant need of the person he or she is dealing with should emphasize the security of an investment, for example, or that the option is sure to generate profits, or that the machine in question is guaranteed not to break down, etc.

3. Need to belong

This person seeks union with others, concretely or symbolically, and needs to feel part of a group.
Arguments: You should sell the area as much as the house itself, the club as much as the services it offers, etc. An astute negotiator would explain that the product in question is highly regarded, and sought after by such and such clientele. In other words do what salespersons are doing when they go on about how much an item is in fashion. Beware that if your buyer falls into the fifth category (self-fulfilment), you will simply be putting your foot into your mouth!

4. Need for recognition

This person cares what others think about him or her, and seeks others' approval.
Arguments: The astute negotiator will emphasize anything that may serve to improve the status of the other person or of his or her organization, and ideally of both at the same time, such as good publicity, positive exposure, etc.

5. Need for self-fulfilment

This person is looking for an original angle, and is open to innovative suggestions.
Arguments: Here the negotiator should underline the originality of his or her approach to the negotiations in question – the fact that what he or she is proposing has never been done before, that no one else has dared to undertake a similar venture and so on.

A game where both players win

A last point on the subject: you don't necessarily lose out if the person you're negotiating with wins. There are many cases where, thanks to a skilful exchange, both parties come out as winners.

It's time to throw out, or at least modify, the old, traditional view – and a false view at that – of winners and losers in negotiations. This perception does not necessarily correspond to reality and, more importantly, does not necessarily correspond to your interests.

You can give the person you're negotiating with a minimum of benefits without spending a penny from your own pocket. For example, you may satisfy some of their needs as expressed on the Maslow scale – perhaps the need to belong.

Who has the Upper Hand?

Use this checklist to work out how you and the other party stand in relation to each other, and to assess the division of power.

1. Is one of the parties able to impose a certain type of behaviour upon the other?

Us ☐   Them ☐   About the same ☐

2. Does one of the parties exercise a control upon a resource sought by the other party?

Us ☐   Them ☐   Neither ☐

3. Is one of the parties in a position of legitimacy (in law or because of a precedent, for example)?

Us ☐   Them ☐   About the same ☐

4. Is one of the parties in a position to help the other?

Us ☐   Them ☐   About the same ☐

Checklist continues ▶

---

5. Is one of the parties in a position to do harm to the other?

Us ☐   Them ☐   About the same ☐

6. Which party needs the negotiations more?

Us ☐   Them ☐   About the same ☐

7. Which party has more options or alternatives?

Us ☐   Them ☐   About the same ☐

8. Which party would you say is the richer, and the more fortunate in general?

Us ☐   Them ☐   About the same ☐

9. Whatever the outcome, would you say that it makes a great difference to your specific situation?

Yes ☐   No ☐

10. Which party has invested the most in the negotiations in terms of money, time and human resources?

Money	Us ☐	Them ☐
Time	Us ☐	Them ☐
PR	Us ☐	Them ☐
Human resources	Us ☐	Them ☐
Other	Us ☐	Them ☐

11. In the light of the above, proportionately, which of the two parties would you say has invested the most?

Us ☐   Them ☐   About the same ☐

Checklist continues ▶

12. Which party would you say attaches the most importance to the current negotiations?

Us ☐   Them ☐   About the same ☐

13. Which party would you say has the most cash available?

Us ☐   Them ☐   About the same ☐

Would you say that this makes a great difference to the situation?

14. Which party has the most personnel available?

Us ☐   Them ☐   About the same ☐

Would you say that this makes a great difference to the situation?

15. If you negotiate in teams, which has the best internal consensus regarding its objectives?

Us ☐   Them ☐   About the same ☐

16. Which party would you say has the best technological infrastructure available?

Us ☐   Them ☐   About the same ☐

17. Which party has the best expertise available?

Us ☐   Them ☐   About the same ☐

Would you say that this makes a great difference to the situation?

18. In the current negotiation, which do you think are the most important sources of information:

Technical facts/information

Checklist continues ▶

In terms of the market
In terms of negotiation
In terms of legal and financial knowledge
Others (specify)

19. Which party has more information available in the following areas:

In terms of technical know-how

Us ☐   Them ☐   About the same ☐

In terms of the market

Us ☐   Them ☐   About the same ☐

In terms of negotiation

Us ☐   Them ☐   About the same ☐

In terms of legal and financial knowledge

Us ☐   Them ☐   About the same ☐

20. In the light of your responses, which party has the best information available?

Us ☐   Them ☐   About the same ☐

Does this make a great difference in your particular situation?

21. Which party has the most experience in this type of negotiation?

Us ☐   Them ☐   About the same ☐

Does this make a great difference in your particular situation?

Checklist continues ▶

22. Which party has the most know-how (technical or otherwise) available?

Us ☐   Them ☐   About the same ☐

Does this make a great difference in these particular negotiations?

23. Which party enjoys the best political support?

Us ☐   Them ☐   About the same ☐

Does this make a great difference in these particular negotiations?

24. Which party carries the most weight in the community?

Us ☐   Them ☐   About the same ☐

Does this make a great difference in these particular negotiations?

25. Which party dedicates the most energy to the negotiations?

Us ☐   Them ☐   About the same ☐

Does this make a great difference in these particular negotiations?

26. Which party attaches the most importance to the current negotiations?

Us ☐   Them ☐   About the same ☐

27. Which party is the better prepared?

Us ☐   Them ☐   About the same ☐

Does this make a great difference in these particular negotiations?

Checklist continues ▶

28. Which party has the most influential business partners?

Us ☐   Them ☐   About the same ☐

Does this make a great difference in these particular negotiations?

29. Between the other party and you, which would you say has the best public image, or inspires the most respect?

Us ☐   Them ☐   About the same ☐

Does this make a great difference in these particular negotiations?

30. Which party would you say carries the most weight with the media?

Us ☐   Them ☐   About the same ☐

Does this make a great difference in these particular negotiations?

31. Which party shows the most creativity in its approach to the negotiations?

Us ☐   Them ☐   About the same ☐

Would you say that this makes a great difference in these particular negotiations?

32. In your opinion, which party has most need of the other?

Us ☐   Them ☐   About the same ☐

Would you say that this makes a great difference in these particular negotiations?

Checklist continues ▶

33. In your opinion, which party has the most attractive alternative available?

Us ☐   Them ☐   About the same ☐

Would you say that this makes a great difference in these particular negotiations?

34. In your opinion which party has the most attractive alternative available?

Us ☐   Them ☐   About the same ☐

Would you say that this makes a great difference in these particular negotiations?

Name the other sources of power that the other party has at its disposal:

Name the other sources of power that you have available:

Draw up a list of your principal sources of power in these negotiations:

Checklist continues ▶

When adding up the total, do not count the questions where you answered that you felt it made no difference in these particular negotiations.

Total Us _____   Them _____   About the same _____

Note that this is still just a checklist, and not a test. This checklist is designed to enable you to evaluate the situation, and to give you an idea of your power quotient. It should help you to review the different variables which might well affect the negotiations.

To enable you to keep certain factors, such as greater capital or more influence over the media, in proportion, we have added the supplementary question: 'Would you say that this makes a great difference in these particular negotiations?'

In certain situations, the fact that the other party has more power need not necessarily pose a problem. For example, if you control the rights to an invention which interests a big Japanese company, the fact that this company has more cash at its disposal than you certainly does not pose a problem. In this case, your comparative lack of cash could be a distinct advantage!

Further, if you run a small estate agency and you are solidly established in your area, it is possible that the financial support that a large competitor enjoys will be of no help to him.

Infallible sources of power

Certain factors almost always generate some power, whatever the circumstances. These are as follows:

● the fact that you have more information on the subject;
● the fact that you have more experience in this type of negotiation;
● the fact that you are better prepared;
● the fact that you show more creativity;
● the fact that you have an appealing alternative.

A sixth factor could be added – the fact that you are prepared to act unscrupulously – but this is not always guaranteed to give you power. In the long term, you will actually find that it's a handicap!

CHAPTER 8

Different Ways to Negotiate

The Three Main Types of Negotiations

So, what kind of negotiations are you going to promote? Generally speaking, you have three options to choose from. You can usually base your decision on your own preferences, and on the observations you've already made about the person(s) you'll be negotiating with.

At the top of the list you'll find the negotiating style which is used most often, because it seems, at first glance, to be the most suited to the human temperament. However, the other two types are becoming more and more common.

1. Conflict/competitive negotiations

You would opt for competitive and confrontational negotiations when you are concentrating above all on attaining your own objectives, without caring too much about what the person you're dealing with will get out of the negotiations.

This is how most people view the negotiating process, but interestingly enough, it is now less popular than you would think. And it is certainly not always the most productive approach.

2. Co-operative negotiations

In this case, the emphasis is placed on the common interests of both parties. It's important to remember that prudence is still the name of the game, since there are those who will take advantage of your co-operation and resort to false representation to increase their immediate gains. A sly operator will lead you to believe that they are all for a spirit of co-operation, and thereby create a climate of mutual confidence where they are able to glean as much information – your bottom line and your alternative plans, for example – as they need to use against you.

3. Problem-solving negotiations

In this type of case, the negotiations are viewed as a problem which must be solved together by both parties: how to find the best way to give maximum satisfaction to both sides? Your guiding principle is that both parties should leave the table with more riches or benefits of some kind.

Which type of negotiation should you choose?

Most good negotiators will tell you that unless you're involved in a one-off deal, with someone you'll never see again, it's always better to arrive at an understanding through co-operation rather than through some kind of under-hand strategy.

In Chapter 9 we'll take a look at ways to prepare a strategy using tactics with a proven track record, and which you can expect to be confronted with in future negotiations.

A strategic choice

In the vast majority of cases the best agreements, and those which are most rewarding in the long term, are those where both parties attack and solve a common problem together, and find a way to satisfy their reciprocal interests. They operate from the following viewpoint:

- What do I have to offer?
- How much is it worth?
- How can I get fair value for what I'm offering?

To choose between the three types of negotiating strategies, you must first make a global evaluation of the situation, by considering these questions.

Global Evaluation

1. How does the other party perceive the situation?

2. How does the situation impress me?

3. What is at stake for me?

4. What is at stake for the other party?

5. Can I identify the main points of contention?

6. What are the principal areas of agreement?

7. What solutions (options, packages and others) would be likely to benefit both parties in these negotiations?

8. What are the major concessions I am prepared to make?

9. What major concessions would I like to obtain from the other side?

10. What restrictions does the other side have to respect?

11. What are my restrictions?

12. What power do I have?

13. Are the bargaining powers divided equally?

14. What power does the other party have?

15. Is communication between the parties neutral, good or bad?

16. What about any common past history – is it neutral, good or bad?

17. Is the possibility of both parties benefiting from the situation neutral, likely or unlikely?

Bargaining or negotiation?

Here's a theoretical question. What is the difference between bargaining and negotiating?

The answer is that in a bargaining situation what one party gains is an outright loss for the other party, without any form of compensation. The pie on the table doesn't change size:

Therefore, both parties have the same objective: to try to get the largest slice possible. This is also the case for a simple sale, where you will try to get the best price. Any decrease in the price goes straight into your pocket in effect, instead of into the seller's pocket. Since the figure for the total revenue is set in advance, what one side gains the other side loses. A relatively equal situation would result in the following division:

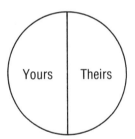

But in negotiations which emphasize co-operation, both sides work to increase the size of the pie:

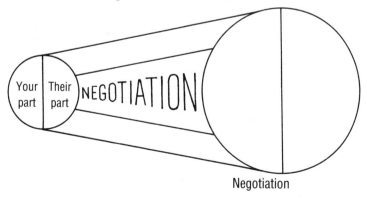

Negotiation

It can also happen that negotiations which are based on this principle of co-operation result in another kind of sharing where one side walks away with a larger part:

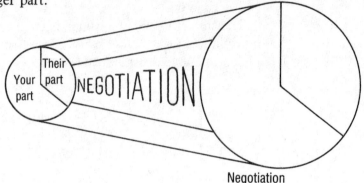

Negotiation

With this in mind, it is sometimes better to let the other party obtain a little more, relatively speaking, if it allows you to enlarge your own portion of the pie as well.

Conflict or co-operation?

Make an overall evaluation of the situation: does the general atmosphere seem tense, likely to turn confrontational, or does there seem to be a common will to face the problem together and solve it? In the left-hand column below are listed the kinds of situations which could lend themselves to conflict and competition. In the right-hand column you will find situations likely to lead to co-operation.

Conflict		**Co-operation**	
Simple stakes	☐	Multiple stakes	☐
One-off deal	☐	On-going business relationship	☐
Rigid negotiator	☐	Flexible negotiator	☐
Concentrated power	☐	Shared power	☐
Neutral or negative atmosphere	☐	Neutral or cordial atmosphere	☐

Tot up the number of ticks you can insert under each column and this will help you to evaluate the nature of your upcoming negotiations.

Timing also plays an important role: although co-operative negotiations may turn out to be more profitable, they also usually take more time. So negotiations which are under some time limit are more likely to be confrontational.

It is important to recognize that there is always some measure of conflict and co-operation in every negotiation and it is just as foolhardy to think that you can completely eliminate the conflict factor as it is to ignore the possibility of co-operation. After all, negotiation is simply the coming together of two parties on a voluntary basis (co-operation) in order to work together (co-operation) to resolve a problem in one way or another (conflict/co-operation). What you need to understand is that it is possible to tip the scales one way or the other by learning how to reduce conflict.

Learn to minimize conflict

The dead ends, sterile bickering, unilateral victories and other such unproductive results that can arise from conflict in negotiation, can be avoided by paying attention to the following factors:

- study the interests and objectives of the other party and try to see things from their point of view;

- during your preparations, determine which solutions, options and packages of options are likely to be advantageous both to you and to the other party;

- during negotiations, emphasize your common interests;

- try to be aware of your feelings as well as those of the opposing side.

Establish Points of Agreement and Disagreement

Now you've identified your objectives and those of the other party, draw up two lists. The first will include objectives on which you both agree, and the second those on which you disagree. List the objectives in order of importance.

The advantage of having this list in front of you during negotiations is that in difficult moments it will help you remind the other party that you do have some objectives in common, so it would be in both your best interests to reach an agreement. Referring to these common objectives lends cohesion to the discussion, tends to moderate conflicts and reinforces the atmosphere of collaboration between the negotiating parties. It also allows you to build on the solid base of your common objectives.

Objectives
Agreed
1. _____
2. _____
3. _____
4. _____
5. _____
Disagreed
1. _____
2. _____
3. _____
4. _____
5. _____

Facing your differences

Try to avoid considering points of disagreement as impassable obstacles. It is often precisely these bones of contention that result in those negotiations which are crowned with success. Relations between people are both difficult and rewarding largely *because* of their differences.

To make your preparations worthwhile, you must confront the main differences between your position and that of the other party head on. If you try to ignore them, they are quite likely to blow up in your face during the negotiations themselves.

Thinking about these differences in a detached and rational way before negotiations have started gives you the advantage of having the time to come up with possible solutions in a non-stressful, relaxed way.

Remember internal differences within your team

Have you ever been on a team where all its members were in perfect agreement about everything? It's very unlikely. A team's cohesion depends on the force of consensus which rallies its different members around one central point. This consensus is sometimes challenged. It's up to you to identify where the dissension is coming from, and to do something about it.

Dissension among the members of the other party

A corollary of this, of course, is that if you're dealing with more than one person (for example with a company or organization), the interests and objectives within that group are likely to differ on one or a number of points. Ideally you should be in a position to identify such divergences.

When exploited properly, the divergences that you detect in the opposing camp could be used to score points. All it takes is for one member of the opposing team to divulge some information at an inappropriate time, or to be convinced that an offer of yours is the right way to go, for the unity of the opposing group to crack.

On the other hand, you should do all you can to ensure the cohesion of your own team by specifying in advance what information should not be divulged before the right time, and which subjects should be avoided. We'll discuss tactics for negotiating as part of a team in Chapter 12.

Evaluate Your Power

Now, make a list of all the advantages you possess in the situation at hand. Leave nothing out: when played at the right time, even the weakest card in your favour can result in substantial gains for you. Next list the advantages of the other party. And don't forget that this list should remain open: you're not aware of everything the other party has going for it, so don't act as if you are.

Power Points	
My advantages	**The other party's advantages**
1. _____	1. _____
2. _____	2. _____
3. _____	3. _____
4. _____	4. _____
5. _____	5. _____

Study the repercussions

At the same time you should also study the possible repercussions of your objectives. What are the short-, medium- and long-term impacts of the negotiations for you, and for your company? A substantial purchase or an important decision implies change and requires that you anticipate the possible consequences.

Legal implications

You should also study the legal implications of the negotiations about to take place well in advance. You should be aware of these implications before negotiations start, since they could very well influence the course of your discussions.

Check out the competition

There's always a market for what you're looking for. It's extremely rare to come across a completely captive market (whether you're the seller or buyer). This means that somebody, somewhere, is offering the same thing or service as you or the other party. Have you checked this out? Can you identify the competition's strong and weak points? Here's another question to ask which can prove very useful when determining the pros and cons of your position: *If I were in one of my competitors' shoes, what would I say or do to persuade the other party to opt for my product?* If you can answer this question it will allow you to predict, up to a certain point, the arguments you may well be confronted with.

Obviously the next question is: *How can I counter these arguments?* And following on from this, begin building on your case by answering further questions like these:

- *What arguments favour my point of view?*
- *What proof do I have?*
- *What printed information do I have at my disposal that could help me impress and persuade the other party?*

'A map is not a country'

Alfred Korzybski, an internationally renowned semantics expert, often used this formula to remind his students that words should not be confused with the realities they describe.

In other words there is inevitably some discrepancy between a description of things and the things themselves. The categories of negotiations we have identified are only models, which means that they don't correspond exactly to reality.

For example, all negotiations, even the most difficult, necessitate a certain degree of co-operation. Without it, discussions would rapidly deteriorate and eventually break down completely. A situation where one party attempts to impose its will totally is as much a negotiation as a totalitarian dictatorship is a democracy! On the other hand, negotiations based on co-operation will always contain some degree of competition.

Choosing the Type of Negotiation

This is up to you. You are always in a position to influence any negotiations in which you are involved. You might, for example, want to emphasize the aspect of competition, thus creating a conflict-type situation. Or you might decide to create an atmosphere conducive to the emergence of co-operative negotiations.

Don't forget that you always have the opportunity to take the initiative and determine the type of negotiations which will prevail. Never underestimate your own influence.

In the next chapter you will discover how to organize your advantages so that they constitute real bargaining power. Once you've decided what type of negotiations you think will serve your interests best, you can start developing your strategy.

CHAPTER 9

Preparing Your Strategy

If you base your strategy on the following principle you should save yourself a lot of setbacks:

Negotiation is a living process.

Like everything living, negotiation is not entirely predictable. Things don't always work out the way you want them to, but this doesn't mean that you will never attain your objectives or satisfy your interests. It is, however, impossible completely to eliminate the unexpected.

You should always work on the assumption that you don't have all the information you require at hand. This will keep your mind alert so that even if, from time to time, you are sure that nothing unexpected can happen, you will still act as if it could. You never know! Strategic planning consists precisely of predicting the unpredictable.

It is also true to say that the most effective strategies are those that are as yet unknown and the best way to deal with them or come up with them yourself is to improvise. In the final analysis, the best tool a good negotiator has is an ability to improvise.

What Is a Strategy?

Before going any further it will be useful to define our terms. Let's start with an extreme view. It has been said that a strategy is like a rain dance: it has absolutely no effect on the weather, but reassures people by making them feel that they're at least doing something!

This radical point of view is certainly accurate inasmuch as auto-suggestion and positive thinking form a large part of what a strategy is.

Suppose that you're determined to complete a certain project. You work fervently, studying the question from all angles; you build a thousand theories, and read everything you can get your hands on which you think will help you attain your goal. You say to yourself:

'I'll start by making such and such a proposal. Then I'll talk about this aspect. Then, at the right time, I'll produce my documentation with such and such information. If I get this reaction, I'll counter it with that argument. Then I'll arrange for someone to call so that it looks like coincidence, and we'll have to continue the discussion over dinner, at which point I'll avoid the issue and talk about other things, just mentioning a certain fact that I know will have an effect. Then if they start using a certain tactic, which they are known to do a lot, I'll call their bluff by . . .'.

What are you doing here? Well, obviously you're developing a strategy! The fact that you're predicting what will take place prepares you for a number of eventualities and by proceeding in this way you are much better equipped to deal with any potential situation. And, psychologically speaking, you have already begun to size up your opponent. You review your forces (your troops), you position them and decide at which moment they'll be most effectively deployed. This game of anticipation serves to condition your mind. And this kind of mental preparation is essential to the success of your work as a negotiator.

Strategy is a delicate operation

A surgeon's work has to be very precise. But he doesn't necessarily decide in advance in what order to use the instruments. However, the surgeon knows that those instruments will be available, and that someone will be there to pass them as the need arises. Obviously the surgeon will study the case in depth before starting the operation itself, so that he has a good idea of what he'll find and how to proceed.

The same applies to negotiations. Everything may go according to plan, but there can also be unexpected circumstances which require immediate attention, and therefore an ability to improvise.

A surgeon in the act of operating on a patient needs a skilled assistant who is familiar with all the instruments. The surgeon decides which instrument to use as he goes along, according to the circumstances. So, who is this faithful assistant that you can rely on during your negotiations? The answer is, 'Your mind!'

Even if you're part of a negotiating team, your mind should always be fully concentrated on every detail of what's going on. Then, when you decide you need a particular 'instrument' – a piece of information, an argument, a strategy or a tactic perhaps – you will be ready to pull it out of the collection of options you have prepared, whatever the circumstances. (Of course, we are not saying that you should always react on the spur of the moment, without taking the time to think things over, simply in order to create an impression of self-confidence.)

The rain dance analogy we used earlier should not lead you to conclude that making a strategic plan is a futile exercise. It is very useful because:

● it prepares your mind, in the same way that physical exercise prepares your body;

● it helps you deal with the unexpected – even though you will always encounter situations which you haven't anticipated, a fact which no good negotiator would deny;

● who can say that a rain dance is entirely 'ineffective'?!

Here is an operational definition for you:

The art of strategic planning consists of exploiting as fully as possible the advantages which you possess.

Tactics or strategies?

There is a tendency to think that the terms 'tactics' and 'strategies' are interchangeable. And up to a certain point, they are: the two terms signify two different steps of the same process, but:

● your strategy is your plan of action in general terms; while
● a tactic, sometimes called a sub-strategy, is a more limited action, designed to allow you to develop your strategy.

Or to take a practical example. Suppose you're building a house. The architect's plans form your strategy. And your tactics are the tools and materials you use to build the house according to your plan.

When you are making your preparations, you are already devising your strategy, although you may not be aware of it at the time. When you set specific and general objectives, when you decide whether to negotiate or not, what are you doing? You are developing a plan whereby you can choose what actions to undertake in order to attain your objectives.

On what grounds do you base your decision whether to negotiate or not? On an evaluation of your strengths and weaknesses, and those of the other party: once again the choice is a strategic one. So you're already thinking in terms of strategy.

It is not possible to provide a set of ready-made plans, guaranteed to work in any situation. Instead our aim is to equip you with tools and materials with which to develop a strategy of your own that really corresponds to your needs. Like the surgeon, you'll have all your instruments ready, together with the skill to use them judiciously at the right time and place.

So, to sum up you have already made a certain number of strategic choices. Among other things, you've determined your objectives, your bottom line and the style of negotiation you prefer.

We will now consider a number of strategic questions, the answers to which will provide you with a framework on which to hang your particular strategies.

Strategic Options

If you are facing an opponent who wants to get as much as possible and give as little as possible in return, you obviously wouldn't answer the following questions in the same way as if you were trying to build a long-term business relationship, where each side must be satisfied in order for the exchange to continue.

Taking the initiative

By taking the initiative you occupy the terrain in some way, by trying to impose your own preferences as to the following.

Time
Are you going to try to arrange for the negotiations to take place at a time which *you* find most convenient, or are you going to try to set up a schedule which is convenient to both parties?

Duration
Is there a time limit, or is it unlimited? Do you have a choice? What about the other party? This can have an enormous influence on the discussions: the party which feels less hurried usually has a strategic advantage although in fact it might not have any real bearing on the issue.

Pacing
The more power you have, the more you can impose your own pace. Will it be:

- rapid?
- slow?
- thoughtful?

Will you also:

- drag things out?
- steadily increase the pace?
- slow things down towards the end in order to gain a few minor concessions?

In general, when engaged in co-operative negotiations, both parties will adjust their pace to suit one another.

Place

Will you try to arrange for the negotiations to take place in a location which gives *you* some advantage (as we'll see later, this type of advantage can be very subtle) or will you try to find a location which is conducive to an atmosphere of co-operation?

Agenda

How will the discussions start? What subjects will be covered, and in what order? Will the different issues be negotiated separately or at the same time? Will they be covered one by one, one after the other or are you going to put everything on the table at once and say, 'Here's what I want!'

Are you going to get right into the important points, or will you start with issues that can be easily worked out? Again, this choice, far from being trivial, can be of crucial strategic importance.

Drafting an agreement

Will you be the one to draw up a first draft of the agreement? If this is the case you would have the privilege of formulating the terms, which constitutes an advantage since you can phrase things so that they are favourable to your interests, even if there are modifications made later on.

Not taking the initiative in any way

You may decide to involve yourself as little as possible, and force the other party to take the initiative. Under these circumstances, it is left to the other party to decide which type of negotiations will take place.

In such cases, you adopt a passive attitude, which consists of following the directions set by the other party. You don't try to promote your opinions as to how the negotiations should proceed.

Since the other party is the one to define the strategic orientation, all you have to worry about is defending your bottom line and manœuvring so that you attain your objectives.

In the great majority of cases, negotiators favour the option of seizing the initiative, except in the three following situations.

• When dealing with a party that is much stronger. But even in this situation it is still almost always possible to exert some influence, however subtle it may be (see Chapter 24 for how to negotiate from a weak position).

• When dealing with someone who lacks experience, and who is bound to 'dig their own grave' as the expression goes. Like a fisherman who remains perfectly still while waiting for the fish to take the bait, you bide your time and create as few waves as possible. And that's probably all you'll have to do to get what you want.

• When you feel confident enough to let the other party take the initiative, knowing from experience that when dealing with that person or organization the negotiations have every chance of succeeding and benefiting both sides.

Strategic Planning

To be able to develop a strategy, whatever it may be, you must have a minimum of bargaining power at your disposal. But you don't need to have a lot of power.

As we've already seen, the art of strategy consists of exploiting the advantages you have to their fullest. Drawing up a strategic plan also means planning for the unexpected. It means eliminating as completely as possible the effects of surprise and abrupt changes in the negotiating situation.

What does the other party have to gain?

One of the best things you can do is to put yourself in the other party's shoes, and not only in order to predict what kind of strategy he or she is likely to use. While planning your strategy you would be well advised to evaluate what the other party has to gain from the situation.

A useful assumption to make is that it's just as important for the other party to gain something (even if it's only a symbolic gain). Why?

Because you never get something for nothing.

You could just keep on plotting and scheming, pulling off a deal here and there and living off other people's foolishness. But sooner or later you are going to run into someone who has something you really want, and who will make you pay dearly for it.

On the other hand, there's nothing wrong with learning to make the most of your position and gain the greatest possible number of benefits from a given situation, which doesn't necessarily mean that you are trying to leave the other side with nothing.

Most good negotiators will tell you that it's almost always preferable to make sure the other party leaves the negotiating table with some kind of gain: this too is strategy of a sort – a long-term strategy, which may pay off only years later. In fact, it's almost a lifetime strategy.

Six Strategic Attitudes

It's not always easy to distinguish between strategies, tactics and attitudes, but it is important to recognize the following attitudes which could all be considered strategic.

1. Timing

Do you have a sense of timing? What it comes down to is simply saying the right thing at the right time, or making the right move at the right time, etc. And it can make all the difference.

Suppose you're involved in negotiations where you know you have a slight advantage. It may not amount to much, but you're aware that psychologically it could mean the difference between success and failure. For example, you may be in a position to add a little extra to the package you're offering, without it really costing you anything.'

The moment to choose to introduce your incentive is the precise time when you feel the buyer is still hesitating and that all he or she needs is that little extra push to make a decision. Just when is that moment? Well, that's where timing comes in. In other words, it's up to you to decide.

It's up to you to decide when the buyer is ripe and when that little extra something will be most effective. All it takes is a certain sensitivity. However, if you offer your incentive too soon, it will no longer serve as a negotiating tactic: the buyer will soon take it for granted and will offer no concessions in return.

2. Calm

If it is essential that you conclude your negotiations by the end of the day or the bank will seize all your assets, what do you do? You do your best to maintain a calm, detached attitude.

If your boss calls to tell you that the corner office you've had your eye on for over a year (and which you were told to forget about) is free, and that it's yours if you want it, what do you do? Well, you don't go overboard with gratitude, but you thank your boss in a calm, friendly, natural way as if you'd been expecting the news any day.

Calmness is a strategic attitude.

3. Patience

Do not allow any of the pressures or the impatience you may feel inside to show, unless, of course, you think that the other party is just taking you for a ride. Always present a calm, patient exterior, even though you may be dying to conclude the negotiations.

The party who is most in a hurry always has less bargaining power than the party who can wait for a better offer to come along. And the more the other party is impatient, the more effective your own patience will be!

Even if you're running out of time, you shouldn't hurry. Examine the issues carefully and never jump in with an answer on the spur of the moment.

It's better to break off negotiations altogether than to rush through a bad deal. You will have your whole life to regret a terrible decision, so why hurry? And don't forget that the side which imposes its pace on the negotiations in fact controls them.

Patience is an essential strategic attitude. A negotiator worth his salt never loses control, and never raises his voice, unless, of course, doing so is part of the particular strategy, or an unalterable personality trait.

4. Stalling

If you never say no, and your negotiations are never completely at a standstill, you come back to the same point a hundred times, even though it's already been discussed, you take a thousand-and-one precautions, and there's nothing the other party can do to make you go any faster, you are using a strategic attitude. This is useful to counter any pressure tactics imposed by the other side, and to control the pace of negotiations, or to eat up the time the other side has to work with.

5. Apathy

Nothing seems to bother you. You are completely detached, whether the negotiations work out or not. Your reactions are stripped of passion, and you appear indifferent to the way that the discussions are going. Apathy can be an effective defence in situations where the other side tries to put more and more pressure on you to make a move.

A variation of this strategic attitude is to appear to be above everything, and to observe everyone else getting excited while you remain absorbed in your own inner world.

The idea behind this strategy is to let the other party know that it would be useless to try and manipulate you. As you'll see, a good negotiator also has to know how to be a good actor!

6. Rapid, brutal transitions

You should do everything in your power not to let yourself be taken by surprise. But there's nothing to prevent you from preparing a little surprise of your own, which may serve to speed up the negotiations. The effect of surprise is especially useful if you want to derail an opposing party which has adopted a competitive style (if there has to be a big winner, why shouldn't it be you after all?). Since the other party will be taken off guard, you will be in a position to take full advantage of the situation.

For example, you may offer a cheque before concluding the agreement; you could change the subject completely; you could present some new information; you could multiply the proposals – in short you add a new twist to the discussions.

So, what purpose can such abrupt changes have? They can push a stagnating discussion forward, and wake up the opposing side.

There was a famous incident at the United Nations when Khruschev banged on his table with a shoe. It was years before someone discovered, by examining a photograph of the event, that the Soviet President was wearing both his shoes when the incident took place! In other words, the shoe he used did not appear by chance. In fact it had come out of a briefcase. Far from being a spontaneous reaction, the move had been carefully planned.

Even if you do get angry during the course of your negotiations, your anger should be measured, cold, controlled and calculated to have a specific effect.

If you must get angry, do everything you can to take a short breather before exploding. Pretend you have a sudden headache . . . anything to get away for a few moments. When you lose control, you allow your weakness to show and you become vulnerable. The other side now knows how to get to you. In other words, they can manipulate you.

A strategic move

Imagine that you have a very high objective for negotiation. The secret is not to hide your ambitions. On the contrary, reveal them proudly. Hold them up in the full light of day. Don't be ashamed to proclaim them to one and all. Nourish them regularly with positive thoughts.

Start by making it clear to others what your ambitions are. They may react with astonishment, since what you want may seem next to impossible – at least that's how they may feel. But the seed is planted, the idea is there and it will take its effect. Time will do its work and your ambition will appear more and more realistic, even to the opposing side.

Good ideas need time to mature, so allow as much as you can. Talk to the other party about your ambitions as often as possible, mentioning them in passing as often as you can. The important thing is that the other party has enough time to get used to them.

If all goes well, they will eventually start taking your ambitions for granted, and even make excuses for not being able to satisfy them completely. Then they may start making concessions – and not in exchange for something you have given up, but for something you haven't given up – your ambitions! In time, they'll start looking for ways to satisfy you. And all because you have raised your own standards and stuck to them.

Formulating Your Strategic Plan

When developing a strategy, you should always begin with the following assumption: *'Either because they can't or because they don't want to, the other party will refuse to give me what I want.'* Therefore, the primary objective of your strategy is to influence the discussions in order to obtain something that someone else doesn't want to give you. There are really only three ways to achieve this result:

- force;
- diplomacy; and
- negotiation.

Force is also called coercion and only applies where your pressure tactics are strong enough to force your adversary to give you what you want (in other words, 'agree or go under . . .').

Diplomacy: in this context perhaps 'cunning' would be a more accurate term than diplomacy, where, after negotiations are concluded, the other party realizes that they've 'been had'. Sometimes they never realize it, but don't get your hopes up, since this is rare.

Force and diplomacy/cunning are not, strictly speaking, negotiating, although they may make use of strategies and tactics. Negotiating means confronting a difference of opinion or one side's needs head on, and *together* trying to solve, satisfy or appease both sides. It means working together to resolve the following question: *'What can we do so that you leave the table with at least your minimum requirements satisfied, and more if possible, while I also fulfil my minimum requirements, and more if possible?'*. Bearing this in mind, take a look at the following questionnaire, together with an explanation of the importance of the questions. The questionnaire is designed to be of practical use to you when you are outlining your strategy. It is repeated in Chapter 14, together with space for your answers, and forms part of our preparation checklist.

The strategic questions

1. Are you going to take risks?
The risk factor plays an important role in negotiations and results can vary in the extreme, depending on whether you adopt a conservative, prudent approach, or whether you're more of a gambler.

At its most basic level, negotiating means taking calculated risks: you are constantly trying to make offers which are as advantageous as possible for you, while at the same time hoping that the other party will see the arrangement as satisfactory as well.

In traditional negotiations, one party tried to offer as little as possible while hoping to gain as much as possible. But at what point does one of the parties decide that he or she can get a better deal elsewhere and withdraw from the negotiations, leaving the other party empty-handed? Generally, it may be assumed that the party willing to take the greater risk is in a better position than the one which is mainly concerned with protecting itself as much as possible.

Someone who makes a proposal or who sells an item is constantly taking the risk of asking too much from the buyer, who could lose interest or find what they want elsewhere. If I ask you for too many concessions, you may decide to break off negotiations. If I don't ask for enough, I risk leaving things on the table that you might have been willing to concede.

A buyer takes multiple risks:

- the delivery arrangements may not be respected;
- the product may not satisfy the buyer's requirements;
- the supplier may not uphold the guarantee;
- after-sales service may be inadequate, and so on.

So the person selling or making a proposal will try to minimize the risks the other party has to take. These risks may be real or imaginary – it doesn't matter. What really matters is what the buyer thinks.

The two fears that most often prevent us from taking risks are the fear of rejection and the fear of failure. Fear of failure is a particularly severe handicap. A skilled negotiator can easily detect someone who is afraid, and knows that such a person can be easily manipulated by playing on his or her fears. Of course, we all have our fears. But what counts is not letting them control us so that we become unable to make decisions.

Never forget that the other party also has reasons to be afraid of failure: one advantage of not thinking only about yourself is that you can feel the other party's fears as well as your own.

2. *Are you going to try and establish a climate of confidence and co-operation?*

You may find it strange that aiming to create a climate of confidence can be considered a strategy: in fact, it is a strategy that in principle should lead to a positive understanding between negotiating parties.

If you do decide to be up front and honest, go all the way. Don't pretend to be up front if you are not sincere. If you try to put one over on the other party, and you are found out, you will not be forgiven. There's a world of difference between just stretching what is considered to be ethical and the out and out abuse of someone's trust.

Perhaps the old-fashioned notion of honour is not so highly valued these days. But it has been replaced by another notion, that of reputation, which is still of value.

3. *What concessions do you plan to obtain?*

You enter into negotiations because you want to obtain something specific. Whatever that is must be clearly established in your mind when determining your strategic orientation.

4. *What concessions are you ready to make?*

Can you come up with any concessions that are minor for you, but that mean a lot to the other party? When skilfully handled, such concessions can result in maximum gains for you. It's up to you to be creative and find out what they could be!

5. *What is your bottom line?*

We covered this question in Chapter 6 when we were looking at objectives: your bottom line represents an essential anchor point when developing your strategy.

6. *What is not negotiable?*

How are you going to make the other party understand just what is negotiable and what isn't?

- Tact and diplomacy?
- An aggressive statement?
- An open-handed attitude?
- Firmness?

The position you adopt *vis-à-vis* your non-negotiable issues will set the tone.

7. *How do you plan to convince the other party?*

There are different ways to get the other party to accept your arguments. What approach will you take?

- Are you going to use persuasion? Are you going to argue? Or both?
- Will you provide written documentation? Audio-visuals? Outside sources?
- What are the strong points of your arguments?
- Will you bring in any experts?
- Will you put together any attractive packages?

8. *Are you going to use any pressure tactics?*

There are different ways to exert pressure, like setting a tight deadline for example. Or having another party interested in negotiating for the same contract. This is a way of exercising your power, and also of assessing it.

9. *How are you going to react to pressure tactics?*

The other party may try to impose a certain rule or condition, or use subtle or outright coercion to get you to make concessions. You should have some idea as to how you will react under those circumstances.

10. *What kind of pace will you favour?*

There are a number of possibilities:

- direct attack or evading the main issue;
- jockeying for a strategic position on each issue;
- gaining individual concessions wherever you can, and putting them together to form an acceptable package.

11. Will you call for a third person to intervene?

Your boss, your wife, a colleague, an accepted authority, an expert, a competitor – there are many people you could bring in to tip the scales in your favour.

You may have heard the story told by Aristotle Onassis which illustrates the use of this strategy.

One day, while he was sitting in a restaurant, a man came up to him. 'Aristotle! It's been so long!' Onassis, a little surprised, replied, 'Do we know each other?' 'But of course we do,' said the man. 'Don't you remember? We went to school together.'

Onassis tried to recall the person, without success. But the man seemed a pleasant enough fellow, and he gave him the benefit of the doubt. The man then adopted an intimate tone, and said something along these lines: 'Listen, since we were in school together, I'd like you to do me a little favour, OK?'

'Go on,' said Onassis.

'Well,' said the man, 'tomorrow at noon I have to close an important deal. I'll be sitting with three men at a table over there, near the bar. If you could just stop by and say hello as you leave, it would help a lot.' Onassis found the idea amusing and agreed to do what the man asked. The next day, as planned, he greeted his old 'friend'. Instead of politely returning the greeting, the man looked angry at being interrupted and said, 'Can't you see I'm busy! I'll talk to you later!'

That man used his tenuous link with the great financier to add weight to his position. Anyone who could tell Onassis to take a walk had to have a lot of power! He made use of a prestigious third person in a very skilful way.

But in fact the person he really wanted to impress was Onassis himself. And not long afterwards, he was hired by the Greek magnate to negotiate on his behalf. He had achieved his primary objective!

12. If you're negotiating as part of a team, how will authority be divided among the members?

We will look at this question in detail in Chapter 12.

13. Are you going to use any surprise tactics?

To create a surprise effect you could, for example, decide to modify your strategy or your arguments mid-way through the negotiations, at the precise moment when the other party thinks that he or she has deciphered your approach and discovered how to counter your tactics. Doing so would effectively derail the opposition, at least for some time.

You could even change your *objectives* up to a certain point: working from position x you might suddenly change to position y. You would make this appear to be a concession when in reality you've been more interested in attaining objective y all along.

Obviously this kind of strategy is more effective if the other party hasn't taken the trouble to make an in-depth analysis of your interests. If, on the contrary, you know that the other has identified your interests accurately right from the start, then it isn't worth pretending to change them.

You can use various forms of surprise. For example, state that a given issue is not negotiable throughout the discussions. Then, when things get bogged down, you drop the issue and somehow justify the change in your position. But make sure that this kind of manœuvre is perceived as an exception rather than the rule.

14. Are you going to do any bluffing?

Prepare yourself. Convince yourself of the *truth* of this bluff. If possible, keep your bluff as close as possible to the truth. Visualize yourself doing what you're pretending to be able to do.

15. Are you planning to overbid?

Define your margin, to what extent can you go? You have to prepare yourself and have a clear image of your minimum – and your maximum.

16. Are you going to talk about the competition?

This question complements the one about using surprise tactics.

You may like to consider the tactics of the storekeeper who keeps a file of newspaper clippings concerning dissatisfied customers of his main rival who had sued the competing store for one reason or another. He shows a few to his potential clients, then says, 'I'm not showing you these to influence your decision. I just want to make sure you're aware of the risks involved if you decide to do business with the guy across the road.'

By doing this he succeeds in planting a seed of doubt in his potential client's mind by giving him the impression that it would be very risky to deal with his competitor. The strategy he is using can be summed up as follows.

- He has skilfully modified his customer's perception of an alternative. Of course, there are always other stores, but in this particular situation he succeeded in severely limiting the field of a prospective buyer who might have preferred doing business with another store in the area.

- By using newspaper clippings instead of just verbally relating the court incidents, he has made use of printed documents to support his position. Doing this went a long way to consolidating his own position: the documents give his claims every appearance or validity.

- He has maintained an air of objectivity by stating that all he is trying to do is to inform the buyer of the facts.

17. What kind of settlement will you seek?
You can conclude the negotiations with:
- a verbal agreement;
- a written agreement, signed by both parties;
- a contractual agreement, including all the clauses;
- a partial agreement (if so what are the specific points you want included?);
- a detailed agreement, or a general outline.

18. What impression do you want to create?
How do you want the other party to remember you? What will they tell others about you – including possible future business partners? This is also a strategic choice which should not be left to chance. Final impressions are always the most lasting.

19. What advantages do you have?
Certain factors can work to your advantage. Have you discovered what they are?

Smart Strategies

After you have considered the 19 questions set out above, the following list of seven smart strategies should help you to make your preparations.

1. If you are thinking about *taking risks*, those risks should be calculated to serve your interests and security.

2. When *putting your cards on the table*, whether you try to establish an atmosphere of mutual confidence or opt for more traditional, competitive negotiations, be honest about what you're doing.

3. As demonstrated in the example given by Onassis, the strategy of *bringing in a third person* should not be overlooked.

4. The *surprise effect* can derail the other party as long as he or she has not analysed your interests too closely.

5. *Discrediting the competition* is another surprise tactic worth considering.

6. The human mind tends to base its opinion of someone on those favourable or unfavourable *final impressions*.

7. Try not to feel any *animosity*: be objective and positive. You'll win the esteem of your business associates if you respect the rules you have defined together.

The Eight Principles of an Effective Strategy

To be an effective negotiator you need to assimilate eight effective principles, and then learn how to apply them in real-life situations. The following are the tried and tested principles of negotiation and sum up what we have already learnt.

1. **Study the difference between you and the other party carefully**
   Contrary to what many people think, it's not necessarily because of common objectives that negotiations come to a fruitful conclusion, but because of the differences between them.

   Take the example of the two sisters and the orange; one wanted to eat the fruit and throw away the peel, while the other wanted to use the peel to make a cake! To find a better solution than simply cutting the orange in half, one had to enquire into the needs of the other, and find out exactly what she wanted. Most negotiable situations have the potential to be beneficial to both parties, if a solution can be found.

2. **In every negotiation, there are convergent and divergent objectives**
   It is important to identify both. Divergent objectives usually pose no problem, since both parties are not after the same thing, and concessions and exchanges are more easily made. But when both parties are after the *same* objective, which is often the case where money is concerned, then by definition concessions become more difficult to make. What one side gains, the other cannot also gain.

   This brings us back to the importance of clearly defining your objectives and and of separating what you want from what you need.

3. **A negotiation is a situation that you can always influence to your advantage**
   Some negotiations are more fruitful than others. Once you are involved in negotiations with someone, if you base your attitude on the assumption that you're working *with* that person, then there are much

better chances of achieving an agreement which is advantageous to both parties.

4. **In any negotiation there are things you win and things you lose**
Too often we imagine that negotiations are solely motivated by questions of money, while very frequently issues like prestige, moral and ethical advantages, symbolic benefits such as recognition, etc, play an important role. It's often just as important to leave the negotiating table with something to be proud of, with your head held high so to speak, as it is to make money, even if what you gain is only symbolic.

5. **Flexibility does not only refer to material gain**
A corollary of the preceding principle, this means that it's possible to concede advantages other than material ones. You should always be on the look out for other kinds of options that could be of benefit or of interest to the other party.

6. **Power alone cannot obtain the same result as negotiation**
Negotiation is far more effective than resorting to pressure tactics. In the workplace, for example, employees have much more respect for a negotiated solution than for one that is imposed on them.

7. **Negotiation depends on the interdependence of both sides**
We tend to forget this aspect. If negotiations are taking place, then both parties *are* interrelated, interdependent and non-antagonistic. This means that *negotiating is a co-operative situation, whether both parties wish to co-operate or not.*
   Therefore, since negotiations are essentially a co-operative situation, it is more effective to respect their real nature and to try and co-operate rather than compete.

8. **Successful negotiations are the result of a series of adjustments and readjustments**
You won't find any ready-made situations as far as negotiations are concerned. For each agreement to satisfy both parties, proposals and counter-proposals must be made and digested. Ideally the situation will develop through a series of mutual concessions and compromises, until both parties agree a settlement has been reached.

Remember these principles when you are preparing your next negotiation strategy.

CHAPTER 10

How to Modify the Other Party's Perceptions

Since negotiating is largely a matter of judgement, one way of orienting things in your favour is to influence, in one way or another, the perceptions the other party has formed of the situation. How can you do this?

1. Establish Your Alternatives

As we've seen, having alternative solutions plays an important role in planning your strategy. Therefore they must be established in a realistic way, since having alternatives tends to give a certain feeling of power.

To make sure you've evaluated your alternatives realistically, you can ask for the advice of a third person who is not involved in the negotiations. Or, if you're working as part of a team, you can use role-playing, a method we'll look at in detail in Chapter 13. You can even resort to playing out the different roles yourself – as you would do when rehearsing your arguments out loud, a technique we'll also look at in Chapter 13.

The importance of carefully exploring the alternatives you have for any ongoing negotiations must be stressed. Your alternatives also serve to determine what can be termed your 'relative threshold'. Past a certain point – below a certain figure – your alternatives become more attractive than the proposals on the negotiating table. The more accurate your evaluation of the alternatives is, the more you will be in a position to know at which precise moment it would be better to break off the discussions and look elsewhere.

2. Modify the Other Party's Alternatives

Once again, don't forget to put yourself in the other party's position. He or she will also have evaluated any possible alternatives to the negotiations at hand, and that's where his or her relative threshold lies. Obviously, the better his or her relative threshold is (in other words, the more choice he or she has of doing business elsewhere), the higher the bottom line will be. It's just simple mathematics!

An important strategic manœuvre consists of modifying the perceptions the other party has of the alternatives. This is what is taking place when you tell a skilled salesman that you can get the same product at a cheaper price somewhere else, and he replies that it's not the same product and gives all kinds of reasons why his product is better.

Or if you're talking about exactly the same product, he will extol the merits of his establishment, its reputation for dependability, after-sales service, etc. He may even suggest that it's sometimes better to pay a little more for fewer headaches, and so on. (This is all true, by the way – after-sales service is important, and you should try to find out if it really is good!)

So this strategy consists of surrounding the other party, so to speak, by making his or her alternatives seem less and less attractive. And as soon as he or she thinks the alternatives are less attractive, the other party will lower his or her requirements as well.

3. If Necessary Say You'll Look Elsewhere!

Are you going to tell the other party what your relative threshold is? In other words, are you going to specify what your alternatives to the current negotiations are?

There are pros and cons to this. On the one hand, specifying your relative threshold sets a kind of limit or deadline. If you do succeed in influencing the other party's perception so that they lower their expectations and consider a better price, then you've made a lot of progress.

But, on the other hand, the other party may use the issue as an argument of their own, by doing the same thing as the salesperson who tells you that the alternative product you've mentioned isn't the same at all. If he or she is skilled in sales, they will always find a way to prove that what they're saying is absolutely true, and that you should forget about buying the product elsewhere.

Yet another result of revealing your alternatives is that in some cases you reveal your bottom line as well. If the other party knows exactly at what point you can resort to an alternative solution, then all he or she would have to do, in theory, would be to offer you just a little more in order to force you into an agreement.

You should therefore let the other party know that:

- your bottom line may be much higher; and
- if he or she allows you to leave the table, the other party will have to look for an alternative too and miss out on an opportunity to make a good deal.

In the final analysis, if you manage to obtain an accurate idea of the other party's bottom line, then to all intents and purposes you don't need any other strategy. All you have to do is propose them in the proper manner for them to accept.

A complementary strategy consists in raising the perception the other party has of your bottom line. As soon as he or she is convinced that you will refuse to go beyond a certain figure, for example, the other party will modify his or her demands accordingly. In fact, it is essential that the other party should perceive your bottom line as higher than it really is.

This is simply a refinement of the ancient art of barter, where you both start high and meet somewhere in the middle.

4. Legitimize Your Position

It is very useful to be able to provide information which legitimizes your position. For example, you can refer to previous cases which are similar and which therefore set a precedent for establishing rules and guidelines.

It's up to you to support your arguments and consolidate your position, which should be very explicit. Add weight to your position with incontestable proofs, official documents, etc. In short, do everything you can to convince the other party that your demands are well founded and that 'what you're asking of me in exchange for what I'm willing to offer is completely justified'.

5. Develop a Critical Path Plan

Instead of mapping out a rigid strategy, work with a critical path plan that takes you from Point A (the present situation) to Point B (your objective). To get there, you have to bring the other party to one of a number of crossroads, and incite him or her to make the decisions that bring you closer to your final objective.

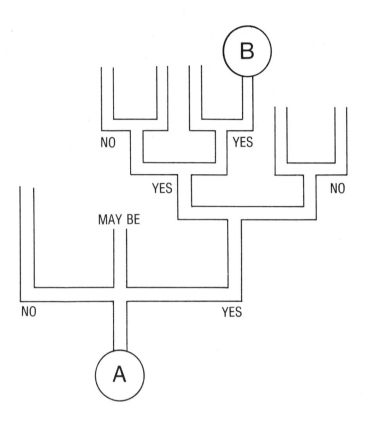

You have to prepare and help the other party make each decision (crossroad) so that you reach B – your objective.

In any case, a minimal strategy is preferable because it provides you with a general direction, and some of the major steps that must be taken during the course of the negotiations.

CHAPTER 11

Get Time on Your Side

Time is a very important commodity for the effective negotiator. Even the time you choose to get involved in negotiations is important.

If you were a buyer for a large manufacturing company, you would try to buy when your supplier's business was a little slow, or when the market was relatively saturated with raw materials, etc. On the other hand, if you are selling, even though you can't really choose the moment, it may help you to know of any deadlines that the buyer has to respect.

Make Time Work for You

A buyer who is under pressure and doesn't have the time to shop around for good deals may be tempted to go straight to his or her usual supplier. This puts the supplier in a very strong position, especially if they find out that the buyer is pressed.

The axiom to remember is: the party which is under more pressure to conclude the deal by a certain deadline has less power if the other party is aware of the situation and can – or wishes to – take advantage of it.

How to Take Advantage of Time

The Japanese are specialists in the art of practising patience. You may have heard the story about the young executive who set off for Japan for a week of negotiations. It was his first important assignment. The first day he was invited to relax after the long journey. The second day he was taken on a tour of the local temples, the third day he was shown an ocean resort.

Every time he asked his amicable hosts when discussions would begin, he was given an evasive answer, 'Oh, we still have lots of time . . .' So the week came to an end and he still didn't have anything to show his employers. He wasn't even close to signing the contract they'd been hoping for. On the final day the young man attempted to bash out some kind of agreement, in response to which his hosts, who'd been aware of his dates of arrival and departure for weeks in advance, politely escorted him to his plane.

In order for him to have taken more advantage of time he should have done one of the following; instead, he tried to rush things at the last minute.

- He could have tried to avoid revealing his departure date.

- He could have bought an open flight return ticket instead of one with a set date. In this way, if negotiations proved difficult and took longer than expected, he wouldn't have been under any excess pressure.

- He could have cancelled his flight and taken another when negotiations were terminated successfully. The extra cost would have been largely compensated for by added gains, since the hosts would have felt slightly indebted for keeping him so long and might have been willing to make more concessions.

Industrial relations

The question of when to negotiate can make an enormous difference in the area of industrial relations. Many different factors can influence these kinds of negotiations. For example:

- the contracts under discussion, their value and duration;

- contracts about to expire;

- the financial health of the company – if it is doing well, management might be more flexible, more amenable to making concessions, but if things are slow, people tend to dig in;

- the period (high or low cycle) of the sector in question;

- almost all sectors of activity are subject to seasonal fluctuations which must be taken into account.

Buyer–seller negotiations

You must determine what the best moment for negotiating is, since timing can be an important power factor. In a buyer–seller negotiation, it is usually the buyer who sets the date for negotiations to take place. Consider ski equipment, or equipment for any seasonal activity, even clothes: many people only make their purchases at the end of the season when everything is at sale price to make room for the new stock coming it. If business is calm, then you're in a buyer's market, which is much more advantageous since owners or sellers are more likely to negotiate and make concessions. If you're trying to negotiate a loan at the bank, you'd do well to study the market. If interest rates are going up, you might be better off making a quick decision (unless, of course, you've been informed by a reliable source that they'll come down in the near future). If you know that each year a certain company has to dispose of its surplus of unsold stock, then you're in a good position to negotiate a price at that time.

The Right Time Means Power

How much time should you spend on your preparations and how much time will you devote to the negotiations themselves? Well, obviously you're not going to spend a few weeks buying a refrigerator. However, it's another matter entirely if you have to equip a large company with a new computer system.

In the same way that you would not call a meeting costing £10,000 in order to make a decision worth £1,000, you wouldn't spend a week negotiating the lease on your flat. The time and energy invested in a negotiation should therefore be proportional to the value of the issue under discussion.

If not, you may suddenly get the feeling you're wasting your time; at which point you may be tempted to make large concessions just to speed things up.

As for knowing how much time you should spend preparing, the answer varies according to your experience of the sector to be negotiated, the complexity of the issues, the divergence between proposals and counter-proposals, etc.

Some negotiators maintain that a good rule to follow is first to predict approximately how much time will be needed for the actual discussions, and then allot the same amount of time for your preparations.

Know Where to Concentrate Your Efforts

The most important moment in any negotiation comes at the end of the discussions. This is, of course, self-evident since negotiations come to a close when an agreement has been reached! But it does mean that you'd better conserve your energy – and your trump card – for the moment that you feel a settlement is about to be reached.

You might have some alternatives which the other party doesn't know about and which weaken his or her position. For example, you may have another client or another supplier in the wings, eager to make a deal with you. Introducing this information near the end of the discussions may help you reach a quick agreement.

CHAPTER 12

The Importance of Teamwork

For very important negotiations, you usually won't be able to do all the work yourself. Even seasoned negotiators find it difficult to deal with more than two opponents at the same time. In such cases it's better to form a negotiating team.

Is Teamwork Necessary?

Just because two or three people in your department want to participate in the negotiations doesn't mean you have to form a negotiating team.

Advantages and disadvantages of team negotiations

- When you negotiate as an individual, you can make decisions without having to consult with other persons. **On the other hand**, you do have to take the time to think about your decisions, causing the other party to wait, which sometimes creates added stress.

- Negotiating on your own excludes any divergence of opinion. **On the other hand**, you can't take advantage of anyone else's advice or support, or of various expert opinions.

- Responsibility is concentrated on your shoulders – you are therefore under more pressure. **On the other hand**, if you're part of a team, the responsibility is spread around.

● Teamwork usually speeds up the preparation stage, and makes it more creative and comprehensive. You have access to more sources of information, and you can resort to brainstorming and role-playing, etc. **On the other hand**, you may not really need these reinforcements.

When deciding whether or not to negotiate as part of a team, ask yourself the following three questions.

---

1. How important are these negotiations?
Do they justify monopolizing the energies of a number of persons? It's up to you to decide whether the negotiations at hand really require a team effort.

Could one person handle the negotiations and get everything done? Even if you have the human resources at your disposal, remember that more does not always mean better.

2. How long will the negotiations last?
Allow yourself a generous margin of error to avoid exposing yourself to any unnecessary time pressures.

Obviously in some cases an agreement can be reached much more rapidly than in others. Usually the better you know the other party and the more familiar you are with the situation, the faster an agreement can be reached.

Work on the assumption that team negotiations generally take longer, and add to that the fact that the larger the team the longer the negotiations are likely to last.

3. What strategy should you use?
Certain strategies favour teamwork, others work better with a single negotiator – it all depends on the situation.

How to Choose Your Participants

Once you have decided to opt for team negotiations, how should you select your team? Ask yourself the following seven questions when evaluating potential team members.

1. Is the person a skilled negotiator?

Although a candidate may have a wide assortment of desirable qualities, if he or she lacks negotiating experience, think twice before including them on the team. The person may have been with the project from the beginning; he or she may even be the owner of the company! This doesn't automatically ensure a place at the negotiation table.

In the case of an expert whose presence is indispensable, make it clear that they are to be an observer and say as little as possible, intervening only when their opinions are required.

2. Is the person competent and knowledgeable about the issues under negotiation?

A true negotiator's position lies somewhere between being an expert who is supposed to know everything about the issues under discussion, and Mister Anybody who, strictly speaking, knows practically nothing about them. But every member of your team should be aware of the stakes and what is going on behind the scenes.

3. Does the person want to be part of the team?

Choosing 'volunteers' against their will would be useless and quickly defeat the object. Always opt for candidates who are enthusiastic and highly motivated.

4. Does the person have enough time?

When discussing the question of time with a candidate, remember that you have to account for time spent in preparation as well as actual time at the negotiating table. It can take days to study and assimilate all the information in a given file.

5. Is the person entirely available?

The candidate has to be mentally available – you are not playing games. Each member – each brain – has to play an active role. A person who is badly prepared can have a disastrous effect on the entire team. Say he or she represents the other party in a role-playing exercise, and completely miscalculates his or her position. He or she may appear complacent and weak, unable to reply to any of your arguments, with no clear strategies or surprise tactics. This lack of preparation can have serious consequences: your team may be lulled into a false sense of security, get mauled at the negotiating table and then wonder what happened! Negotiating effectively is not a simple question of time and energy. A participant should play an active role by trying to come up with original solutions, pertinent information about the other party's position, attractive packages, etc.

In short, intelligent participation and innovative thinking are also important qualities of a good negotiator. A person who is preoccupied, whose energy is being consumed by various problems other than the ones under negotiation, is not 100 per cent available for the work at hand.

6. What role will he play?

If you can't find a specific role for a candidate, why make them part of the team at all? Every member must have a specific function, and be integrated into the group's framework as a whole. (We will look at how to divide the various tasks later on in this chapter.) Only include persons who are indispensable: you don't need any 'interested observers' on the sidelines.

7. What can you eventually expect of the candidate?

In other words, does he or she exhibit a measure of enthusiasm for the impending negotiations? Simply put, a team without enthusiasm is like a cake without yeast – it just doesn't rise to the occasion! Of course, you need a good dose of realism too. But enthusiasm can't hurt your cause. On the contrary, it's hard to beat a team that's well prepared, has high ambitions and a reasonable amount of bargaining power, especially if the team spirit if there.

How Large Should Your Team Be?

Once you've opted for team negotiations, you have to decide how many people to include. A small, well-trained team is better than a large, unprepared one where members interrupt each other and get in each other's way.

You can't always add to the number of members of your team, but you can reduce it.

In principle, a smaller team works more efficiently than a larger one. Experience will dictate what works best for you, but the theory is to try to make your team a little smaller than that of the other party. Ideally, have one less in your team. Never create the impression that you're trying to crush your opponent by sheer weight of numbers. This isn't a free for all! Effective negotiation requires intelligence, creativity and presence of mind, not muscle and force. Research has shown that teams with numerical superiority actually tend to rely on that advantage at the expense of vigilance and creativity.

Now that you've decided who is to be on your team and the size of it, let's look at ways of transforming a simple group of people into an effective negotiating team.

How to Build Your Team

What makes a football team a winning side, apart from the star players, who can't do it all on their own? The answer is, cohesion.

On the negotiating field you need an overall strategy, where each member of the team has a specific role to play. And the players should usually know each other pretty well, and be aware of each other's strengths and weaknesses. Off the field you need good communication and a sense of solidarity and support among team members, both during the difficult and the good times.

Solidarity is indispensable

Unexpected initiatives on the part of one team member who has decided to play the valiant knight should be prohibited, just as actors are not allowed to improvise in a Shakespeare play: they risk throwing their colleagues completely off track, leaving them uncertain about which course to follow. In other words, individualism in a negotiating situation can be catastrophic.

A good way to make up for the lack of cohesion in a newly formed team is to tackle the intense work of preparation together. In this way, team members will get to know each other and respect the rules of the way the team works. At the same time the group will develop its own internal dynamics and spirit and take on a life of its own.

When the file on the upcoming negotiation is already complete, the research done and the data assimilated, the team should be put through the following steps.

Team Preparation

1. Hold an information session, where each member is given a copy of the file on the upcoming negotiations and information on the other party.

3. Then have a period where members work individually, digesting the contents of the file and assimilating as much information as possible.

3. Hold one or a number of working sessions for the group as a whole, where subjects like objectives, deadlines, bottom lines, etc, can be discussed. This is an opportunity to adjust your strategies and tactics to suit the situation.

Use these occasions to:

- delegate tasks (see below);
- get team members to brainstorm and engage in role-playing;
- fine tune your team.

Use this time to decide how to communicate among yourselves. For example, who will get the ball rolling, how you can let a team member know that you want them to remain silent, or that you want them to speak out, etc. Try to develop a code, along the lines of a rugby team, using signals to identity your instructions.

Delegating Tasks

Who's going to do what? The great advantage of teamwork is that you can concentrate your efforts in one area where you already have some expertise, or which you find stimulating. There are, of course, a number of ways in which tasks can be delegated. Here is one example.

The leader

If a team is to function as one body, then it needs a head. In this age of the 'me-generation' and democracy, we sometimes have a problem with the role of 'the leader' who takes hold of the rudder and steers the boat.

But in negotiations you need a captain. And there can be only one. Work on the basis that the leader can be the only negotiator on the team, and consider the other members as resource persons. If not, you risk running into conflicts, and you won't be able to synchronize your efforts and strategies.

On the other hand, the leader does not necessarily have to be the person with the most important position, hierarchically speaking. This can even end up working against you, if the other party finds out. They may then decide to talk only to that person, since he or she is the one who controls the purse strings.

The leader should be more of a spokesperson: the one who does most of the talking, making proposals, presenting arguments and counter-arguments, refusals and agreements.

The first officer

The first officer's job is to answer certain specific questions, and to sum up the terms and proposals being discussed around the table. This person is also responsible for helping the leader out whenever a problem arises. For example, if the leader can't answer a question, this person should take over until a satisfactory response is found. The first officer may also be asked to provide more details on a given subject or proposal, or to act as a diversion by answering a question in a rhetorical way. This gives the leader more time to think, without having to ask for an adjournment, which is not usually practical.

The observer

As the title indicates, the observer observes the proceedings, takes notes and then briefs the other members of the team about his or her findings during breaks in the discussions. Although this is a secondary role, it is important and by no means easy. A skilled observer can read between the lines and is aware of the subtle nuances and details which may seem insignificant, but which could make all the difference in the final analysis. It may just be a certain habit, or some kind of body language – nothing should be overlooked. To simplify things, this member of the team should not speak during the discussions, but should concentrate completely on observing and interpreting what he or she sees and hears.

This is a good position for a less experienced negotiator to hold. It's an ideal way to learn by watching how expert negotiators handle various situations.

The expert

Experts are necessary in certain cases. You're much better off bringing in your own expert than relying on the other party to do so. Always make it clear to the expert that he or she is not to talk about your organization in any way, either at the table or away from it, since he or she could unwittingly divulge some information that might harm your cause.

Who Says What?

Be very clear about which subjects are to be avoided, and which are to be discussed. Also by whom, and when. Doing this will counter a possible tactic of the other party, which could consist of isolating the most inexperienced member of your team and asking something like, 'and what have *you* got to say about this point?' when a delicate issue is being discussed.

Enforce the law of silence

Some people just can't hold their tongues. They don't necessarily give away any secrets, but they are incapable of listening to other people talk without putting in their own two penn'orth.

The problem is that a negotiation is not a conversation. So if a person is uncomfortable not participating in the discussions, it might be better if he or she weren't there. Negotiations are not casual get-togethers – they're not the right place for trying to impress people or imposing your personality.

Some people find silence, not verbal exchanges, stimulating. They can't bear silences that last too long, and end up saying something that could ruin your chances.

The Importance of Attitude

There's not much that a well-prepared team with high ambitions and a reasonable amount of bargaining power can't achieve if it has the right kind of team spirit. So what exactly *is* the right kind of team spirit?

The first questionnaire (Questionnaire A) will help you identify the qualities which are desirable in the members of a negotiating team. There is no marking system against which to tot up your answers, because the various qualities are like apples and oranges – they cannot be interchanged. It's up to you to think about your answers and evaluate the respective qualities needed for each member of your team, in light of your answers.

For example, if one potential member of your team lacks a little humour, but has a strong sense of solidarity, would you include that person or not? Probably, you should. Team spirit is much more important than a sense of humour.

On the other hand, a short-tempered person, with deep prejudices, would not make a good negotiator. Nor would persons with an alcohol problem, or with marital problems, at least while their problems persist.

We can say that an ideal team member would get 'yes' answers to all the questions except the last two and we take for granted that the candidate in question has already favourably impressed you with his or her talents as a negotiator.

It may also be interesting to evaluate yourself as a potential team member!

The second questionnaire (Questionnaire B) is designed to help you evaluate not only the individual members of your team, but also the team as a whole.

You will notice that the two questionnaires overlap on some points. This is because the questions apply both to individuals and to the group as a whole.

Questionnaire A: The Team Member

Yes No

1. Can he/she take a lot of stress without losing control?

2. Is he/she able to assimilate a given situation rapidly and effectively?

3. Is he/she able to come up with alternatives?

4. Can he/she remain objective under most circumstances?

5. Does he/she know how to handle pressure, wherever it comes from?

Yes No

6. Can/he/she remain calm, no matter what the circumstances?

7. Does he/she have a sense of humour?

8. Does he/she have a creative approach? Is he/she capable of making intelligent compromises?

9. Does he/she know how to listen?

10. Can he/she keep quiet, even during long periods of silence?

11. Does he/she have a pleasant personality?

12. Does he/she have a tendency to lose his/her temper, get upset easily? Is he/she often in a bad mood?

13. Does he/she enjoy working as part of a team?

14. Is he/she likely to exhibit a sufficient degree of solidarity with the rest of the group?

15. Is he/she the kind of person who likes to show off, without considering the consequences?

16. Is he/she capable of overcoming his/her personal prejudices (of sex, class, race, position, etc.)?

17. Is he/she able to moderate someone else's anger?

18. Is he/she likely to remain tactful, no matter what the circumstances?

19. Is he/she likely to respect team discipline?

20. Do his/her appearance and manner coincide with the style

21. Is his/her general health good?

Yes No

22. Is he/she a smoker?

23. Does he/she have any personal problems (alcohol, drugs, depression, marital problems, etc.)?

Questionnaire B: The Team as a Whole

Yes No

1. Do team members voluntarily suggest working together?

2. Do members encourage creativity in other members?

3. Are they able to accept ideas suggested by others?

4. Are they able to evaluate the impact of their proposals (in other words, to analyse feedback)?

5. Does the leader of the group tend to make decisions on his/her own when things are going well, and to look for support only when things are going badly?

6. Do team members tend to see the negative side of things?

7. When the team has a brainstorming session, do the results generally provide sufficient food for thought?

8. Are orders and directives respected?

9. Does the code you've set up for discreet, internal communication work well?

CHAPTER 13

Role-playing

You're at the White House, in the president's famous oval office. A group of men in their shirtsleeves are busy studying piles of documents and files. The atmosphere is tense. You can feel that something important is about to take place.

Suddenly, one of the men asks the president a question. Seated behind his imposing desk, he hesitates for a fraction of a second, and then answers, speaking slowly and precisely. When he finishes, a second man asks another question, which the president answers with ease. This is followed by a third question. A man, seated at the back of the room, is taking notes.

The president stops speaking for a moment and leans towards one of his aides, who whispers a few words in his ear. The president then answers the third question. It's obvious that he's repeating what he's just been told to say by his aide. This is followed by more questions.

The men asking the questions are all part of the president's staff. In a few minutes, the leader of the most powerful country in the world will face the best journalists in the country at a press conference. All he's doing is getting ready. His aides are racking their brains to find the most provocative, difficult and unexpected questions they can think of.

They're playing out the press conference themselves. In other words, they're role-playing.

They try to discern what questions the journalists are going to ask, and then come up with suitable answers which the president learns by heart. It's as simple as that!

Then the president tries to repeat the answers in as natural and spontaneous a way as possible (including the little jokes and anecdotes that make his responses seem so 'real'). The president must find it amusing when one of the journalists asks a question they think is especially provocative, since he's already got the answer prepared in advance!

The president's aides are responsible for preparing the files, doing the research and studying the habits and special characteristics of each of the journalists, so that they can predict what kinds of questions are likely to be asked.

It is easy to understand how an ex-actor did very well in this most prestigious of jobs, for a period of eight years!

Role-playing Is Serious

Don't be misled by the term 'playing'. Role-playing is not a game. It is a technique to help you learn, predict and plan. This very adult activity is one of the most sophisticated methods of predicting how the other party is going to act and react. The technique allows you to:

- test your arguments

- test your strategies and tactics

- anticipate the other party's arguments

- anticipate the strategies, tactics and surprises the other party may decide to use

- simulate the arguments you plan to use

- develop a scenario of the way you'd like things to go

- observe your reactions, as well as those of the other team members

- correct your arguments whenever obvious incongruities arise (and they always do!)

- establish a degree of objectivity (not so that you will be more likely to agree with the other party, but so that you can predict his or her moves better)

- put your nerves to the test.

In fact, role-playing is an exercise in anticipation. It's a rehearsal, a run through, a bit of living theatre where you get the chance to practise the role you will have to assume during the actual negotiations.

So, if the other party is planning to take you by surprise, they'll have to come up with something really good. And many of the people you'll be dealing with just won't make the effort to do this, counting as they do on a kind of natural inertia which has allowed them to surprise people in the past, with the minimum of effort. What they don't know is that you've got a method to combat this kind of manœuvre!

Put yourself in the other party's place

Role-playing is the best way to gain an understanding of the other party's position, objectives and interests. It allows you to see things from the opposite perspective. And on another level, you get to see yourself the way the other party sees you.

Those who you face in role-playing – who represent the opposing party – can tell you what impact your arguments and strategies have, just how much of a surprise one of your surprise tactics is, and so on.

After the role-playing session, make a careful evaluation of everything that was said and done. Then sum up your performance and the effectiveness of your strategy. If any animosity resulted from the role-playing exercise, do your best to work it out. Take note of:

- which of your preparations were most useful
- which strategies worked best (on both sides)
- where your performance was and was not successful.

Role-playing should uncover problems and gaps in your position and it will indicate your weak points.

Who plays the opposition?

It is often a good idea to use persons who were candidates for the negotiating team, but who weren't chosen for one reason or another. This gives them an opportunity to blow off some steam. Role-playing may be a game, but don't forget that the participants are not always completely innocent! There are various things at stake here – in some cases public credibility is involved, and points can be scored for and against. If a person is extremely accurate in his or her predictions of the reactions and strategies of the other party during role-playing, his or her credibility and political sense is likely to receive a healthy boost.

Some candidates may have been ruled out because of their character defects: perhaps they get angry easily, or tend to get caught up in bickering over minor issues, etc. This is a good opportunity to test your team's nerves when faced with such behaviour.

If a number of you are involved in preparing for the negotiations, start by having everyone from within do the exercise before calling in people from outside.

On the day the role-playing exercise is to take place, don't discuss it beforehand with your colleagues. Don't exchange any information. Just act as if nothing special were to take place.

Should you create a hostile climate?

It's important to simulate the actual atmosphere likely to develop during negotiations, even if it isn't overly friendly. Some negotiators even suggest that it's necessary to create a hostile atmosphere during role-playing exercises.

Not all negotiating situations are hostile, far from it, but it is always a good idea to prepare for the worst.

Such simulated hostility can be a good thing, as long as it doesn't carry over outside the context of the role-playing and affect working relations between team members.

Don't destroy your opponent

Our prevailing attitudes contribute to creating situations. Suppose you start the negotiations feeling like you're backed up against a wall, convinced that the other party is determined to get as much out of you as possible. Your attitude will be defensive, less confident, etc. And this attitude is inevitably going to influence the other party.

If you are wrong, the person you're negotiating with might say something like: 'Well, there's something going on here I don't understand . . .'. He or she could tighten up his or her own position, taking a step back to observe more and participate less. It's a simple question of protecting him- or herself.

In short, you put your opponent on the defensive too.

You'll probably notice his or her change of attitude (more or less consciously) and interpret it as confirmation of your suspicions. And if you were wrong to begin with, you've lost an opportunity for both of you to benefit, since your relationship will have already taken a turn for the worse, and the atmosphere will be one of hostility and suspicion.

As we have already said, prepare for the worst but plan for the best! It's up to you to study the opposition and set the proper tone for your role-playing exercises.

Some people recommend exaggerating the obstacles to create more hostility during role-playing. For example, prohibit smoking, ask one member of the team to break the rule without the others knowing, express disagreement forcefully and be hard to get along with.

These kinds of ploys are effective ways of evaluating the psychological resistance of your team members. But remember that, strictly speaking, this kind of resistance doesn't have much to do with the ability to negotiate a fruitful and profitable agreement.

Negotiating On Your Own

Are you practising on your own? There's nothing to stop you from assuming both roles yourself. Make sure no one can hear you: they may wonder what's wrong with you! That's exactly what happened on more than one occasion to Aristotle Onassis, who was heard talking, sometimes shouting at someone, although he was known to be alone in his office! In fact what he was doing was arguing first for himself, and then for his opponent.

Make your own movies!

Buy, rent or borrow a video camera and observe your responses, and the way you speak in an objective way. This can be of great help when analysing the strength of your arguments, and seeing if the tone you adopt is really effective. If you can't convince yourself, you have to assume that you'll have trouble convincing other people! Imitate Ronald Reagan, ex-president of the US and practise until the tone and the accompanying gestures – not to mention the substance of your argument – is just right. You can use this method to practise how to avoid answering questions as well. It's just as important to learn how not to answer a question as it is to answer one!

Once you've drawn up your arguments and strategies, practise presenting them out loud. This forces you to use not only the right words, but the right gestures and intonations as well. Do this not so much to learn what you have to say by heart, but to be totally relaxed when you say it.

The mistakes you make in practice probably won't be repeated when the actual negotiations take place. You'll also be more fluent, having already practised what you're going to say. You won't have to pay as much attention to what you're saying either, which will give you more opportunity to observe the other party.

If you don't have access to a video camera, try using your spouse, or perhaps a friend, to assume the role of the other party. Or you could try using a mirror!

And if you start to feel a little ridiculous in front of your mirror, spouse or video camera, just think about any people who excel at anything – sports stars for example – and remind yourself that they do a lot more than simply perform on the big day. They spend most of their time practising, because as the old truism goes, practice makes perfect.

How to Get Ideas

You probably know people who always seem to come up with bright ideas, who seem to find an original way of looking at almost any situation.

Have you ever asked yourself how these people seem to generate a constant flow of great ideas, instead of being limited to one every now and then? We tend to rationalize the question away by saying that they're just more intelligent than we are, or more creatively inclined, etc. Such explanations assume that the quality is innate, like some kind of bonus bestowed on certain people at birth.

In fact people who regularly come up with great ideas are often no more intelligent than you or I. The difference is that they cultivate a state of mind which is conducive to the birth of original ideas. In other words, they have a method. They may be intelligent, certainly, but they don't have to be exceptionally brainy.

All this leads us to the technique of **brainstorming**. The aim of the game is to provide you with a rich harvest of new ideas that should help you find the best negotiating strategy for a given situation, and solve any problems or weaknesses that arise in role-playing.

Use the hidden resources of your brain to find ways to persuade the other party to find suitable arrangements, packages, new and interesting proposals and solutions that could benefit both parties, as well as to develop an effective and powerful strategy. Our logical mind can furnish us with a host of acceptable ideas, but it lacks that special light, that flash of intuition which is capable of producing a radically new and effective approach.

In other words, you have to cultivate the soil of your mind if you want to see new and creative ideas grow!

The 10-step brainstorming checklist

The rules of the game are simple – and fun! Brainstorming can be an enjoyable activity that relaxes you while you build up your file in preparation for negotiations. Here's how to proceed.

1. You can conduct a brainstorming session alone, or with a number of people. The important thing is that you feel at ease with the persons you've chosen to help you. Don't include more than eight people: if

you do, some of the participants may lose interest and undermine the entire process by remaining silent and intimidating the other participants.

2. Choose a location where everyone feels at ease. If possible, it shouldn't be the place where you conduct your regular meetings. However, if that can't be avoided, do something to modify the atmosphere and make it more relaxed, like bringing in some food, using first names, changing the seating arrangements, etc.

3. Get the group to participate in choosing a chairperson to ensure that the rules of the game are respected.

4. Describe the rules of the game:
   - participants have to come up with the greatest number of ideas possible, as wacky or strange as they may seem
   - make it understood that during the session none of the ideas presented will be judged and evaluated. There will be no approval or disapproval – only complete neutrality. The evaluation phase comes later.

5. Set a time limit, say 5 to 10 minutes.

6. State the problem in question.

7. Open the floor for ideas. The chairperson writes the ideas down on a blackboard. You can also use a tape recorder or video camera. However, it's helpful to write the ideas down anyway, so that participants can see them and use them as a springboard for finding new ideas. Also, displaying even the craziest ideas will encourage the other participants to let go, and it is this feeling of freedom that results in creativity and originality. Encourage humour, which can be of great help in overcoming inhibitions.

8. During the evaluation phase which comes next, examine the ideas with a critical eye. Don't expect too much – most of the suggestions made will be useless. It sometimes takes 20 or 30 ridiculous ideas before you find one that can really work. Consider this as part of your research: an idiotic suggestion may spark something that could suit your needs exactly. Choose the suggestions which seem most interesting, without emphasizing who was responsible for them.

9. Look at the list of suggestions you chose and, as a group, try to improve them and develop viable strategies based on them.

10. Keep only those ideas which can actually help resolve the problem at hand.

CHAPTER 14

A Preparation Checklist

Use these checklists as your reference file when you prepare for your next negotiating session. It is important to proceed in this structured way if you want to be an effective negotiator.

- If you write down your objectives, as well as areas of convergence and divergence, you can specify what you want, and what you can give in return. This forces you to clarify details which you may not feel like confronting.

  When you confront issues head on then you are conducting a 'reality test' which could save you considerable amounts of time, effort and money. By using the checklist, you dispel any uncertainty and confusion which may surface during the discussions themselves – and sometimes even afterwards!

- Once your objectives are down on paper, it's easier to evaluate them objectively. In other words, you gain extra perspective.

- If you're working as part of a team, the checklist will help to clarify each member's role and avoid discrepancies. This results in a clearly defined consensus and reinforces the group's collective strength.

- The checklist will serve as a reference point throughout the negotiations, preventing you from being thrown off track by the other party.

- The checklist will also help you draw up a post-negotiation evaluation of your performance, and write a report on it (if and when required).

The questions will not always correspond to your situation. But take the time to cover them all; it's a simple way to make sure you haven't left anything out. You can add your own questions to the checklist if required.

I General Questions

1. **What are the main issues in the negotiations at hand?**

   _____

   _____

2. **What are the main stumbling blocks likely to result in conflict?**

   _____

   _____

3. **In a single sentence, can I identify my interests as far as this deal is concerned?**

   - Short-term interests _____

   - Medium-term interests _____

   - Long-term interests _____

4. **What are my objectives?**

   First Objective _____

   Maximum _____

   Minimum _____

   Benefits? _____

   Disadvantages? _____

   Financial impact? _____

   Value? _____

   Legal implications? _____

   Second Objective _____

   Checklist continues ▶

Maximum _____

Minimum _____

Benefits? _____

Disadvantages? _____

Financial impact? _____

Value? _____

Legal implications? _____

Third Objective _____

Maximum _____

Minimum _____

Benefits? _____

Disadvantages? _____

Financial impact? _____

Value? _____

Legal implications? _____

5. *Ideally* what would I like to get out of these negotiations?

_____

_____

6. What do I *absolutely* have to get out of these negotiations (in other words, what is my bottom line)?

_____

_____

Checklist continues ▶

7. **What are the objectives of the other party?**

First Objective _____

Maximum _____

Minimum _____

Benefits? _____

Disadvantages? _____

Financial impact? _____

Value? _____

Legal implications? _____

Second Objective _____

Maximum _____

Minimum _____

Benefits? _____

Disadvantages? _____

Financial impact? _____

Value? _____

Legal implications? _____

Third Objective _____

Maximum _____

Minimum _____

Benefits? _____

Disadvantages? _____

Checklist continues ▶

Financial impact? _____

Value? _____

Legal implications? _____

8. **What are the main points of divergence between my objectives and those of the other party, as I have just defined them?**

_____

_____

9. **Are there any points of convergence?**

_____

_____

10. **Which issues can only be bargained for (what one side gains the other side loses)?**

_____

_____

11. **What might the bottom line of the other party be?**

_____

_____

12. **What packages could benefit both parties?**

Package 1 _____

Advantages for me _____

Advantages for the other party _____

Checklist continues ▶

Package 2 _____

Advantages for me _____

Advantages for the other party _____

Package 3 _____

Advantages for me _____

Advantages for the other party _____

13. **What concessions am I ready to make?**

_____

_____

14. **What concessions do I want to obtain from the other party?**

_____

_____

15. **To my knowledge, are there any pressures or restraints that may incite the other party to agree to a settlement?**

_____

_____

16. **What about my own pressures and restraints?**

_____

_____

17. **Am I under any time pressures that could influence the course of negotiations?**

yes ☐   no ☐

Checklist continues ▶

If yes, what are they?

_____

_____

18. **Is the other party under any time pressures that could influence the course of negotiations?**

    yes ☐   no ☐

If yes, what are they?

_____

_____

19. **What are my trump cards?**

    _____

    _____

20. **What trump cards might the other party have?**

    _____

    _____

21. **What are my weak points?**

    _____

    _____

22. **What might the other party's weak points be?**

    _____

    _____

Checklist continues ▶

23. What are my alternatives in the event no agreement is reached?

Best _____

Second best _____

Acceptable _____

Worst _____

24. What are the other party's alternatives in the event no agreement is reached?

Best _____

Second best _____

Acceptable _____

Worst _____

25. Is there a third person who could influence the course of the negotiations?

yes ☐   no ☐

26. If yes, who and to which party's advantage?

_____

_____

II Determining the Type of Negotiations in Progress

1. What are my impressions of the other party?

_____

_____

2. What is the other party's general attitude? Mentality?

_____

_____

3. What style of negotiation does the other party seem to favour?

_____

_____

4. How am I perceived?

_____

_____

5. In my opinion, is the other party's general approach to negotiations based on:

co-operation? ☐   conflict? ☐

6. Is he or she likely to change this attitude?

yes ☐   no ☐

Other remarks _____

7. Do I perceive the situation as one of:

co-operation? ☐   conflict? ☐

Checklist continues ▶

8. In my opinion, the communication between the parties is:

good ☐   bad ☐   neutral ☐

9. What makes me think this way?

_____

_____

10. Based on past history (assuming you've already had business relations with this party) the general climate between the parties is:

good ☐   bad ☐   neutral ☐

11. The chances for *both* parties benefiting from the situation are:

good ☐   bad ☐   neutral ☐

12. Are the stakes:

simple? ☐   multiple? ☐

13. Is this a one-time deal, or an ongoing business relationship?

one-time ☐   ongoing ☐

14. Am I dealing with a flexible or rigid negotiator?

flexible ☐   rigid ☐

15. Is the division of power entirely in the hands of one party, which may decide to take maximum advantage of it?

balanced ☐   unbalanced ☐

16. In light of the previous questions, are the negotiations more likely to be based on:

conflict? ☐   co-operation? ☐

Checklist continues ▶

17. **In light of the previous questions, can I assume that there is an equal division of power?**

    yes ☐   no ☐

18. **If no, is the division of power:**

    in my favour? ☐   in the other party's favour? ☐

19. **Still in the light of the previous questions, is the general climate:**

    good? ☐   neutral? ☐   deteriorated? ☐

20. **What negotiating style seems to be prevalent in the other party?**

    _____

    _____

21. **What are working relations like in the other party's organization?**

    _____

    _____

22. **How have their past negotiations worked out?**

    _____

    _____

III Tactics and Strategies

1. **What strategy will I use during the course of these negotiations?**

   _____

   _____

2. **Do I have an alternative strategy?**

   yes ☐   no ☐

3. **If yes, what is it?**

   _____

   _____

4. **What tactics can I use?**

   _____

   _____

5. **Can I identify three strategies the other party is likely to resort to?**

   (1) _____

   (2) _____

   (3) _____

6. **From what I know, what tactics are the other party like to use?**

   _____

   _____

7. **Who are my competitors in this situation?**

   _____

   _____

Checklist continues ▶

8. **What are the strong points of the competition?**

_____

_____

9. **What are their weak points?**

_____

_____

10. **What arguments could get me to change my mind, if I were in the other party's shoes?**

_____

_____

11. **Are there any counter-arguments?**

_____

_____

12. **What are the arguments in favour of my point of view?**

_____

_____

13. **What proof do I have?**

_____

_____

14. **What documented material do I have which could impress and convince the other party of my point of view?**

_____

_____

IV The Other Party

1. **What power does the other party have?**

   _____

   _____

2. **Does he or she have to consult with someone else before concluding an agreement?**

   yes ☐   no ☐

3. **What are the sensitive points of both the person I'm dealing with and the company he or she represents?**

   _____

   _____

4. **Has he or she succeeded in past negotiations?**

   yes ☐   no ☐

5. **How have past litigations involving the company I'm negotiating with been resolved?**

   well ☐   badly ☐

6. **What do I know about the other negotiator's habits?**

   _____

   _____

7. **What are his or her political preferences?**

   _____

   _____

Checklist continues ▶

8. **General portrait of the person I'm dealing with:**

   - How long in present job? _____

   - Tax bracket? _____

   - Professional history? Successes, failures, other companies worked for, etc.

     _____

     _____

   - Part of town lived in? _____

   - Own house or rent payer? _____

   - Marital status? _____

   - Hobbies? _____

   - Kind of car? _____

   - Preferred food? _____

   - Favourite restaurants? _____

   - Favourite wines? _____

   - Favourite holiday spots? _____

9. **What are the other party's needs according to the Maslow scale (based on your own intuition and grasp of psychology):**

		weak	strong
(1)	Physical survival	☐	☐
(2)	Security	☐	☐
(3)	Belonging	☐	☐
(4)	Need for recognition	☐	☐
(5)	Self-realization	☐	☐

   Checklist continues ▶

163

10. How can I satisfy this person more than anyone else?

_____

_____

_____

V Strategic Questions

1. Are you going to take risks? If yes, what are they?

yes ☐   no ☐

_____

_____

2. Are you going to try and establish a climate of confidence and co-operation?

yes ☐   no ☐

3. What concessions do you plan to obtain?

_____

_____

4. What concessions are you ready to make?

_____

_____

5. What is your bottom line?

_____

_____

Checklist continues ▶

6. **How are you going to make the other party understand just what is negotiable and what isn't?**

   _____

   _____

7. **How do you plan to convince the other party?**

   _____

   _____

8. **Are you going to use any pressure tactics?**

   yes ☐   no ☐

   If yes, what are they?

   _____

   _____

9. **How will you react to pressure tactics?**

   _____

   _____

10. **What kind of pace will you favour?**

    _____

    _____

11. **Will you call for a third person to intervene?**

    yes ☐   no ☐

Checklist continues ▶

165

12. **If you're negotiating as part of a team, have you determined how authority will be divided among the members?**

_____

_____

13. **Are you going to use any surprise tactics?**

yes ☐   no ☐

14. **Are you going to do any bluffing?**

yes ☐   no ☐

15. **Are you planning to overbid?**

yes ☐   no ☐

16. **Are you going to talk about the competition?**

yes ☐   no ☐

17. **What kind of settlement will you seek?**

_____

_____

18. **What impression do you want to leave the other party with?**

_____

_____

19. **What advantages do you have?**

_____

_____

And Finally...

Once you have completed the checklists you should also draw up a list of all the questions you wish to discuss with the other party and before you close the discussion make sure that you have covered them all to your satisfaction.

This is useful because anything which is left out of the discussions now will probably be omitted altogether, since it's not a good idea to try and reopen negotiations once an agreement has been reached. You open yourself up to losing more in the long term.

Points to discuss with the other party

1. _____

2. _____

3. _____

etc.

CHAPTER 15

Final Preparations on the Day

When the day of negotiations finally dawns you'll want to be in top shape. If you have followed the advice given in this book so far you should be well prepared for what is to follow. Here are some final hints to help your preparations on the big day itself.

Your Energy Cycle

Everyone has a personal energy cycle. Do you know the time of day that you're most alert, most awake, least susceptible to the stress of fatigue? Many people have more energy in the morning. If you're working as part of a team, try to discover which part of the day most members seem to be at the high point of their energy cycle.

Even when you have to travel, try to make sure that the schedule of the negotiations corresponds to your energy cycle.

Avoid fatigue

Be organized and get lots of rest. It's very important to apply the principles of an ordinary healthy lifestyle in order to stay calm and alert.

Try to avoid fatigue as much as possible: it diminishes your faculties, undermines your self-confidence and destroys your patience.

Fatigue can cause even the most experienced expert to commit serious errors. You will be more vulnerable to pressure, and more likely to succumb to arguments demanding a quick decision.

Being tired can also result in your losing sight of what is essential.

Sometimes the other party will spend an interminable amount of time on secondary issues, and turn the negotiations into a marathon in an attempt to wear you down before the deadline expires.

A useful strategy for combating fatigue is always to have one member of the team in reserve, fresh and rested, who can step in when things drag on for too long. This will help to discourage the other party from trying to wear you down.

Don't play Superman

Avoid negotiations that go on all night, even if your image of a seasoned negotiator is someone who, with sleeves rolled up and a thermos of coffee on the table, can continue for days and nights on end without stopping. A negotiation isn't a marathon: such a situation might test your endurance, but it probably won't produce very positive results.

If you don't feel well, postpone the start of the negotiations for a few hours. It's useless to enter the fray if you're not in top shape. Try to find someone to replace you for a few hours (which won't always be easy) or ask for an adjournment. The repercussions of such a move will be less serious than if you made some terrible mistake because of your state of health.

You should also 'negotiate' the times you'll be breaking for meals. Try to stick as closely as possible to your normal routine (as well as that of the other team members).

Some Helpful Hints

Don't react to negative insinuations

Some people will try to throw you off track by alluding to certain subjects that they know are likely to upset you. They might ask questions which are meant to irritate you by touching a sensitive nerve:

'How are your children?' (when you haven't seen them for years . . .)

'Well be at it late again tonight. I guess your wife won't be too happy.' (you've been having some marital problems . . .)

'You'll be late for dinner again.' (you've been late for everything for the past three days, trying to hammer out the important issues . . .)

Concentrate

Before an important negotiating session, no matter what the circumstances, take the time to concentrate your mind and prepare for what is about to take place. Consider practising relaxation plus visualization in order to programme your subconscious. The best time to do such preparation is when you are about to go to sleep or just as you awake. When you are in this state of mind, your mental images have a stronger effect on your subconscious. For more on relaxation and positive thinking, see page 291.

Spoil yourself!

If you have to travel to negotiate, go business or first class if you can. Consider the higher price to be an investment in your company. Being comfortable and travelling in a relaxed environment reduces the risk of fatigue and will put you in a much better frame of mind.

And there's nothing like travelling first class to boost your ego and self-confidence. It helps compensate for the fact that *you're* the one who has to go to the trouble of travelling instead of the other party.

Don't start the negotiations as soon as you arrive. Take time to rest up and relax.

Don't try to have fun

You'll have plenty of other chances to amuse yourself. But this is an important moment, so you should concentrate on it. Think twice before accepting invitations to taste the nightlife of the town you're visiting. It may be part of the other party's strategy to appoint a member of their team to wine and dine you until the early hours while they get a good night's rest. The likely effects of all this living it up on your negotiating ability can be well imagined.

Eat well

This doesn't necessarily mean you should eat a lot! You don't have to eat more to negotiate well, but neither do you have to be content with fast food and sandwiches. The negotiating timetable should allow sufficient time for eating in a relaxed atmosphere.

Avoid planning sessions that continue after a heavy meal. Digestion causes somnolence and reduces your concentration. If you have no say in establishing the timetable, which is often the case, then you should consider the following.

● Eat light food: you'll be more alert. As we have already said, a full stomach usually relaxes you and reduces your concentration. Avoid foods that are difficult to digest. Eat fish and chicken instead of red meat if you can.

- If you have to have a steak, make it small. Or stick to salads. It's educational to watch someone polish off a huge rib steak and a glass or two of wine, and then try to negotiate! They'd be better off going to sleep!

- You may even consider keeping yourself slightly hungry. Save eating until after the papers have been signed. Then you can dine and drink to your heart's content! But in the meantime, you need all your faculties fully alert and your sixth sense – intuition – is adversely affected by heavy eating.

- Don't drink any alcohol, for the same reasons. In a negotiating situation, even a glass of white wine at lunch is too much.

- Try to wait 20 minutes between the main course and your dessert, or better still don't have any dessert at all. Have a piece of cheese instead. Sugar complicates digestion and slows it down considerably. That little piece of pie can sometimes prove to be very costly!

- Finally, this is not the time to forgo your daily workout routine, whether you jog, swim, do yoga, etc. On the contrary, being in top physical condition is more important than ever!

Be prudent about invitations

Decline to attend elaborate dinner parties and entertainment (carefully) planned in your honour if you can.

For example, perhaps you arrive at night, and preparations are to begin the next morning. You are invited out to one of the best restaurants in town. What do you do?

You should decline as politely as possible, on the pretext that you still have a lot of work to do (actually you'll be going to bed early). But you add that you'll be delighted to accept once the negotiations are over. If the dinner doesn't materialize then, you can be pretty sure it was just a trap in the first place.

If you are tempted, find out if the principle negotiator from the other side is supposed to be there or not. If not, you can then be sure it's a trap! Or, if you can't refuse without being impolite, or if the other party insists, try to observe the rules for eating outlined above: eat lightly and not too close to your bedtime.

So here you are, ready to face the opposing side. In Part III we will look at how things should proceed during the negotiations themselves.

HOW TO BE AN EFFECTIVE NEGOTIATOR

CHAPTER 16

How Do *You* Negotiate?

Test yourself by answering the following questions.

Yes No

1. In my discussions with business partners I always work on the basis that I'm ready to negotiate.

2. The outcome of a negotiation is decided at the moment an agreement is reached.

3. Whenever I can make a concession that doesn't cost me anything, I do it voluntarily.

4. When the other party is in a bad position, I get the most I can out of the situation.

5. When I leave the negotiating table with the lion's share, I'm not shy about letting the other party know I've won.

6. I let the other party know early on that they're dealing with a skilled negotiator.

7. I involve outside people (the other party's competitors, other sales representatives, etc) during the course of negotiations.

Yes No

8. During negotiations, I let the other party ask the questions, preferring to speak as much as possible.

9. I let the other party guess what my main objective is.

10. In negotiations, honesty is more effective than skill.

11. I always allow a comfortable margin between my objectives and my demands.

12. I like to get the other party to become less concerned with his/her own objectives.

13. When negotiations are concluded, I always give away a little extra.

14. The most important thing is what is said, not where it's said.

Now count up your points:

1. Yes=1 No=0		8. Yes=1 No=0
2. Yes=1 No=0		9. Yes=1 No=0
3. Yes=1 No=0		10. Yes=1 No=0
4. Yes=1 No=0		11. Yes=0 No=1
5. Yes=1 No=0		12. Yes=1 No=0
6. Yes=1 No=0		13. Yes=1 No=0
7. Yes=0 No=1		14. Yes=1 No=0

Results

Between 10 and 14 points: Not everyone has a knack for negotiating. But with a little effort you can improve dramatically.

Between 6 and 9 points: You're already doing pretty well. And now that you've taken an interest in negotiating, you'll be able to radically improve your performance and increase your revenues.

Between 0 and 5 points: You're already applying many of the principles of effective negotiation. If your knowledge is intuitive, you're a born negotiator. And when you start methodically to apply the principles in this book, the sky's your limit!

Comments

This questionnaire was based on the 10 major principles of negotiation as outlined by John Winkler of the London Institute of Marketing.

Each of the principles and the comments made here will set the agenda for Part III of this book.

1. *In my discussions with business partners I always work on the basis that I'm ready to negotiate* – No

Negotiate as little as possible, and only about minor issues. This might seem like strange advice to give people who are just starting a negotiation. Obviously the question has its subtleties. Note that we didn't say, 'Don't negotiate' but 'Negotiate as little as possible'.

The other party will do everything possible to get you to make major concessions, while your aim is to make only minor concessions in order to gain as much as possible. Ideally you shouldn't have to make any concessions at all to get what you want.

The key to understanding this question is flexibility. If you are in a weak position, you wouldn't want the other party to abuse its power. Therefore, when a negotiating situation arises, don't be overly severe, even if you're in an advantageous position this time. 'He who lives by the sword shall perish by the sword' still holds true.

There's always the possibility of having to deal with the same person on another occasion, but with the tables turned. This principle of not negotiating is therefore quite a paradox: its value as a rule lies in your ability to break it at the right time.

2. *The outcome of a negotiation is decided at the moment an agreement is reached* – No

Always be as well prepared as possible for the start of the negotiations. Even when negotiations last for hours and even days, it does seem that a strong first impression is often the number one factor: it seems that often everything is decided in the first 15 minutes.

So make sure that you create a clear, positive and constructive impression from the outset. In fact this is precisely when it's most important to project your desire to see the situation resolved in accordance with your objectives.

3. *Whenever I can make a concession that doesn't cost me anything, I do it voluntarily* – No

Don't give things up too easily. This may seem elementary, but you should remember this, even if the concessions don't cost you anything. Why? Because if he or she doesn't have to work for it, the other party may not think the concession is worth anything, and won't be likely to give you very much in return . . .

4. *When the other party is in a bad position, I get the most I can out of the situation* – No

Don't abuse your power. If the other party is in bad shape, help him or her out, unless you're planning to leave the country or change careers. This is not only because of your altruistic outlook on life. Business relationships are built up over time. It's much better to make someone a good business partner than an enemy.

Even if you're not planning to continue doing business with that person, you'll still have one enemy less to reckon with . . .

5. *When I leave the negotiating table with the lion's share, I'm not shy about letting the other party know that I've won* – No

Be modest in your triumph. As with Question 4, it's not a good idea to abuse your power. It serves no purpose to destroy someone just to show how superior you are. If you're tempted to boast, ask yourself why. The vast majority of effective negotiators will agree that the most successful negotiations are those in which both parties feel they've come out a winner.

6. *I let the other party know early on that they're dealing with a skilled negotiator* – No

Don't seek the approval of the other party. Once again, negotiations are not the time or place to get rid of your frustrations or prove your superiority. If the other party thinks you're too skilled, they might hesitate in doing business with you, afraid of losing out. It's much better to gain the other party's confidence and be appreciated for your true value.

7. *I involve outside people (the other party's competitors, other sales representatives, etc) during the course of negotiations* – Yes

During negotiations it's perfectly acceptable to talk about other people, including the competition. You should let the other party know that he or she is not the only one with whom you can do business. There's nothing wrong with quoting a competitor's prices, for example, or with informing the other party that you intend to meet another supplier later on, to discuss the same subject.

8. *During negotiations, I let the other party ask the questions, preferring to speak as much as possible* – No

Learn how to listen attentively. If you're constantly talking, you won't have any opportunity to sound out the other party: you won't know what they want, or if what they want is compatible with what you want.

Who do you think controls the negotiations? All other factors being equal, the person asking the most questions is in control of the situation.

9. *I let the other party guess what my main objective is* – No

Get the other party used to accepting your main objective. Give him or her a chance to digest what you'd ideally like to gain from the negotiations. It isn't always possible, of course. If the other party reacts with horror when you name your price, you'll probably have to make some adjustments.

But don't hide an objective because you think it's too ambitious (as long as it *is* relatively realistic). Let the other party know what it is. Make it a part of your life. In the face of such determination, there's a good chance that he or she may start seeing the objective as quite acceptable, and try to find ways to accommodate you.

10. *In negotiations, honesty is more effective than skill* – Yes

A person's word is sacred. Especially when it's your own. Integrity is a powerful negotiating tool when dealing with serious people. If you don't inspire confidence, you'll always be faced with nervous people, difficult to convince and reticent to conclude an agreement with you. And this is another reason not to display your skill as a negotiator.

11. *I always allow a comfortable margin between my objectives and my demands* – Yes

Give yourself room to manœuvre. This is a classic principle: if you have to quote a price or a figure, allow yourself a margin of error.

12. *I like to get the other party to become less concerned with his/her own objectives* – No

Nourish the other party's hopes. It would be futile to try and get the other party to forget his or her objectives. Don't think for a moment that he or she has only sat down at the negotiating table to make you happy. If the other party sees that you are taking their objectives into account, you may succeed in getting him or her to modify them so that they correspond with your own.

13. *When negotiations are concluded, I always give away a little extra* – Yes

Always leave the other party with a favourable impression. At the very last moment, in a burst of spontaneous generosity, you make a minor concession which the other party isn't expecting. This is your 'gift'. If you haven't been overly (and uselessly) severe during the negotiations, then this gesture will contribute to your being remembered as a pleasant person to do business with. And more than that, your gift 'buys' the other party's respect, since the final impression is almost as important as the initial one.

14. *The most important thing is what is said, not where it's said* – No

Prepare the terrain beforehand. Don't leave anything to chance. Everything concerning the negotiating environment should be thought out in advance, from the size of the table to the decor of the room to the refreshments that will be served. The three most important things in negotiations are preparation, preparation and preparation!

It's an accepted fact that the person who is better prepared will win at the negotiating table.

To Sum Up

Remember these principles.

- Negotiate as little as possible, and only about minor issues.

- Be as prepared as possible for the start of the negotiations.

- Don't give anything up too easily.

- Don't abuse your power.

- Be modest in triumph.

- Don't use the other party as a gauge of your talent or skill.

- During negotiations, there's nothing wrong with talking about competitors.

- Learn to listen attentively.

- Get the other party used to accepting your ambitions.

- Your word is sacred.

- Always allow yourself a margin of error.

- Take the other party's hopes and objectives into account.

- Leave the other party with a favourable impression.

- Prepare the groundwork in advance.

Now we are ready to see how a negotiating session should proceed.

CHAPTER 17

How to Open Negotiations

If you've never taken part in an important negotiation before, you might by now be asking yourself the following questions:

- How should the negotiations start?
- Who speaks first, and about what?
- At what point do the parties spell out their demands?

One thing is certain, **the start of the negotiations are decisive**.

The Opening Rites

Role-playing is a part of every negotiation. The more important the negotiation is, the more elaborate will be the roles being played out. The ritual of opening a negotiating session differs, depending on whether the parties are multi-nationals, heads of state or private individuals.

If you have an appointment with your boss or department head because you want a pay rise, for example, you're going to have to explain why you've come. And you should do this in a way that places your request in a favourable light. You might, for example, begin talking about your last successful project. You would not want to mention any mistakes you might have made.

There's always some role-playing involved. Ideally you should be the one to do it, although it's generally up to the party who is hosting the negotiations to open the discussions.

No two negotiations are ever exactly alike, so you'll have to adapt the way you introduce the issues according to the circumstances. You would not proceed in the same way if you thought that the negotiations were going to be competitive and involve a lot of conflict, as you would if you felt the atmosphere was likely to be one of co-operation and mutual respect. In the latter case, of course, you would be more open and friendly.

Preliminaries

Don't just jump in – allow a little time for things to warm up. Introduce the people around the table, with the usual courtesies. Introductions give you an opportunity to find out if the persons at the table are the persons you expected to be dealing with, especially when you don't know them personally.

- Are the persons you expected present?
- Are there too many of them? Too few?

Sum up the situation

The host then gives a brief summary of the situation, including any pertinent background information. If you are the host, it's your move. If the other party delivers the summation, and you think the facts are being distorted, correct them on the spot, or at least get your version on record as quickly as possible.

In fact, everyone has a tendency to interpret facts to their own advantage. There's nothing unusual about that. If we didn't have differences of opinion, there would be no need to negotiate!

The background information should be kept more or less simple according to the situation. But don't overlook the importance of this phase of the negotiations. This is the time when you can:

- make sure both parties are present for the same reasons
- find out if you're on the same wavelength
- agree on the facts, more or less. If you don't agree, at least you're aware of the fact from the outset
- find out if you're speaking the same language
- observe and get to know each other.

In your summary you should really be saying, *'What is the reason for this meeting?'* By introducing your version of the facts, and presenting the background information you place the negotiations in context. But don't be tempted to get into too much detail. This is the moment to decide who will take notes during the discussions.

Try to set the tone, and lay out a broad indication of what you think a final agreement could look like. Formulating a proposal always gives you a slight advantage.

Propose an agenda/timetable

A well-prepared agenda is one of the keys to negotiating effectively. It's like suggesting a 'menu' for the negotiations.

When preparing your agenda you should carefully consider the following questions.

A Negotiating Menu

1. What are you going to discuss and in what order?

2. What are you going to start with?

3. What issues are to be included?

4. What will be omitted?

5. What is the most important issue?

6. What do you propose to deal with first? The most important issue? The least important one?

7. What kind of progress do you foresee? Subject by subject? Groups of subjects?

The person who proposes the agenda in a sense reveals his or her position, priorities, preferences and, above all, gives the other party an idea of the strategy he or she plans to use.

When they see your agenda, the other party can react by preparing themselves accordingly. You're the first to get your feet wet, since the agenda you propose obviously will fit in with your strategy (however, you can always resort to surprise tactics by introducing new subjects during the course of the negotiations).

If an agenda is imposed on you – you don't have to accept it! When you're the visitor, you have to follow the other party's lead during the preliminary stages, but never hesitate to add your two penn'orth to the discussion. If you allow yourself to be taken advantage of right away, you may pay heavily for it later.

Here are some questions you should ask yourself if the other party is proposing the agenda.

- Have any questions been left out that I absolutely must have discussed?

- Does the agenda include questions which I consider non-negotiable?

- What does the agenda reveal about the other party's strategy?

- What are the other party's priorities likely to be?

Plan Different Scenarios

During your preparations, take a look at different possible sequences of events. To develop a scenario, use file cards to write down a number of probable scenes. You can then play around with the order, until you come up with the one that's best for you.

You may want to plan a number of possible scenarios in this way, and decide later which is the best one to adopt. Each scenario should include your own arguments, and your responses to the various proposals the other party is likely to make.

Try to vary the way you deal with the preliminaries and organize the agenda, especially if you negotiate with the same people on a regular basis. If you don't, you risk becoming totally predictable.

So controlling the agenda can be considered a negotiating tactic just like any other. If the other party draws up the agenda, pay careful attention and make sure it suits your needs.

Some Possible Agendas

There are different ways you can proceed. Here are a few choices, since there isn't one single, ideal way which works in all situations and it's a good idea to have several different ways of proceeding at your disposal.

Push

You start with the important issues.

This prevents you wasting time on secondary aspects of the negotiation. Doing this also lets the other party know what your priorities are and allows him or her to prepare him- or herself accordingly.

Procrastinate

You begin with less important issues.

These can serve as bargaining chips later on. Laying possible concessions out on the table in this way is conducive to an atmosphere of co-operation. You keep your trump cards for the end, introducing them at the moment they are likely to be most surprising and therefore most effective.

Assemble

Here you put together groups of issues on which both parties agree, forming packages which are likely to lead to an agreement.

Classify

Classify issues according to what they're about. For example, put all financial issues on one side, and all other issues on the other.

Sort

You review all the issues to be negotiated with the other party and decide if there are any that can be settled quickly.

Select

You suggest dealing with one issue at a time, in an order to be decided by you as you go along. Most negotiators will refuse to accede to this formula since it gives the person controlling the agenda a great advantage – the other party has no time to prepare arguments and proposals. You should not accept this formula if it is suggested to you!

Consult

You prepare an agenda in advance and fax it to the other party for consultation. You can then revise the schedule after receiving the other party's comments.

Concede

You start by putting a certain number of points on the table that you're willing to concede, in order to build up your credibility.

It works like this: because of the concessions you're making, the other party will have to make some concessions in return. If you opt for this route, don't give up too much too easily! Make the other party earn what you're prepared to give – tire them out a little!

This approach can be slightly risky in that the other party may become used to your making concessions, sometimes without asking very much in return. So use it with caution.

Soften them up!

Do you think the other party is looking for a quick and easy victory, as so many people today are? Well, you can play along for a while, throw out some bait, let the other party win on a few minor issues and get them lulled into a false sense of security. Then, when the issues that are really important to you arise, you harden your stance. This is especially effective if the important issues are to be covered towards the end of the negotiations.

What if the other party starts out by being tough and hard as nails? In that case don't concede anything easily at the outset, and try to wear down the other party before you get to the more important issues later on.

Appetizers

You start by dealing with a number of issues which you think both parties can easily agree on. This creates an atmosphere of co-operation, where both sides get used to agreeing.

If you find that the other party is blocking all your proposals, no matter how unimportant, then you can deduce that he or she is jockeying for control of the situation, and that you're probably in for a long and arduous session.

The initial phase of a negotiation is important, not because any of the main issues are resolved, but because it's here that the tone is set for the negotiations as a whole. If your attitude differs radically from that of the other party, experience has shown that it is only during this initial phase that there's a chance of making any changes. It will be too late if you leave it until later on.

Getting Off to a Good Start

Forget the past

Make an effort to clear your mind of any negative residue from previous negotiations. If, for example, your last meeting ended in failure, don't associate that failure with the negotiations now in hand. Try to avoid starting with the attitude that the same thing is bound to happen this time around.

If the previous round of negotiations was crowned with success, however, adopt the attitude that this round is completely different, and that there's no guarantee things will go just as well. You must avoid resting on your laurels and even double your vigilance.

Pay attention to trivial information

Before the actual negotiations begin, pay attention to anything the other party says, both to you and among their team members. People tend to forget that even though the negotiations haven't officially started, it is important to be on your guard and say as little as possible.

The other party may drop some bits of trivial information, which are seemingly unimportant, but which can take on added weight and significance when placed in their proper context.

'I hope things go well this time,' says one member of the opposing team. The phrase 'this time' could mean that past negotiations have been less than satisfying, that they need to reach some kind of settlement this time round, and would be willing to make a few more concessions (which is what you will try to verify as the negotiations progress).

'I reserved a room for two days,' could actually mean, 'I think we can settle these issues in two days or less' or 'I have another meeting in two days, so we'd better work quickly.' Are two days enough for you? Remember the tactic of patience used so effectively by the Japanese.

'Yes, we've been having a good year, but our predictions were even higher, and we have a lot of unsold stock on our hands.' You therefore have some idea of the real value of the unsold stock, which the other party may try to use as a bargaining chip.

Keep an eye out for details, for looks exchanged between team members. Do they seem confident of winning? Are they worried about something? Are they relaxed and calm? Or nervous and in a hurry to get started?

Be very careful about the possibility of a bluff: a shrewd tactic is to drop some seemingly insignificant bit of information which is actually *meant* to put you on the wrong track. Politicians are experts at this kind of strategy.

If you're dealing with skilled negotiators, you'll notice that they're probably very business-like, and that they don't reveal much about anything before the negotiations start. In such cases it's pretty futile to try and guess what's going on in their minds: you'll be met with a solid and studied poker face, developed over years of practice, making any intuitive guesswork impossible.

Also, don't be taken in by a seemingly unorthodox approach. Assume that, until you have proof to the contrary, the other party is highly skilled and in control.

Without having to resort to ESP, the other party's general attitude can be informative. You can sometimes deduce whether or not the other party is hoping for a fruitful outcome.

- Are they smiling?
- Are they talking freely?
- Do their gestures seem relaxed?
- Do they seem tense and nervous?

Create a diversion

During the preliminary phase you may want to tell a few jokes or a funny story which doesn't really have anything to do with the subject of the negotiations. However, make sure that there is no doubt in the other party's mind of the seriousness of your approach. You are just aiming to relax the atmosphere a bit, and observe how the other party reacts.

This kind of little 'performance' gives you a chance to affirm your talents as an actor, to test out how the other party reacts and increase your self-confidence. It will also help you to get an idea of the atmosphere that is likely to prevail throughout the negotiations. How does the other party react to your little anecdote (which appears to be off the cuff, but which has actually been carefully rehearsed!)? Are they clearly waiting for you to get it over with so the bargaining can begin? Or do they seem willing to proceed at your pace?

If they don't smile at all you may conclude that the negotiations to follow are likely to be pretty arduous, unless human relations are not a strong point of the other party's psychology. All this is subject to interpretation, of course. There are many people who smile a lot during the preliminary stages, but who seem to forget completely how to smile once the actual discussions are under way. And remember that it's not necessarily the people who seem disagreeable at this stage that you have to watch out for. You may have a little trouble reaching an agreement with them, but at least you know where you stand.

The really dangerous people are those who disguise their true motives with a crocodile smile, who seem to agree with everything, and who say they are all for co-operation. This is the kind of person who could suddenly turn around and hit you with an ultimatum at some critical point in the negotiations, when he or she feels they've got everything they can out of you, and before you have a chance to work out your side of the deal.

Be diplomatic

Be relaxed and calm when you introduce the issues, even though you may intend to attack and play tough later on. It's best to start things rolling gradually.

Perhaps you think that by starting off in an aggressive, intimidating way you can establish your authority and put yourself in a position of force. However, this tactic often tends to backfire since the other party usually toughens up very quickly and digs into an inflexible posture of defence.

In the very first exchanges (approximately the first three minutes) of negotiations, which set the tone for the rest of the discussions, it's a good idea to show restraint and preferably adopt a pleasant attitude.

You're now ready to get to the heart of the matter. In principle, it should take less time to deal with the preliminaries than it took to read up to this point in the chapter!

The Summing Up

During this information session, you should make sure that both you and the other party are on the same wavelength. It's not unusual for two parties to realize at this stage that they don't agree as to the reasons which brought them to the negotiating table in the first place.

Depending on the context of the negotiations, you should decide here just how open and confident you can be, how many issues will be dealt with and in which order. You should preferably present those issues where there is already some agreement or convergence of opinion first. This gives both parties some common ground to work on, and this is a good thing since both parties have come together because they want to reach an agreement of course, even in the most difficult negotiations. So it's best to introduce and develop the issues in a way which would allow the other party to react favourably to your proposals.

Then deal with the differences of opinion one by one, starting with the least important. Then introduce possible areas of discussion.

Dealing with Delegates

What do you do at this stage if the person you were planning to negotiate with bows out and sends a second-in-command to replace him or her? First you find out if the person delegated has the power to make decisions on his or her own. You could call the original party directly to find out, if necessary.

If the delegatee does not have full power, deal with the secondary issues and save the main issues for a second round. By doing this you don't antagonize the delegatee unnecessarily (he or she might be present for the second round as well), while planning for further negotiations so that you don't waste time in this round discussing issues which can't be decided.

CHAPTER 18

How Effective Negotiations Proceed

The Six Stages of a Formal Negotiation

It has been suggested that all negotiations are comprised of six major stages, and experience confirms this in the vast majority of cases. Here they are.

1. Both sides present their positions, and justify them

In short, both sides put forward their arguments, or defend their position. This is when divergences become most apparent. You get some idea of how far apart the two parties are, as well as an indication of the general climate in which the negotiations are to take place.

2. Next, both parties evaluate their respective positions, deciding what chance they have of influencing each other

This process is often one of trial and error, where the parties try to sound out what maximum concessions are likely to be made. What you are trying to do is alter the other party's perception of the situation so that they understand you won't concede anything of importance without getting a fair and equal return.

3. Together, or separately, the parties look for areas of agreement

Once both parties have stated their positions and measured their respective powers, they get to work (either together or separately) to try to find solutions or areas of possible compromise. This is when you study the options, proposals and counter-proposals, looking for common ground where agreement is possible.

In cases where competition and conflict dominate, both parties will present ready-made solutions. Each side tries to impose the solution which is most advantageous, while refuting the opposing position.

In a co-operative situation, on the other hand, both parties view their differences as a problem to be solved together in an approach called 'joint problem-solving'.

4. Time for adjustments

Here concessions are discussed, whether reciprocally or not. This is the time to exchange, compromise and manœuvre.

5. Solution ... or not

Following the discussions, a solution is either adopted or not, depending on the pros and cons put forward during the discussions.

6. Closure

Before leaving the table, the situation is summarized. Although a total solution may not have been found, a professional negotiator will always make sure to list any positive results the meeting may have produced, and to indicate the parties' intention to work together in future or not.

If a solution *was* found and the negotiations ended in agreement, then the situation is recapitulated and both parties proceed to make a firm commitment, based either on a verbal agreement or a written contract.

Don't forget that, as a general rule, the really important issues are often settled at the very end of the negotiations.

What About Improvised Negotiations?

Not all negotiations can be organized in this way, especially when the situation is more informal. Negotiations often take place in restaurants, in offices, on the golf course, in a waiting room, even in corridors. Obviously you have to adapt to the circumstances at hand. But the more important the negotiations are, the more they are likely to resemble the model described above. You may not have a formal agenda to work with, but you still have to decide on an order for your discussions.

It is also the case that if you want to give the impression that the negotiations you're involved in are, in fact, important, then all you have to do is proceed in the manner described above!

In any case, most negotiations, however informal, resemble the model at least schematically, and you should be able to recognize the various stages described in our model as they occur.

How to Proceed Effectively

We will now consider the rules you should follow when you finally take the floor to outline your point of view.

Avoid being too familiar

By keeping your presentation somewhat formal, you maintain a certain margin of manœuvrability in your relations with the other party. There's always time to get more friendly later on, if the situation is favourable. And being formal adds a serious aspect to your image, the importance of which should not be underestimated.

If you have to argue – structure your arguments

In some circumstances your presentation will resemble that of a lawyer pleading his or her case. Here you must be sure to include all the arguments in support of your position. To do this you may want to prepare a speech which contains all the facts and figures you need to justify your arguments.

In any case, you should always make an effort to structure your initial presentation. You can organize it in one of four ways.

1. History   You explain what steps have been taken in the past to bring about the present situation.

2. Sectors   You group your proposals according to subject and cover the issues one by one, with supporting arguments that point to the conclusion you desire.

3. Description   You describe the situation or the product in detail, emphasizing its advantages and/or inconveniences, depending on the case.

4. Comparison   You compare the present situation or product to other similar ones, citing precedents, examples of previous agreements, etc.

Be clear

Use precise terms to outline your proposals. It can be extremely frustrating to discover that after two hours (or two days!) of discussions, a term that has been used frequently has not been understood.

For example, for an employer the term 'restructuring' could simply mean reorganizing the company's services, without any significant effect on the employees. But for a union representative, the same term might automatically imply lost jobs.

Be brief

Avoid making long presentations. By talking too much, you risk boring the other party. Also, you may give away more information than is absolutely necessary. So, speak as little as possible.

If you must make a long presentation, divide it into sections, almost like the chapters in a book. Try to make it interesting and stimulating. We'll look at some ways to do this later on.

Establish areas of agreement

In general it's not in your interest to reveal all areas of agreement at once. Lead up to possible agreements progressively. If you're facing a seasoned negotiator, you may have to reveal these areas more rapidly, since he or she will be more likely to know the difference between a final and a negotiable offer.

But, in most cases, you should hold back when establishing areas of possible agreement, until the discussions are well under way. Doing this makes the other party earn the agreements, instead of having them handed over on a silver platter. He or she will then be less likely to try and get you to reduce your demands.

Know your own power

Condition yourself! Impress your mind with the advantages you possess in the situation at hand. Above all, do not minimize the importance of your power at the outset of discussions. It's precisely at this point in the discussions that people tend to lack confidence, and to worry about the gaps and weaknesses in their strategy.

To avoid creating a negative image of yourself, stick to this rule:

'For every doubt I have, I will list one of my advantages'.

Reaching an Agreement

What can you do to gain the other party's consent in as many situations as possible?

- **Always present your proposals by emphasizing any benefits they may have for the other party**

Don't think only about what *you* want to get out of the negotiations. Remember that if you want the other party to agree, you have to come up with proposals that they find attractive as well.

- **Present your interests first, and gradually lead up to establishing your position**

This is very important. It's much easier to discuss objectives when a climate of exchange prevails. Establishing your position calls for the other party to establish his or her position as well.

From then on, each side tries to distance the other from their initial position, while pressing for the adoption of their own proposals. This is nothing less than a power struggle, with all that implies in terms of tension, latent hostility, etc. But if you begin by presenting your objectives, both parties can work to find a common position that is advantageous to both sides. Why? Because you'll both be trying to answer the following question: *'How can we both satisfy our demands?'*

- **Establish a relationship based on confidence**

This is very important since it allows both parties to communicate information and ideas much more easily. Since at least a minimum of trust is necessary to reach a negotiated settlement, you'd do well to generate a positive climate right from the start.

Remember that you should be trying early on in the discussions to get the other party to modify his or her position in favour of a solution which you have proposed, and which you consider beneficial to both sides. Therefore, do everything you can to prevent a polarization of positions at the outset of the negotiations.

- **Gather as much information as possible**

Whether you acquire the information before or during the negotiations, the more you know about the other party's interests and objectives the better your position will be to find areas of agreement and to make decisions. It's not possible to gather all the information you need before the negotiations begin, as we've already seen. Some more information will always be revealed during the course of the negotiations themselves.

The following rule is a simple one to follow: *'Listen and ask questions'*.

- **Make sure the other party does not lose face**

How can you get the other party to accept a proposal which holds no advantages for them, even though they might have to resign themselves to accepting it?

The importance of this point cannot be over-emphasized, and not only where co-operative negotiations are concerned. Always allow the party to feel they have performed honourably. So many negotiations break down, when all that is required to reach a successful conclusion is to formulate things a little differently, so that the party at a disadvantage could sign the agreement without losing face.

- **Try to involve the other party as much as possible when formulating proposals**

This is especially important when the discussions are likely to be difficult. It's much easier to accomplish this if the two parties have common interests, although their positions may differ. In this way, the other party is implicated in formulating proposals right from the start, and does not feel that they are being imposed.

This means that it's better to outline your proposals long after you have communicated your interests. Then the other party can suggest changes and adjustments, and can accept or refuse individual proposals. Research concludes that **the feeling of participation in formulating a proposal is the single most important factor when the time comes to accept or reject a proposal**.

By involving the other party in formulating the proposals, you set them on a path which leads naturally to their adoption for the following reasons:

- as he or she is, in a sense, the proposal's co-author, he or she is as responsible as you for its success or failure

- the proposal respects the essential requirements of the other party, since he or she has had his or her say in its formulation all along

- the other party's need for recognition (for the importance of this see Chapter 7) is satisfied, facilitating agreement

- it prevents the other party from losing face, especially over issues that may seem minor to you but are significant to him or her.

- **Give the other party time to think**

In other words, don't expect an immediate answer every time you make a proposal. You wouldn't want to feel hurried into accepting anything either. So, give the other party enough time to think before making a decision.

Once again, it's better to avoid presenting a formal agreement, saying,

'Sign here, please!' Not many people appreciate this kind of behaviour, and you might end up throwing a spanner into the works if you try it.

You're better off making proposals which aren't too structured, where there's still room to incorporate additions and make adjustments. This is yet another reason for doing your homework and clearly defining what your interests are: you can then appreciate a variety of ways in which they can be satisfied, instead of having to stick to one set of proposals.

Who Makes the First Offer?

When two negotiators begin their dance, it's better if one of them leads. In other words, who makes the first offer?

Which of the two will take the plunge and say, 'I want this . . .' or 'I'd like that . . .' and 'I'm ready to pay such and such an amount . . .'. For various reasons, making the first move is often seen as a sign of weakness: the other party has a momentary advantage at that point, since they are in a position either to respond positively or attack. Speaking out first also allows the other party to discern what your priorities are, and what your strategy may be.

Contrary to popular belief, it is actually often best to speak out first because:

- it gives you an opportunity to alter the other party's perception of the situation, which can very useful

- starting the negotiations by presenting a demand or a figure which you've arrived at yourself defines the high-end limit of the discussions

- it shows self-confidence, since you're ready to reveal some information

- it also shows that you are ready to trust the other party, and that you expect your trust to be respected in return.

Although it is often advantageous to take the first step, don't reveal too much information. Don't give everything away (another advantage consists of keeping some information hidden). The other party need not necessarily know what issues you consider most important, i.e. the ones you absolutely insist on negotiating. If he or she does, he or she may take advantage of that information by over-valuing those issues, and making you pay dearly for them.

The first offer

If you're making the first move, you have to steer your proposal between these two rocky points:

- an offer that's too conservative, and
- an offer that's way too high.

At one extreme you risk quoting a lower figure than the other party would pay, while on the other you may have to adjust your position considerably, giving the impression that your position is extremely flexible and open to a lot of concessions.

If the other party isn't well prepared, of course, your initial offer could influence the way they perceive the situation. In other words, you could lower their expectations, and exert a subtle influence on their position.

What do you do if the other party makes an offer that's much too high?

Suppose the other party expresses a demand first that is much too high. They are asking too much. How are you going to react?

You should avoid tying up the discussions by constantly referring to the issue of this inflated, initial figure. Doing so would eventually serve to fix the price in your mind, something you don't want to happen. That inflated price could become the main reference point around which the rest of the negotiations revolve. Even if the other party lowers the price a little, it would still remain much higher than what you expected to pay. Once the discussions are anchored to this base, changing it becomes very difficult. That's why you have to react immediately. Your options lie somewhere between the following two procedures.

1. Make an immediate counter-offer which is as far off the mark as the other party's (on the opposite side of the scale, of course). When you have two offers on the table, the natural thing to do is to cut the difference in half, which works if the other party has allowed himself a sufficient margin of error, and if your initial offer is not below his bottom line. You would have to calculate your offer accordingly.

   This limits the range of discussions to somewhere between the two figures. If the other party refuses to contemplate your counter-offer, and also refuses to negotiate, then at least you save yourself a lot of time and trouble – and in some cases money.

2. Break off negotiations. Don't wait to get bogged down in endless bickering. Leaving the table immediately may result in the other party

adjusting their demands. You also demonstrate your capacity to stand firm, which is excellent for your image and your reputation.

Establishing a Position

Opening offers are crucial because they influence the entire negotiating process from that point on. They indicate where your demands are situated, and may also contribute to altering one or other party's perception of the situation.

As we have seen, if your initial offer is too low, you risk insulting the other party and destroying any chance of an agreement. If it's too high, you may be giving away more than was hoped for. This leaves you with two possible situations, depending on how well you prepared your case, and on the accuracy of the information you've been able to gather so far.

1. Make the initial offer if you have a good idea of the other party's price range, or if you think you know what the other party expects from the negotiations.

   This prevents the other party from making an initial offer which is highly inflated, and which places the rest of the discussions in a context which is disadvantageous to you.

2. If you have a good idea of the price range involved, and if the difference between the two parties is relatively minimal, then you can start the discussions by making an offer within an acceptable range of the other party's expectations. This 'acceptable range' depends on your market, but could range from below 3 to around 30 per cent.

   To get over this hump, some negotiators make an initial offer which is much too high or low, but they let the other party know that the figure is negotiable, and that they are completely flexible.

Work on the other party's perception of the situation

Research has shown that the very first figures mentioned in the course of negotiations have a tremendous influence on the debates that follow. If a buyer starts off by making a very low offer, the seller will always retain that figure in his or her mind. If a seller starts with a very high figure, the buyer will tend to use it as a reference point throughout the discussions and will think that any reduction he or she achieves is a success. But perhaps someone else is selling the same thing for a lot less and only when considered in relation to the opening demand is the buyer making a good deal!

Sometimes both negotiators aren't sure what they can get out of a given situation. If that is the case, it's up to you to make an offer that you consider very advantageous. In this situation also, experience shows that a negotiator's perceptions can be strongly influenced by an inflated figure, presented at the start of the negotiations.

Negotiating parties often have a very vague idea of what the opposing side might demand. This is especially true when the item under negotiation cannot be priced according to some fixed market value (even for cars and houses subjective evaluation plays an important role in determining the final price), so that the parties have to rely on comparative pricing which is often inaccurate. Therefore, a separate evaluation has to be made for each case, and this creates an opportunity to influence the other party's perception of the situation.

When You Have to Make an Important Proposal

Should you demand a lot? Will your price be too high? Will your demands be too severe? Make sure you're doing the right thing while the other party still has a chance to get used to your objective. Although you shouldn't be overly aggressive, you should present your demands firmly and clearly.

- Start with a preliminary meeting, during which you outline your intentions. Then, when the second meeting takes place, the other party will have had a chance to get used to the idea.

- Don't get into too much detail. Set your bait by asking a few harmless questions to make the other party think and sometimes worry. Try something along the lines of:

> *'Have you thought about selling your company?'*
> *'What would you say if our two companies opted to merge?'*
> *'The situation isn't easy, but imagine what would happen if . . .'*
> *'And what would you say if by chance we were able to pool our assets a month from now?'*
> *'Have you ever thought about changing sectors?'*
> *'Haven't you ever been bothered by that awful house across the street?'*

The idea here is to bring up a subject without seeming to do it intentionally. Then, when you make your proposal, the other party won't feel attacked: no, this isn't an out-and-out takeover; no, you're not trying to get him out of the picture completely, etc. Dropping a few hints before making a radical proposal gives the other party time to get used to the idea.

Discretion is essential

If the other party knows you have a deadline he or she is much more likely to drag things out until the last minute, knowing that you won't have any time left to sound out the competition.

Say you want to purchase a laser printer for your computer so that you can prepare a professional-looking report for an important client. On Wednesday you meet with the sales rep and say, 'I need the printer by Friday at the latest, because I have to use it to prepare an important report.'

The sales rep then knows that you need that printer quickly, and a skilled rep will be able to dissuade you from looking at the competition.

But maybe the rep is in a hurry to sell? Remember that we all have our deadlines to make. Maybe his boss warned him that if he didn't make a sale that week he'd be laid off. And if he gets a commission, he might be willing to cut it down a little just to make the sale . . .

If you had this information, you'd be in a very advantageous position. But the sales rep isn't going to say anything about it, knowing he'll lose any advantage he might have. In the same way, you shouldn't reveal any information either.

In some cases the other party will try to gain information by asking questions like:

'How soon do you need it?'

'When do you want to start using the machine?'

'Is the machine you have still working? Because if you're not in a hurry, I have a new model coming in next week . . .' And you're likely to reply, 'Next week! Oh, no, that's too late!' and give the game away. Watch out for this!

A skilled negotiator can find a host of advantages in all kinds of seemingly harmless remarks. So it's always a good idea to think twice – or even three times – before saying anything, even if it seems unimportant.

Acquiring information is crucial in negotiations, so, conversely, you should always be in control of the amount of information you give away.

CHAPTER 19

Top Negotiating Techniques

There are so many things to remember if you want to improve your performance as a negotiator. This chapter contains some useful tips gathered from the world's top negotiators which you should read and study before each important negotiation.

Get Used to Reacting Quickly

If you're dealing with someone very creative, who suddenly springs a package on you that looks interesting, but which you find difficult to evaluate accurately, what should you do?

You should always be prepared for such an eventuality by keeping your mind sharp and your powers of concentration finely tuned. It isn't always possible to wait before making a decision. That's why it's so important to prepare your file before negotiating. If you've carefully evaluated the alternatives beforehand, you're less likely to be taken by surprise when the other party makes a new offer.

Create an Impression of Progress

It's always gratifying for both parties to feel that you're making progress, that things are moving along. You can create this impression by recapitulating from time to time, emphasizing the issues on which you've been able to agree. Do this especially after you make a concession so that the other party doesn't think you're walking away with all the advantages.

Get the Other Party to Say 'Yes'

Learn to formulate your demands so that the other party has to respond with a 'Yes'.

– *'Would you like to discuss our options?'*
– *'Do you think we could come to some kind of agreement that would include these issues?'*
– *'If we could introduce certain other issues, do you think we could find some area of agreement?'*

Slowly but surely the other party will get used to answering in the affirmative, so that when the time comes for you to make your final proposal (hopefully the one that will lead to an agreement) he or she is more inclined to accept it.

Present Positive Arguments First

Present only the positive outlines of your proposals at first, trying at the same time to predict any negative reactions the other party might have, and to answer them before they become concrete objections.

Ignore Exaggerated Demands

A problem arises if the other party proposes an inflated figure at the outset of negotiations: even though both parties may know that the figure is only a shot in the dark and is bound to be modified significantly, it nevertheless has an effect on the discussions and evaluations made during the course of the negotiations. If the other party makes an extremely inflated offer, there are two ways you can react, depending on the character of the person you're dealing with.

- If the other party has a threatening attitude: counter-attack immediately by making an offer which is just as exaggerated.

- If the other party is just being overly optimistic: pretend you didn't hear the offer. Ignore it. Instead of allowing the inflated figure to influence you, make a counter-offer which is reasonable and which you can defend.

Manage Your Munitions

You don't have to provide a complete list of all the benefits the other party will obtain by accepting your proposals right away. Spread things out a little. Give the other party time to unwrap one of your little 'gifts' and savour it before offering another, and another, and another, and so on.

Of course, the word 'gift' is not meant in a literal sense. After all, you'll be wanting something in exchange. But do try to make the other party aware of the value of each concession you make, so that you can use them to overcome any points of resistance, one by one. In this way you win, step by step. Great negotiators always proceed this way.

In more competitive negotiations, refrain from using your strongest arguments until a critical moment has arrived, instead of wasting them in the opening rounds.

Don't Be The First To Yield

The party which makes the first important concession is likely to come out at a disadvantage when the final settlement is reached. This is even more true if you give something up without getting anything in return. Try to modify the way you present your offer so that the other party has to make the first move, or select certain points which you think will be more attractive. Don't be in a hurry to make concessions (see Chapter 21 for more on this topic).

The Time Factor

When negotiations start, look at your watch. Be aware that you should make at least a minimum of progress in the first few hours. If not, you may find yourself involved in long, drawn-out discussions that lead nowhere.

Studies have shown that in negotiations where no obvious progress is made during the first few hours, a final agreement is not likely to be reached either. If that's the case with your current negotiation you may be better off postponing the negotiations for some other time.

Pacing

Don't try to move too fast, looking for an easy victory. Even if things seem to be going smoothly, don't hurry. Above all, don't give the impression of wanting to speed things up towards the end. The other party may think you're trying to bully him or her into making a hasty decision.

Verify Deadlines

In many cases deadlines of one kind or another are used as a pressure tactic. It may be due to the competition, a third person, etc. It really doesn't matter. A deadline can also take the form of an ultimatum in some cases – a proposal or an offer that only lasts for a certain time. The result of imposing deadlines is that it accelerates the pace of the negotiations and calls for more rapid decision-making.

Don't let yourself be overly impressed by time limits. In many cases they're simply tactical manœuvres. Find out just how rigid the limits really are, and if they can be extended or not. Sometimes you'll take a break to think things over, and when you return to the table you find that the deadline has been mysteriously withdrawn. It's much better to come to a well thought-out agreement than to bash something out in a hurry because of a deadline.

Take Notes

Every time you make or obtain a concession, write it down. Even with the best intentions, it is sometimes easy to forget one point or another. Also note any modifications in the other party's position, as well as any concessions he or she has made. Try as far as you can to record the way proposals and concessions have been formulated verbatim. This makes them easier to analyse during breaks, and prevents any discrepancies from arising. Ideally you should appoint someone to take notes, since keeping an accurate record of events often requires the complete attention of one person.

Don't Exhibit Your Enthusiasm

This is elementary. Once an extremely fruitful and co-operative negotiation is over, both parties may wish to express their satisfaction. Before a conclusion is reached, you should never demonstrate your affection or satisfaction. Wait for the right time and place for the following reasons.

• If you appear overly satisfied you risk arousing the other party's suspicions. He or she may wonder if you wouldn't have accepted a lower price.

- If you are too enthusiastic about the other party's product or proposal, he or she may be tempted to raise the stakes, or forget about a concession or offer made previously.

It's unfortunate, but that's the way things are. Even if you think you've made a great deal, you still shouldn't exhibit your satisfaction. Save your euphoria for your friends and family!

Make a Show of Your Independence

If you think that a proposal or concession is not being accorded its true value, you have to choose between continuing the negotiations and perhaps seeing your bargaining power dissolve into nothing, or leaving the table. In situations where you can find the same item elsewhere, for approximately the same price, remind the other party that you have alternatives. If there is still no change in his or her attitude, then you should take the more radical course and simply leave.

Decoding

Never reject a negative reaction outright. On the contrary, take time to study it carefully, since some refusals are actually hidden indications of alternative routes you or the other party may wish to pursue. See if you can read between the lines in the statements on the following page.

Find the Meaning

1. We're not going to negotiate prices.

2. This is open for discussion.

3. We prefer not to discuss this issue at the present time.

4. This is not usual practice.

5. I can't see how you're going to achieve this.

6. We'd find this very difficult to accept.

7. These are our usual terms.

8. I'm not qualified to discuss this.

9. We couldn't produce this amount in so short a time.

10. Our assembly line is not equipped to meet this kind of demand.

They could be saying...

1. *We're ready to discuss other aspects of the situation.*

2. *The issue is negotiable.*

3. *We'll discuss this tomorrow.*

4. *Convince me.*

5. *Explain some more.*

6. *It's possible.*

7. *They are negotiable.*

8. *You'll have to meet with my superior.*

9. *I'm ready to negotiate quality standards.*

10. *But it can be arranged.*

Read Signals which could Translate into Advantages

Certain signals indicate that things are going well for you. Learn to recognize them.

- Any allusion to deadlines.

- An indication to the effect that the competition no longer plays a role. This could mean that you have exclusive control of a given commodity, that your terms are the best around or simply that the other party has already invested too much time with you to back out.

- Judgements which are favourable to your point of view from other members of the other party's team.

- Anything the other party offers which is to your advantage.

Avoid Making Judgements

We sometimes tend to judge the other party, interpreting his or her little idiosyncrasies, tastes and attitudes in an unfavourable light. Don't fall into this trap. Try to be as open minded as possible, and avoid making value judgements about the person(s) you're negotiating with.

Of course, if you know for a fact that you're dealing with an out-and-out con artist, then you have to be sure to protect your interests and evaluate every proposal extremely carefully. And in future try to do business with more reputable people – negotiations are difficult enough without the extra stress of worrying about the other party's honesty!

Put Yourself in the Other Party's Shoes

Don't get entrenched in a position and then hope to persuade the other party through pressure tactics and rhetoric. Try to see the situation from the other party's point of view. This doesn't mean you have to agree with him or her. But doing this reduces the risk of engaging in pointless dialogue, and gives your proposals more impact, since they take the other party's interests into account.

Present your proposals with the other party's point of view in mind and emphasize the ways in which he or she will benefit from them. However, don't leave out the ways your own interests will be satisfied, or you will only arouse suspicion and doubt: altruism is not a common characteristic when hammering out a business deal!

The other party should clearly understand how the agreement is going to benefit you as well. But accentuate the fact that both sides will come out winners. All things being equal, most people tend to favour deals where both sides have something to gain.

By setting an example and taking both sides into account, it is also likely that the other party will do the same for you.

Expressing Your Emotions

Knowing how to stay calm doesn't mean letting someone walk all over you. If you want to let the other party know that you feel uncomfortable, that you have the impression you're being led up the garden path or that you would prefer to deal with someone a little more conciliatory – well tell them!

Don't say, 'You make me uncomfortable . . .' or 'You're a thief!'. It is much more difficult for the other party to ignore or contradict something you feel than something you've already made a judgement about. Saying, 'I find your price a little expensive . . .' is always better than, 'This is too expensive.' Even if you know it is too expensive, you still have to be diplomatic if you hope eventually to get what you want. If not, you risk offending the other party and he or she may break off the negotiations.

Expressing Disagreement

If your opinion differs from that of the other party, you should be able to express your disagreement without antagonism. There are various ways of doing this.

- You can explain the reasons for your disagreement, although this isn't strictly necessary. We all like to understand what's going on, and have a lot less trouble accepting things we understand. Explaining your position may also encourage the other party to modify his or her proposals so that an agreement can be reached. You could refer to the limits you have to respect (budget, authority, time pressure, etc).

- Any effort to reaffirm areas of common agreement which have already been established will make it easier for the other party to accept your differences of opinion.

- Qualify your objections: you may reject certain points of a proposal while accepting others. This opens the door to a possible compromise, which would have remained closed if you rejected the proposal entirely.

- If you have to say no, do it gently, without being aggressive. Your refusal will be accepted graciously, and you'll be perceived as a thoughtful, prudent negotiator instead of an enemy.

- Reject the proposal, not the person making it. The other party should not be made to feel that there's anything personal about your refusal.

Always Remain Calm

Avoid personal attacks and injurious statements. This may seem obvious, but some people are particularly gifted at feeling out your weak points, which they will attempt to exploit at the most inopportune moments.

Don't let these cheap shots disturb you. Never raise your voice, even if the other party is shouting at you. It's not your responsibility to educate people, and it's too bad for them if they don't know the difference between a negotiation and a shouting match.

If you have a hot temper and the other party finds out about it, you'll never be completely safe against a manœuvre calculated to make you lose your cool.

Don't Overdo It

Is business good? Don't boast about it. Be modest. This will help you avoid taking unnecessary risks which you might attempt if you let success go to your head, and start thinking that you can handle any situation, no matter how difficult. It's useless to try to be a crowd pleaser.

Silence Is Golden

To the extent that negotiating is a business of words and communication, you must be able to hold your tongue and remain silent at the right time.

Silence is extremely important when a proposal is being made. Most people can't stand silence. So, if someone makes a proposal and you don't say anything, or if you pretend to be thinking about it, they may interpret your silence as a sign of disapproval or lack of interest, and will, in many cases, add other concessions to the package to make it more attractive.

Some negotiators use the technique of remaining silent for precisely that reason – to gain more concessions. If you outline a proposal and the other party doesn't say anything, what do you think? You assume they are not interested, that they want more.

You tell yourself that their silence means that the proposal isn't nearly good enough, and that you'll have to make a better offer. Because of your uneasiness about the other party's silence, you agree to modify your proposition. So they have achieved what they want without saying a word!

Take Your Time

The importance of being able to react quickly, and also to come up with interesting new proposals on the spur of the moment has already been stressed, but the converse also applies.

It's just as important to take your time and not to let yourself get rushed into things. Think before you make a commitment, no matter how long it takes. Knowing how to hesitate and refusing to make quick decisions is a tactic in itself. And pays off in the end. Taking your time is an advantage under most circumstances.

Some people won't take the time they need to think things over because they want to impress everyone with their skill and intelligence. They think they're in the movies, where a tycoon enters a room and says, 'How much? Twenty million? I'll take it!'. There are few people around who can make decisions involving millions of pounds in a few seconds. And they can only do this because they really know their markets or they've carefully studied the situation before negotiating. They've already done all the thinking they need to do about the situation. They've pondered over all the angles. So when a proposal comes up which they've already decided is profitable, they're naturally in a hurry to sign before the other party realizes their mistake and changes their mind.

However, many people want to present an image of someone who is strong, who knows what they're doing, who's in control of the game. Overly concerned with appearances, they want to be admired as someone who doesn't hesitate for an instant, and above all as someone who has the power (or cash) to get whatever they want. But you must never let yourself feel intimidated, and always take the time you need to think things over. Especially since doing this can be more profitable than you may realize (see 'Silence Is Golden' above).

Negotiating on the Telephone

Avoid negotiating on the telephone whenever you can. In principle you should conduct your business dealings face to face. It's a lot easier for someone to say no over the phone and you can't read the reactions of the other party to your proposals. However, if you have no choice, here are some rules to follow:

- Be well prepared.

- The person making the call is always ready. The person receiving the call sometimes isn't. Try to be the one to make the call. You'll be prepared, you'll have your arguments all thought out and the file in front of you. If you get a call when you're not ready, invent some pretext and say you'll call back later. Then take the time to prepare your case.

- When you're waiting for an important call, have the file containing all the information you need right there in front of you.

- In certain cases you have to know how to delay the conversation; for example, when you want to check out the competition, or when you aren't fully prepared. Use your secretary or answering machine to filter your calls. By not answering you can put things on hold for a certain time.

  If the person you call is always 'in a meeting', it's quite likely that the same delaying tactic is being used on you!

Negotiate with Their Friends and Spouse

During a negotiation, remember one thing: in a sense, you're also negotiating with the people close to the other party. He or she may talk to his or her colleagues or friends, and they'll want to know all about how things are going. The other party will have to convince all these people that he's doing a good job. The other party's reputation is on the line, and he needs concrete arguments to support his position.

It's up to you to provide them.

If you don't, the other party will try to get them by force, since he absolutely must be allowed to feel proud of the way he has conducted the negotiations.

So you might as well provide the trophy yourself. Emphasize the advantages the other party is obtaining by negotiating with you – the quality of your product, the long-term advantages, etc. You can even create the impression that he or she imposed certain conditions which, in fact, are to your advantage.

So, even though they didn't succeed in getting a fantastic price, the other party can report all kinds of other, secondary advantages which you were willing to concede, and can hold their head high. This principle can be summed up as follows: *always convince the other party that they are an excellent negotiator.*

In fact, if you manage to convince the other party that they are a better negotiator than you, you'll actually be the one to benefit because they will be less suspicious of you.

And you don't always have to make substantial concessions to do this. A skilled car salesperson always knows just when to throw in that rear wiper or that clock radio: these little extras are calculated to seduce the buyer. Even if the value of the extras is tiny compared with the overall price, the buyer will use them to justify the purchase and convince him- or herself that he or she has made a good deal.

That's why it's important to be creative: the more these little extras and bonuses, and special concessions add up, the more attractive your offer becomes. It's the whole package that counts, and not the value of each separate item.

Always Negotiate!

Whatever the situation, never assume that failure or loss is inevitable. Fight for your rights! Once you're prepared, and armed to the teeth, your opposition often seems just to melt away. You know your rights, your position, your advantages, your alternatives. You've visualized your objectives, you've covered any possible objections . . . and hey presto! You get what you want almost effortlessly!

Is it because of the determination you project? Is it because the other party knows right from the start what you're made of? It's probably a bit of both because when you're mentally ready for something to happen, the chances are that you will be able to deal with it much better. You almost feel disappointed because you didn't have to fight harder! Well, there are always bigger rivers to cross!

However, you should always be suspicious of negotiations that proceed too smoothly. Obstacles won't disappear just because you're applying this method! Be wary of deals that seem too good to be true.

How to Get Out of Tight Spots

Inevitably, during the course of your negotiations, you'll find yourself in some very tricky situations. Here are some strategies you can use to get the negotiations back on track.

Negotiate a Problem – Not a Position

This is especially true when you want to orient the negotiations towards co-operation rather than conflict. But in almost any situation, if you can concentrate on the various aspects of a problem instead of on your position, it will make things a lot easier. By doing this you avoid making your position the central issue of the negotiation. In other words, your ego or image is no longer at stake, as it is when you have to defend your position.

Your main interest lies in solving the problem, and by proceeding in this way you have a much better chance of finding a solution. What's more, you can always revert to your initial position if nothing better is offered. But your position is not the issue at stake. If you can involve the other party in the problem-solving, then you've already won some points (and so has the other party).

Dealing with Animosity

With or without cause, the other party may develop a considerable amount of animosity towards you. It's usually better not to react in kind – doing so would only worsen the situation and make it much more difficult to reach an eventual agreement. Let the other party express his or her grievances, all of them, without interrupting. Just allowing the other party to get his or her negative feelings out in the open will do a lot to help smooth out the problems.

When You Reach an Impasse

1. Above all, remain calm. Be patient. Do everything you can to avoid giving in to stress.

2. Try to understand how the problem developed: is it a question of attitude, circumstances, past events, etc? Dig deep. You will react differently depending on the nature of the problem.

3. Observe yourself. Is the deadlock a result of your being so intent on attaining your objectives? We always tend to assume that the other party is at fault. So, it's very useful, once again, to imagine yourself in the other party's shoes. If you conclude that your attitude may very well have contributed to the problem, then you may be able to find a way out of it.

4. Suggest taking a break. Fatigue and tension lie at the bottom of many situations that at first seem unsolvable. Sometimes a few hours, or even a day of rest is all that is needed to revitalize your energy and re-evaluate your approach. When you get back to the table you'll probably be able to come up with additional information, or a new and original proposal.

5. You may suggest changing your location for a while. Sometimes having a drink somewhere (stick to fruit juice!) can do a lot to ease the tension. The aim – and it isn't absolutely necessary to leave the room to achieve it – is to create a better understanding, a better climate in which differences can be resolved. You can also admit to the validity of certain of the other party's arguments – it doesn't help much to reject everything he or she suggests.

6. Offer to talk one on one with the other party's chief negotiator. In the absence of certain assistants whose frame of mind is negative, or who are throwbacks to the old-fashioned style of negotiation (win–lose), you may be able to make a lot of progress.

7. Suggest a brainstorming session to try and come up with solutions to the impasse.

8. Try to see both sides of the problem, and set yourself up as mediator.

9. Take a step backwards to get out of the dead-end street you're in and suggest that you deal with another issue in the meantime. This is, in fact, a variation of taking a break.

10. Suspend negotiations and suggest that one or the other party call when they think they've found a solution to the impasse. Obviously, resorting to this strategy may simply end the negotiations, if neither party is able to come up with a solution before a certain deadline (which should, in fact, be specified). Also, you should be aware that this tactic implies a certain power struggle – who will call whom first?

11. Suggest a solution. This can be delicate – you don't want it to be perceived as a sign of weakness on your part, or as a concession you're making in response to a difficult situation. In such cases you can:

   - indicate that it was your eventual intention to show flexibility on one or another of the points that are causing the problem
   - make it clear that you're not willing to make the concession without getting something in return
   - also advise the other party that you could break off the negotiations if there is no reaction to your proposal.

12. In a situation where conflict is imminent, impress the other party with the value of your arguments, your advantages and the power you have. Make it understood that you're perfectly capable of defending yourself, but that you're ready to co-operate if the other party is in any way conciliatory. You can even place a conditional offer on the table. But never give the impression that you're backing down from a threat.

What About Total Impasse?

In some cases, negotiating is so difficult; the parties' interests seem to conflict so completely; tempers are so exacerbated that it seems absolutely impossible to reach any kind of agreement. This is often the case when ideological conflicts are involved.

It seems like it will be impossible to get anywhere, but there is an approach which often works in these situations. It's sometimes possible to ease antagonism by appealing to superior values: the good of the country, for example, or the children, the environment, etc. The important thing is finding a value which is greater than the conflict, which transcends it and gives both parties an opportunity to find some common ground on which they can agree.

By appealing to higher values, you gain a wider perspective of the situation, and you can set yourself up as a kind of mediator, making proposals which both parties can support, even if they're only abstract principles or ideas. When both sides support the same idea, there is already an agreement in principle – a foundation on which an accord can be built.

Here are some other values which you may call upon in these situations:

- the importance of the relationship between the two parties
- equity
- the advantages of reaching an eventual agreement
- the very fact that it's better to *negotiate* than to enter into an out-and-out conflict.

The rest depends on your powers of persuasion.

Dealing with Intimidation

Intimidation is often effective, owing its success to the simple fact that most people haven't taken the time to sit down and think seriously about it.

You are bound, from time to time, to meet up with people who try to impose their will on you in order to get what they want. You should be prepared to give as good as you get. Even if you have the gentlest disposition in the world, if someone tries to rip you off, you have to be ready to defend yourself – you have to know how to turn the tables to your advantage.

Threats and bluffs

'If you don't do what we demand, we'll break off the negotiations, there will be no more deliveries, we'll stop payments, we'll start doing business with your competitors.' This is an example of an unbridled threat, which resembles waving a gun in the face, with no fear of reprisal, no courtesy and no offer of a peaceful solution. It is clearly the intimidator's desire to show his or her power, and to make you believe that he or she is in a very strong position.

How should you react to this kind of tactic? It all depends on the circumstances, and on who you're dealing with. Is the other party really going to act on those threats?

- If you have good reason to believe that the other party is only bluffing, then you can call their bluff and tell them to go ahead and do what they say they are going to do.

- You can ignore them completely. Don't take the threats seriously, and don't let them bother you.

- React immediately by being aggressive. As soon as the other party calms down, you can become less aggressive and proceed as if nothing has happened.

A good rule to follow in negotiations is, 'forgive, but never forget'. Make it clear to the other party that you won't just let things pass. Make use of appropriate reprisals if someone tries to intimidate you or pull the wool over your eyes. If this happens, fight back until the other party realizes their ploy won't work. Then, when you feel that they have made sincere and honourable amends, you may let the other party know that, while you will remain vigilant, you are prepared to forget such impropriety and co-operate in further discussions.

Acting in this way will produce much better results than adopting a vindictive attitude, which will only serve to make the objectives you both seek more inaccessible.

If these measures do not produce the desired results, then inform the other party that he or she either puts a stop to the intimidating behaviour or you will not continue. You must absolutely refuse to become a victim.

If *you* are the party doing the intimidating (if the circumstances really justify such behaviour) you must be absolutely sure that you will carry your threats out if necessary.

Verbal Intimidation

This tactic is most often used to provoke women, but everyone has fallen victim to it at one time or another. You're talking about something, expounding a point of view or answering a question. Suddenly someone at the other end of the table interrupts you and starts talking more loudly than you, as if they are trying to drown you out. The person keeps talking without stopping, mixing up all your proposals without giving you an opportunity to correct or explain anything. They twist everything you've said, making contentious insinuations and thinly veiled threats. What should you do?

It's useless to get angry. In fact, that's precisely what the tactic is trying to achieve. The answer is to frustrate the aggressor by not giving them the satisfaction they seek. Continue talking calmly, without showing the least sign of being upset. You can ever lower your tone a little, and ignore the 'noise' coming from the other side of the table.

What you're saying may be practically inaudible, but your attitude, so calm and collected, will make your opponent's antics appear infantile, ridiculous and demonstrate a complete lack of maturity. Your opponent will usually end up feeling embarrassed and become silent, unless he or she is the one to lose control, in which case he or she may start shouting, making all kinds of absurd accusations and outrageous statements. If this happens, face the person and wait until they stop to catch their breath. Then quickly say: *'I don't think this is the right time to discuss these issues, but if you like we can add them to our next meeting's agenda.'*

This will give you time to prepare your counter-arguments and gather your thoughts before the next meeting, by which time the other party may have completely changed their attitude.

Or you could try saying something like: *'I didn't realize that in coming here today I'd have to deal with this kind of problem. But if there's something bothering you, I'm prepared to listen as soon as you calm down.'* Often the simple act of listening helps to calm someone whose attitude seems to border on the hysterical.

If the other party persists despite your efforts, don't submit. Get up and walk out, saying you'll be ready to resume negotiations when they have calmed down.

Verbal intimidation is not a negotiating tactic in the proper sense of the term. It is more like an outbreak of a disease, against which you must know how to protect yourself. Fortunately such situations don't occur very frequently, but you may find some people who persist in applying these outdated and entirely unproductive methods.

Aggression and Personal Attack

Only very mediocre negotiators resort to personal attacks, threats, insults and other unsavoury tactics. This kind of climate will generally fail to provide conclusive results. But since you have no control over the way the other party behaves (at least not directly) you may sometimes find yourself in a position of having to defend yourself against attacks.

During the course of negotiations you may find yourself personally attacked, your integrity questioned, the truth of your proposals denied, etc. What should you do? There are a number of ways of reacting.

- Ignore it. You heard nothing. Move on to the next issue without making a case out of the attack. There's nothing more frustrating for an aggressor than to see their prey carrying on as if nothing were the matter.

- Take it as a joke. Let the other party know that you consider their behaviour to be a momentary and temporary lapse of courtesy. What the other party has said is so far off the mark that it's not even worth talking about.

What is insidious about such malevolent attacks on your honesty and/or goodwill is that they plant a seed of doubt, since it's generally impossible to prove your innocence. A single accusation, *even if it has no truth to it whatsoever*, can tarnish your credibility and your reputation. Don't fall into the trap of protesting your good faith, your complete innocence in the matter, etc. If you bite the bait, if you play the game, you'll only dig yourself deeper into a hole.

Such accusations are designed to get you to lose your temper. If the tactic does not produce the desired result, the other party (your adversary in this case) will drop it and try something else. So be on your guard.

And when the right occasion arises, don't be afraid to provide proof of your good faith through some concrete gesture. If the other party is also acting in a spirit of good faith, they will recognize your gesture and respond positively. If not, you may decide to resort to more aggressive tactics yourself, when the time is right.

The Tyrant

This person abuses his or her power to tyrannize others. You should obviously avoid dealing with such people whenever you can, but you can't always avoid it. Some sectors of business are unfortunately more prone to the use of pressure tactics than others. If you have to deal with such persons, you'll need to know how to defend yourself.

There are three ways in which people usually react when they are faced with persons who abuse their power. Which would most likely be your reaction?

1. Would you react with violence?

In other words, you call the other party's bluff. But what if the threats are not a bluff?

- You place yourself in the position of having to play the same game, a game where the other party may be more comfortable than you, since they started it (this is not necessarily the case).

- You risk escalating the violence, which may explode.

2. Would you play a weak card?

It's always risky to count on someone else's compassion. You may simply become their next victim.

3. What if you don't react at all?

As before, you act as if nothing's happened. You allow neither their words nor their attempts at intimidation to affect you. This is the preferred alternative, which shows neither aggression nor weakness. Aggression always feeds on the reactions of its object, a little like a sadist who gets more excited the more his victim protests.

By not reacting to insults and aggressive tactics, there's a good chance they'll just sputter out and die. Also, if you refrain from reacting, the attacks will have much less effect on you. In any case, this is the right time to bluff the other party out by pretending that you're not in the least concerned.

Learn to show your teeth

Know your rights, and the alternative you may have recourse to, and don't hesitate to mention them if necessary in the course of discussions. You may say something like:

'I imagine you're aware of the fact that a judge would find your remarks somewhat disturbing . . .'

'I remember a similar situation which ended very badly for the person who tried to use such arguments.'

'Since I wanted to understand the ins and outs of the situation, I consulted my lawyer.'

Most people, as soon as they hear the words judge, lawyer or court case, tend to become a little more careful about what they say. Fear of legal reprisals has its positive side!

Be natural. Practise maintaining a neutral, detached attitude, as if you found the other party's abusive contortions banal and boring. You could also recount a little story about nothing in particular, which begins with, 'My lawyer said to me the other day . . .'. The point is to let the other party know that you're on intimate terms with a lawyer, on whom you can call at any time.

If *you* are being threatened with some kind of lawsuit, you can react in the same way – by referring to a lawyer or judge who is on your side.

In other words, if pressure is being applied to force you to do something, don't count on that pressure easing up on its own. It's up to you to react in a way that will get rid of it by 'showing your teeth'.

Practise inertia

If a tyrannical opponent is trying, more or less subtly, to force you to do something, an effective counter-measure is simply to put up a show of passive resistance. You say neither yes nor no, you become very evasive and refuse to conclude anything.

Then, over the next few days, you become very distant and difficult to reach. You don't return calls, or you return them at lunchtime, when you know the person will be out of the office. You no longer agree to participate in private meetings.

CHAPTER 21

Developing Your Arguing Power

It is important to know how to argue effectively in the negotiating arena for various reasons. Here are three to consider.

● First, there is no absolute truth. Even if you have arguments to hand which seem to you to be irrefutable, you cannot stop there. You cannot, for example, be content to 'put the facts on the table' and let them speak for themselves. In contrast to what people often think, facts do not speak for themselves – you have to make them talk.

● Secondly, there are a certain number of arguing techniques you can learn which will allow you to reinforce your presentation and your case.

● Finally, you may be confronted by strategies of negotiation which could cause difficulties for you. If you recognize them, and if you use them yourself from time to time, it will obviously be much easier for you to de-rail them.

What Is Argument?

To define the word argument, you could say it is the opposite of persuasion. In principle, persuasion appeals to the emotions and feelings of your adversary, while argument takes place mainly on a logical basis. Argument appeals to reason, or to what *seems* to be reason (be careful here!).

The basic idea of argument, some say, is to play up your own points and minimize the importance of those of the other party. Certainly, this tactic is almost inevitable in the negotiating situation.

However, argument works best in a negotiation situation when the general level of communication is good – in other words, where the negotiation depends on co-operation rather than competition. Top negotiators would agree that the impact of argument is greater, the better the atmosphere in which the negotiation takes place, and the better established the lines of communication.

When you prepare your argument, therefore, remember just one thing. When you argue, the aim is the *same* as when you persuade; you are trying to break down the resistance – indeed, the hostility – of the other party, so that you can progress towards your objectives.

Obviously, the more you offer appealing alternatives and attractive bargaining points, the easier the argument becomes, for it no longer relies, in this case, only on words!

The aim of argument is to reason your case well and to convince the other party of the validity of your position. This will help him realize that it would be advantageous for him to share your point of view.

You will be able to argue even more sincerely if you genuinely want the other party to leave the negotiating table with more than he had when he arrived.

Who Speaks First?

When you are in a position where you have to *defend* and argue your point of view, let the other party speak first.

Letting him present his side of the argument will give you a chance to find out what his advantages are and also to include some powerful answers in your own presentation.

Listen to him very carefully. By doing this you set the tone, and you can subsequently make your own presentation without being interrupted. This is very important because of the point we will look at next.

Organize Your Argument

It is useful to know what type of logic you are going to use to convince the other party. There are a number of approaches, and you should be aware of them. Here are brief definitions.

Deduction

What is true of a group is also true of each of its members. The classic example of this is:

All men are mortal.
Socrates is a man.
Therefore, Socrates is mortal.

You could adapt this argument as follows:

This consortium is solvent. This business is under the administration of this consortium, therefore this business is solvent . . .

Induction

If a large number of members of a group share a characteristic, it is very likely that the other members will share it too. For example:

This consortium is in difficulty. This business is run by this consortium, therefore this business might well be in difficulty too . . .

Analogy

A particular situation is similar to another. In certain circumstances, this and that happened. Since the same circumstances prevail again, the outcome may well be the same. For example:

This business shows the same characteristics as another, which reacted in a certain way. The market behaves more or less in the same way; the outcome of a similar operation could well be the same.

You should always try to identify the significant differences, if there are any.

Hypothesis

'Let us suppose that we decided to go ahead with this project. What do you think would happen? Suppose that . . .'

Here is a technique that is frequently used to frighten: 'And if we didn't get this credit?' 'And if our suppliers abandoned us?' 'If the bank withdrew its credit', etc.

Whichever type of logic you have decided to adopt, make sure that you can always defend it to the other party. This means that you will be in a position to predict the stance and reactions of the other party. Will he lend a sympathetic ear to your words or will he try to undermine each one of your arguments? If you apply your chosen type of logic to the situation you will be able to test the ground in advance. Since the rules of the role-play game consist of giving each other a rough time, if your argument collapses under the blows of a friendly battering ram, you can always go back and rework it without actually having lost anything. In fact, you will have gained!

Prepare the Order of Your Arguments

The order in which you present your lines of argument should not be neglected either. There are lots of different techniques you can use, but here is one I recommend.

- Use a strong argument first. These put the other party on the defensive. Right at the beginning, you are taking up a position of strength, and you show that you are someone to be taken seriously.

- Then, present the weaker arguments. Just because they are 'weaker' does not mean that they are not justifiable. Make as much of them as you can without trying to give them any categorical order.

- And, finally, come in with the 'sledgehammer' arguments. This is the moment to put forward the arguments which will have the greatest impact upon the self-confidence of the other party and on the solidity of his position.

This strategy is useful. The other party is not easily going to sweep aside the weaker arguments, because they are made early. And we are used to considering what comes first as being very important: it is, in principle, *more important* than what follows.

Obviously, by using his or her judgement, the other party will be able to see quite well which of your arguments are the most convincing. But he or she must work out their order of importance him- or herself.

Put forward as many minor arguments as you can: the other party will have to perform mental gymnastics to be able to follow you and he will probably be trying to find all the answers in his head at the same time.

Following weak points with very strong points is a significant tactic. After some 'weak' arguments, the other party's attention might wander a little. Suspecting he has heard everything, in his mind he may be considering your first points again, thinking that they are the most important to you.

Then, without any noticeable transition, without changing tone, you weigh in with the arguments that are *really* important to you. If the other party is not concentrating properly he may feel slightly frustrated at his poor evaluation of your line of argument!

What is more important is that straight away he will think of you as someone he has to watch carefully. You have reinforced his perception of your power in the negotiation. This always has to be better for you.

If, on the other hand, you present your weak arguments at the end, *after* the sledgehammer points, the other party sees straight away that they don't really deserve an answer. So, he concentrates on the strong points and tries not to waste time on minor points.

Now do you see the advantage of a seemingly 'disorderly' presentation?

Let the other party do the work

It is important to keep arguments of equal strength together. Do not give in to the natural temptation to classify them and to organize them into different categories.

Make the other party concentrate on several types of fact at once, and make him move from areas where the evaluations are more objective to ones where the evaluations are rather of a subjective nature (for example, switch between arguments which are factual and those which are based on values).

However, if this technique is used by the other party, always take some minutes to sort out his arguments, but don't draw attention to what you are doing. You will find it easier to deal with the facts first, then with the questions of principle.

Do You Know How to Reply to an Argument?

Every day we respond to arguments. Without realizing it, we make use of certain tactics and strategies which can be identified, analysed and deliberately reproduced.

It is always possible to manipulate the situation in such a way that your answers will be effective in reinforcing your power.

To start with, you do not have to follow the order of the other party's arguments. Reorder them into weak and strong points, and principal arguments, as you did for your own lines of argument.

First, attack the strong points

Reject them without dwelling too much on the details, but keep one or two points for the end.

Get through the trivia

Mention the points of detail in passing, saying that you consider these points to be of secondary importance (do not call them 'minor', though) and that you would like to return to them later.

Move on to the *pièce de résistance*

Continue by saying something like this: 'What particularly struck me in your presentation was the part where you spoke of . . .', and then talk about the principal arguments.

Keep your answers to one or two of the other party's strong points for the very end. The other party will think that you have not brought them up because you have nothing to say about them. He may then be off his guard, already concentrating on basing a new line of argument on these very points.

Finish with the dessert!

To wind up, add one or two strong arguments to your answer. Do this quite casually, as if it is understood that for your adversary himself these were just details: 'As for the question of . . ., that can't really make much difference, because . . .'

Don't go over the top. Quickly cover your line of argument on the points without entering into detail.

The stronger your rejection of a point, the more the other party is likely to be impressed by the fact that you are not going on about it. Try to act as if the point scored seems so unimportant to you that you do not even bother to count it.

If that point comes back on to the table, you are then free to develop your theme, to show that you have plenty in reserve and that you do not lack valid arguments.

Reinforce Your Line of Argument

Try to present very strong arguments in a casual way, as if they were not important moves in your game, but simply rejected ideas or passing thoughts: 'I was thinking – it would always be possible to get in touch with your competitor, but, after all, you and I have a good working relationship and I'm sure that we can come to an understanding.'

Let the other party know that you have an alternative without putting yourself in the delicate position of making threats.

Next, push the other person into a corner without seeming to touch him at all. In other words, explore the alternatives which are available to him by showing that they are dead ends. 'You could always think of this and that possibility. But you have surely realized that that would put you in just as bad a position because of this and that.'

Always take care not to fall into the trap of believing or showing that you know about all the other party's alternatives. Behave as if they were still a part of the game which has escaped you. Not to the extent of losing your confidence, but enough so that you remain alert at all times – even when everything seems to be going well.

Obviously, the better your preparation, the more you will be able to foresee the other party's arguments, the counter-arguments that he is likely to use against your line of argument and the answers that you can give. Work through the checklist on page 239.

In Chapter 22 we will look at more ways of rejecting the other party's arguments.

How to Counter an Argument

What Is Countering?

Countering is the action by which you show that the other party's line of argument does not stand up. You can 'counter' in several stages, and there are as many ways to counter as there are individuals. However, there are some extremely useful precepts you should consider.

First of all, it is in your interests to listen very attentively to the other party so that you understand his position well. (We will study this point in more detail when we look at feedback.) Then, it is up to you to give validity to your point of view. This is the countering phase.

You may sometimes find it difficult to put forward your point of view in a valid way and to counter the arguments of your adversary. Here are some clues to keep in mind.

Don't counter everything

Be satisfied with taking up only the most important points. If the other points are brought up as a matter of course, this can show that the other party is running out of steam, and that he is short of arguments.

You can then concede that the other party is right on one or two minor points, but always be careful to bring up your important points again: 'On that point I admit that you seem to be right, but it must be said that it doesn't have much to do with the basic question, which is . . . And on the subject which specifically concerns us, I think that we agree that (and you then give the opinion that you have already successfully put forward).'

Foresee the objections

Here is a chance to double your score. When you anticipate an objection, you can also mention it immediately after giving your point of view: 'You're going to tell me that I could always bring my prices down, but I would say to you that in that case we could not provide such a good service . . .' In this way, of course, you counter the objection yourself, before the other party has the chance to reinforce it in his own terms or to supplement it with one or two ideas.

I should give a word of warning here: be careful not to go so far as to give the other party any arguments to use against you.

Anticipate counter-objections to you

Your line of argument is going to raise a counter-argument which you will try to refute as well as you can. During your preparation, you should have anticipated the following:

- Objections to your line of argument. Note them point by point.

- Counter-objections. These are the arguments that you can use in opposition to the objections of the other party.

- Counter-counter-objections. If possible, go so far as to anticipate a line of argument in the face of counter-objections. This could be described as being really well prepared!

Of course, having said this, you are not always obliged to respond to an argument. You can:

- ignore the objection, as if it really does not deserve to be brought up again; take up your argument again as if it still has its initial strength;

- bypass the objection; take it up again saying, for example, that it is not really anything to do with the case in question.

How Do You Counter Difficult Arguments?

You are in a negotiating situation. The other party has just played his ace. You would like to be able simply to sweep his argument aside, but here you are, his argument seems absolutely irrefutable. All you can say is that it does offer you a challenge.

So, are you going to admit that the other party is right?

Before answering 'Yes' or 'No', think about this: is your style of negotiation one of co-operation or competition? According to the type of negotiation in which you are involved, your answer to this question will not be the same.

Co-operation

Give yourself a little time to pause for thought. In the heat of a discussion, it is easy to get carried away. Ask yourself what your goal really is.

If it is a matter of negotiating an understanding which will be favourable for both of you, perhaps the time has come to show your goodwill and to recognize the strength of the other party's argument.

In this case, it is better to choose another point where you think the other party might be weaker. You must not admit a concession without gaining another in return. Besides, in a discussion, it is usually recommended in principle that you *never* admit that you are wrong. But, during a negotiation, not recognizing your faults may actually undermine your credibility.

You know how painful and pointless it is to try to discuss things with someone who never admits his faults. Reserve this type of discussion, therefore, only for those who themselves never admit that they are wrong: this is called the 'mirror technique'.

But suppose that you want to start up the negotiation again. Well, you can weigh in with something like: 'On this point, I must admit that you are definitely right. But, on the other hand, on the question of . . ., it seems to me that you are in complete agreement with me.'

You have just struck two blows with one stone. You have elegantly extricated yourself from a difficult situation, and you have advanced the negotiation, while winning a reciprocal concession at the same time.

In competition

Obviously, in a tough negotiation, it is not in your interests to give ground easily. There are different things you can do.

Method 1. Question the other party

Ask for more details. Asking questions will allow you to gain time and you might discover a detail which will give you a way of starting up the discussion again. If you have done your preparation well, you may already have a suspicion that the line of argument in question would come up.

Your questions should seem to be quite innocuous, and at the same time they are never really neutral, as they direct the thought from one side to the other. It is sometimes said that power belongs to the person who asks the questions.

Clever questions can quietly undermine the confidence of the other party, to the point where he might lose trust in his argument.

Method 2. Carry on regardless

Act as if you did not hear, as if what the other party said wasn't very important. This is not a very sophisticated technique, but it may be all you can do in an extreme case.

Method 3. Listen!

Make sure you have properly understood what has been said to you, and take your time before replying. An attempt at a reply is always better than silence. This is why you must make sure you have really understood what the other party is saying.

Method 4. Argue against the reasoning, not the position

When you are arguing with the other party, avoid criticizing his position as such. Instead, concentrate on the reasoning which motivates him to adopt this position.

For example, if you are dealing with a tenant who is refusing to accept a rent rise, talk about the general question of the rise in the cost of living, the repairs that you have had to do, and so on, rather than attacking him because he doesn't want to pay. Ask, 'Do you have any particular reasons for opposing this rent rise?' If the answer is that it is too expensive, do not immediately say 'No, it's not too expensive!', but ask why, again.

If the tenant answers that it's because he cannot pay any more, the problem is not the same as if he were saying that the lodgings are not *worth* the rise (this is what might be said to you anyway).

Method 5. Relax

This is not the moment to be tense or nervous, or to strain yourself to listen harder. When you are nervous, you are more likely to hear what you *want* to hear, jump to conclusions and to think the worst of the other person.

Recognize Your Mistakes

Must you recognize your mistakes or not? Should you admit them? Opinions diverge on this subject. I think it largely depends on the situation in hand.

In a situation of conflict, when you know that the other person is going to see any concession on your part as a great victory, and that any concession will look like a sign of weakness, it can be better *not* to admit your mistakes. On the other hand, if, for example, you realize that you have been given false information, it is usually better to admit it, and to ask for an adjournment in the light of the new facts that have arisen.

It is essential that the other party does not feel justified, after a mistake on your part, to doubt all that you say.

Learn to Identify Inflated Arguments

Be on the look-out for tactics which give the *impression* that the other party's argument is stronger than it really is. There are several ways of doing this. Sometimes the truth can be twisted to diminish your arguments. It is useful to think about the main distortions that the truth can suffer when someone wants to 'puff up' his or her argument. If you are aware of these techniques you will be able to identify and counter them more easily.

Counters which aren't counters

Some people appear to be countering an argument when they are simply rejecting it. Replies such as 'Not on your life!', or 'That's absolutely wrong!' or 'There's absolutely no question of that' are not arguments, but statements of principle. Unfortunately, one doesn't always think of simply asking: 'Why?' or 'Why not?'. If you ask a question it puts the onus on the other party to prove his or her case.

Specious examples

Specious examples are justifiable, but they do not apply in your particular case. They have been 'stretched' outside their field and should be deemed irrelevant.

False logic

Every day, we come up against false logic and it is not always easy to identify it. Here is one well-known example:

Asses are mortal.
This man is dead.
Therefore, this man was an ass.

Seen in this way, the problem of false logic becomes obvious – it is not only asses that are mortal.

But, if we say: 'This businessperson has failed in this enterprise. You are a businessperson, therefore you are going to fail too', the false logic is less obvious. But all businesspeople are *not* the same and it is up to you to prove that you are different.

There are also 'magic causes': 'The explosion happened just at the moment when he put on his crash helmet, therefore it was the helmet which caused the explosion!' Or, the outcome is seen as the cause: 'Each time women's hairstyles become short the government is threatened. Therefore, women should be forbidden to have short hairstyles.'

There are loads of falsely logical arguments, and there is no room here to list them all. Suffice it to say that you must always be in your guard and avoid letting yourself be carried away by facile arguments.

Never hesitate to ask 'Why?' and 'Why not?'.

Circular arguments

To prove the argument you are putting forward, you repeat the same idea twice: 'This machine is the best. See, it's written in our brochure.' Or: 'Our firm always chooses the best experts. This expert is therefore the best since we chose him.'

Again, watch out for such claims and refuse to accept them.

Labels

Labels often serve to repudiate arguments. The effect is very quick and long-lasting. 'You plan to be financed by this businessman? But he is a megalomaniac (or an eccentric, or a member of the Communist party, and so on)'. 'Don't listen to him, he's just frustrated, jealous.' Without specifying any reasons, you seek thus to dishonour a person, a position or an argument.

Always ask the other party to explain *why* and *how* this label has been applied as it dishonours a person and devalues his arguments. This will give rise to two very different types of answer, which will affect the way you proceed.

'Why is he a megalomaniac? Well, because everyone says so!' *or* 'Because it's well known!'

'Why do I say he is a megalomaniac? Listen, I can name at least four people who got involved with him on grandiose projects which never saw the light of day.'

The law of the greatest number

This is an argument that is equally commonly used: 'Everyone does it, so you do it too.' For example, since everyone uses aerosol cans, you can do the same. In fact, 'everyone' thinks that the use of aerosol cans does not pose a serious ecological problem, therefore there is no reason not to use them.

You may have noticed that parties are often organized in just this way: 'Everyone will be there, we can't possibly not go.'

This is also the way in which great financial frauds are set up. All the banks lend to a clever negotiator, which gives him an exceptional credit rating, and so it goes on – at least until the day when no one wants to lend him money any more. Don't be so easily fooled.

Avoid Scandalmongering

You may be drawn in to discuss stories about a competitor, for example. You create a shoddy kind of 'solidarity' for yourself, using a third party who is not present and cannot defend himself. Avoid this kind of thing and try to stand apart. It's a suspect technique and the results generally leave you with a bitter taste in your mouth.

The False Choice

You are given two possibilities to choose from. You do not like either of them. But perhaps there is an alternative? The answer is to avoid getting bogged down.

Have you ever been stuck in the snow in a car? You may know that the last thing you should do is make the wheels spin round at top speed. The snow packs hard and you cannot move. Instead, you should try gently to move forward slightly, then straightaway put the car in reverse, back up gently and go off forwards again as soon as you get stuck.

The idea is that, as you move forwards and backwards, you have more chance of getting out than if you stop and start.

The same goes for argument. If you come into conflict with the other party on a particular point, avoid digging yourself into a hole. Pass on to another point which is easier to sort out, come back to the contentious question and again, as soon as you start to get stuck, pass on to something else. In other words, try to make gradual progress in the negotiations.

As soon as you have made some good progress, bring up the controversial point from a new angle. Approach it in a different way. Put your creativity to work. Do not allow the discussion to stagnate. It is much better to move on a little and come back to the point afterwards. And when you do that, avoid basing your arguments on a single issue.

Trust Your Instincts

Certain lines of argument sometimes leave even expert negotiators feeling a little confused, with the impression that they are missing something. It can often happen that you think you have missed the point, or that you haven't properly taken in the information presented to you.

If you feel that you are a victim of confusion don't immediately assume that it's *you* who has been misunderstood. The strategy to adopt is quite simple: ask questions. Perhaps you are dealing with a confused person, whose own analysis of the situation is, in fact, very weak. Perhaps the other person has managed to change the subject, or is mixing up different levels of information, and so on. He could also have dodged part of his reasoning, precisely because it is a little weak.

Always avoid letting yourself be dragged into a maelstrom of information and arguments without asking questions.

The test which follows will help you to evaluate the strength of your argument, and of your preparation. When you have prepared your arguments, use the test to review the different points of your reasoning.

Test on Preparing Your Argument

	Yes	No
1. If asked exactly what I want to convince the other party of, can I answer straight away?		
2. Have I established my argument properly?		
3. Can I say whether my reasoning is based on deduction, induction, analogy or whether it is causal? (If yes, say which.)		
4. Can I base each argument on facts?		
5. Do I have concrete examples to illustrate my points?		

Yes No

6. Have I prepared striking examples, impressive images, pithy phrases?

7. Have I anticipated any objections that might be raised to my arguments?

8. Have I prepared an answer to these objections?

9. Have I identified the weak points in my argument?

10. Do I have satisfactory answers to these weak points?

11. Do I have a list of secondary points which I could concede?

12. Have I identified some of the arguments that my adversary might bring up, and am I prepared to counter these arguments?

13. Am I am relatively confident that my arguments will have the power to sway my adversary?

TOTAL

The more yesses you score, the more solid your argument will be.

CHAPTER 23

Getting and Making Concessions

The art of negotiation is indissolubly linked with the art of making concessions. The word negotiate comes from the Latin *negocio* which means commerce. This gives us the following relationship: *negocio*=commerce=exchange. In the final analysis, negotiating is, to a large extent, the art of knowing how to exchange concessions. If you watch two seasoned negotiators at work, you'll notice their skill at evaluating and exchanging concessions. This sometimes happens with a simple nod of the head.

The problem with concessions is that they can incur losses on two levels: both material and image. That's why you should always avoid making concessions at the start of a negotiation; for example, when you're not likely to get anything in return.

Lead the Concession Dance

First, let's look at the classical type of progression. If you ask for £120 per item, and I offer £110, then we will work progressively towards a mean figure of £115. And as I get closer to my bottom line, I will reduce the increments between my offers.

For example, the first concession I make may be to offer £112, an increase of £2. However, the next time I'd only go to £113, followed by £113.50, then £114, £114.25, £114.40, £114.50, and so on.

The closer I get to £115, the harder it becomes to get me to move, because I'm getting closer to the price I'd really like to pay. And I'm going to do everything I can to stay above my bottom line, which is the absolute maximum I'm willing to pay (in this case £116).

So, the corollary to this type of progression is that the smaller the increments become, the closer the other party is to their bottom line price. And it's always good to know how much the other party is willing to pay.

Making a concession calls for a concession to be made in return. In fact, as we have already discovered, you should know in advance which concessions you're willing to make: this should be an integral part of your preparation work. In other words, you should add ballast (concessions you're prepared to make) to your ship when planning your strategy, and then drop the extra weight at the appropriate time.

Learn to adjust your offers

In many cases, it is enough progressively to adjust an offer in order to reach an agreement. This is why you must thoroughly investigate your options and alternatives during the preparation stage, considering factors like the size of an order, delivery requirements, payment conditions, after-sales service, etc. Any factor which can be added to the original proposal and which can be used to justify the price being asked is likely to be helpful in reaching a final agreement.

Don't be the first to concede

You should do everything in your power not to be the first one to concede an important point. The psychological victory to be gained by the other party is too great. If you absolutely *have* to concede, then you're probably not in a very good position to begin with. Try to obtain an equally important concession as soon as possible, arguing that you have demonstrated your good faith already, that you've already given up a lot, etc.

Letting go

Some deals just aren't worth the effort and you should realize this as soon as possible. If the discussions just don't seem likely to turn in your favour, then you should take a close look at your alternatives, and don't hesitate to excuse yourself and break off the negotiations. This should not be considered a failure – negotiations which are broken off in time sometimes turn into successes.

How to Make a Concession

When preparing to make a concession, you have to define its limits.
Ask yourself these questions:

'Do I really have to make this concession, or do I have enough power (in the form of alternatives, etc) to stick to my initial position?'
'What do I want in exchange?'

- Don't wait until the last minute to determine what you're willing to give up, and what you absolutely refuse to cede. Doing so is risky and frequently leads to errors of judgement. During your preparation stage, you should decide what you will eventually be willing to give up, and at what price.

- Do not make concessions under pressure or too rapidly. Wait for conditions that are relatively favourable. Making one concession from a position of weakness can result in your being forced to make a host of other concessions later.

- State your position: you're not making this concession free of charge. You simply play your card, making it clear that you will withdraw the concession if a reasonable counter-offer is not forthcoming.

- Explain why you're making the concession, but don't forget that it is a concession and not an adjustment. This means, for example, that if you have to undertake negotiations with another party, the concession will be retracted. It is therefore applicable only to the discussions in progress.

- If the concession is some form of ultimatum signalling the end of negotiations (*'This is my final offer...'*) make sure the other party understands that you've reached your limit, and that past this point the discussions will be very difficult. If your offer isn't accepted, and you still want to make a deal, you can get around the ultimatum by adding a condition (which may be only symbolic) that will modify the situation from your point of view (*'Unless you agree to...'*).

Remain flexible

An inflexible negotiator is a contradiction in terms. Nevertheless, many negotiations break down precisely because one or both parties refuse to give an inch once they've established their positions.

Put a time limit on your concessions

When you offer to make a concession, you are not obliged to leave it on the table indefinitely. The other party should be made to understand that the offer is conditional – that you expect some movement on their part, like an equally important concession in return – and that if they don't you're prepared to withdraw it.

In this way you don't end up giving concessions away. At the same time you let the other party know that the point is negotiable, if an offer of equivalent value is made in return.

Make an accurate evaluation of everything you give

Calculate the cost of each concession. If you can't set a price in pounds and pence, don't sign. If, for example, a figure is to fluctuate with variations in market values, you may find yourself in a difficult position later on. If such an eventuality is unavoidable, you can protect yourself by insisting on a limit: *'We will accept any hidden costs, but only up to this specified amount . . .'*.

How to Get a Concession in Return

Look for the happy medium between wasting excessive amounts of energy defending a point of secondary importance to you, and giving away too much by adopting an overly open-handed approach.

Force the other party to work for what they get. If you give things away too easily you will arouse suspicions. So, even if your concession is valid, objectively speaking, the other party may start wondering if he or she is being taken for a ride when he or she is not asked to do anything to earn it.

Make sure you always get something in return for a concession, even if it doesn't cost you anything. This may seem to be elementary. But what is the aim of an unscrupulous negotiator? Obviously to get as much as possible without giving anything in return. So, whenever you're asked to make a concession, develop the reflex of asking yourself: *'What am I being offered in return?'* If you can't determine what this is, you're better off waiting until a more interesting proposal arises.

The myth of splitting the apple in two

You offer £100,000, the other party is asking for £120,000. He then suggests that you split the difference, and you agreed on £110,000. However, there is nothing which obliges you to proceed in this way, even though common sense and an equitable settlement may seem to favour such a solution.

- Who is to say that this equitable figure is not simply an artificial amount based on the other party's over-evaluation of its initial position?

- Why do you have to agree? Simply because someone suggests that you do?

Cutting the apple in two is just one way of overcoming the impasse created when neither party is willing to budge from their respective positions. But this is precisely the moment when you should promote and add weight to your arguments. There are different ways to react, depending on your position in the negotiations.

- you can increase the value of the item in question to justify your refusal to meet the other party's offer half-way

- make it understood that you have certain constraints which prevent you from going beyond a certain figure (budget, authority, etc)

- make a counter-offer. *'Listen, I can't go as high as 50 per cent, but I can make an effort to settle for 33 per cent of the difference'*

- if you decide that the only way to reach an agreement is to accept splitting the difference, then simply make a counter-offer to pay half of what will finally be acceptable to you.

In the above situation, if the other party proposes a £2,000 reduction, would you up your offer by £2,000 as well? This would be the same as agreeing to cut the apple in half, which is not absolutely necessary even in a climate of co-operation.

Get the other party used to making concessions

If you can, get the other party to make a few minor concessions at the outset of negotiations. This will lay the groundwork for obtaining more important concessions later on.

If you allow the other party to sail through the greater part of the negotiations without making any concessions, it will be much more difficult to get them to make concessions later on in the game. Because of your generosity, the other party will rightly assume they are in a superior position where they don't have to concede a thing, and rightly so.

Always emphasize the value of the concessions you make: this will allow you to ask for more in return. And, on the other side of the coin, you must always try to play down the value of any concessions made by the other party.

When a demand is refused

When you are informed that a certain concession is impossible due to budgetary constraints, precedents, etc, adopt the viewpoint that the refusal may very well be a tactic designed to force you to modify your unilateral position. When this happens:

- investigate the alternatives – would another arrangement be more profitable?

- could you modify your offer to accommodate the other party's demands without making any significant concessions?

Give up less and less

In principle, the further along you are in the negotiations, the closer you are getting to your bottom line. It therefore follows that the concessions you are willing to make should get smaller and smaller. This tells the other party that you're approaching your limit, and that he or she must therefore work all the harder and offer more in order to make you change your position.

In the next sections we will be looking at some techniques you can use to win the concessions you want to gain.

Techniques for Getting Concessions

The salami technique

This well-known approach involves 'slicing up' what needs to be negotiated into sections, so that you can treat each part separately.

Also called the 'nibbling' technique, the strategy is to try to win many small concessions on a large number of points. The hope is that the concessions accumulate until, in the end, appreciable gains have been made.

This tactic has another useful effect, which is to wear out the enemy by making him spend a lot of time thinking about minor points. It should be mentioned that this strategy serves just as well in defence as in attack.

It won't be an outright winner every time, but the process can be effective in certain situations, notably when you know that you are going to have to strike a bargain.

The snare

This technique involves using a diverting manœuvre to distract the other party's attention away from your real aims. For example, I put forward some objectives – genuine or otherwise – which require substantial concessions on your part. The more I insist, the more I put pressure on you to give me something which, basically, I do not really want.

The advantage that I gain from this technique is to get you used to inflated, if unrealistic, demands. In your eyes, I seem to be extremely demanding and difficult to satisfy.

To your relief – and to make you 'owe' me, all I have to do is to come down on my fictional demands (they are fictional in that I do not really value them). If I'm really clever, I could even make you see this as a concession on my part, and use it to snatch one or two concessions from you in return. And I will have had them for nothing!

The other advantage is that I can pass off as a secondary objective that which is really my *true* aim. And I can pursue it while giving you the impression that it is nothing but a stop-gap, filling in because I had to drop the thing that really interested me.

Inflationary demands

Another approach is to ask for much more than you really want or you can reasonably expect to gain.

The procedure seems at first glance to be absolutely classic, but the idea is as follows: while the negotiations are going ahead, you drop certain demands, in exchange, of course, for substantial concessions. 'Good, OK, we'll drop the delivery times of 48 hours, and we'll wait a week as you've requested. On the other hand, we would like the possibility of short-term finance; we would also like you to give us an option on the new model which is coming out in the autumn.'

In effect, you are exchanging the demands you know to be unrealistic for concrete concessions . . .

However, how should you react if you feel that someone is using this very tactic against you? (See page 225.)

How to Tell if They Are Bluffing

Start by asking yourself two questions.

1. *Am I lacking any information?*
If the details you have put together on the other person have in no way

prepared you for such an avalanche of demands, could it be because you are badly prepared?

2. *Is this a tactic?*
No, you don't really realize this straight away, especially if the demands are well balanced. They may well appear to be legitimate demands. Perhaps the other person is seeking to make you have doubts about yourself in order to make you re-evaluate your demands and bring them down. (This is a common manœuvre.)

Now you need to ask the other party questions. Is it wishful thinking, or is the person person really in a position to impose such conditions? You will only need to ask a few pertinent questions to distinguish one from the other.

- 'What are you able to offer in exchange for such demands?'

- 'Do you think we will be able to sort all this out in one (or in ten) sessions?'

If You Really Cannot Concede

Negotiations are just beginning when the discussions get bogged down over an issue which you really can't concede. What do you do?

You should suggest getting back to the issue at the end of the negotiations. You then have two options.

1. The first option

The first option is, during the discussions, to keep mentioning the various points on which you *have* agreed to make concessions. You have been generous, but not overly so, and you made the other party work for what they got.

You're finally approaching the finish line. Like a horse putting on a last burst of speed as he senses the end of the race and home, the other party becomes a little impatient and wants to conclude the agreement, especially since things are looking very good for them because of the care you've taken to pave the way for a mutually advantageous settlement. The other party thinks that all they have to do now is convince you to lower your price a little . . .

'I'm really sorry, but the figure isn't negotiable', you say when the other party brings up the question of price. At this stage in the negotiations, your

answer can only be taken to mean that you've thought everything out thoroughly and have still decided that you will not yield.

Here too, all the other concessions you've already made will influence the way your refusal is accepted. You may want to review them one more time, showing the other party that you're not really that greedy after all!

In the light of the work that they have already put in, the other party will think twice before throwing it all away at this stage.

2. The second option

The second option is to make very few concessions on any other issues throughout the negotiations, apart from some merely symbolic ones. Then, when the contentious issue comes around, you change tactics and offer a number of concessions in return for the price you want.

In other words, you exchange concessions on negotiable issues for concessions on non-negotiable issues. Everything depends on your strategy and the way the other party perceives that:

- you really do want to negotiate, and you're ready to concede on a number of points, but

- you simply cannot concede the point in question.

So, what is the other party going to do? They've invested considerable time and energy, they like the rest of the package and the way you've been dealing up to now . . . Well, they could always start the whole process over again with someone else. That is a possibility that can't be counted out. But consider the following.

- You have almost reached an agreement: therefore you can count to some extent on the principle of human inertia working in your favour!

- If things break down, the other party will have to deal with someone else, and who knows – the next person may be worse than you are!

- A relationship already exists between the two of you. You've shown yourself to be understanding and flexible on a number of issues, so the relationship is positive. If they refuse, will you be willing to do business with them in future? Here again, the principle of inertia acts in your favour.

So, if you've set the stage properly, the other party should think twice before breaking off the negotiations and looking elsewhere.

To be sure you've done everything possible, see if you can answer the following questions in the affirmative. If so, you have a good chance of succeeding even if, in fact, you refuse to negotiate certain issues.

Yes No

1. Have you given the other party good reasons for conceding the point you want them to?

2. Are you able to summarize these reasons clearly, and make them seem attractive?

3. In other words, have you respected the principle that someone who negotiates with you never leaves the table empty-handed?

It's worth repeating that **you must do all you can to postpone non-negotiable issues until the end of the discussions**. And remember that it's preferable to make the other party earn the concessions you make, even those you are willing to give up, unless the climate is extremely co-operative.

If you have an ongoing business relationship, you can expect to find the ball in the other party's court at some future date. The best – and the most lucrative – business relationships are founded on an ability to give and take concessions on both sides.

Learn to stonewall

You must learn to make the other party respect your position, even if it's an artificial one, well above your bottom line. You must be able to convince the other party that **you are immovable**.

Of course, it's important to:

- be flexible
- know how to make concessions
- be able to put things in perspective
- and put yourself in the other party's shoes.

But these skills will only be handicaps if you don't *also* know how to make the other party understand that you are absolutely inflexible and immovable on certain points. When you say: *'I will not go lower than this price'* or *'This point is not negotiable'*, you have to say it with enough conviction absolutely, completely and entirely to convince the other party that you mean it. In other words, you have to know how to stonewall.

One of the best ways to stonewall is to introduce some exterior consideration to support your position. This defence tactic can be used against almost any kind of attack (except out-and-out force, of course).

To ensure that you don't give in, make a commitment to a third person so that you won't be able to change your mind. For example, you've set a ceiling on the amount you want to spend to acquire a certain asset. It's easier to stick to the figure you've decided on if you take out a loan for say £100,000, and if you know you won't be able to get a penny more. That figure represents your maximum budget.

You may enter into extensive negotiations, but you've set your maximum expenditure at £100,000. So, you know that if the seller tries to get you to pay £110,000, he's going to meet with a wall of resistance, *'I just can't – it's absolutely impossible'*.

You could also defer to some exterior authority; your boss, for example, or your board of directors, your bank manager or even your spouse. This gives you some margin of manœuvrability, but at the same time forces you to remain within strict limits. And if the other party is in any way reasonable, they will do everything they can to settle on a figure which is within a budget you can approve, unless they want to get into lengthy negotiations on other issues or with your superiors.

Actually you can be flexible and co-operative on some issues, and inflexible on others. Your commitments and the defence of your position become all the more reasonable when the other party realizes that they aren't due to a mean streak in your character or to any bad will on your part, but are your real limits. Simply stated, some issues are negotiable, others aren't.

To be effective, your commitment must be concrete, visible and credible.

- **Concrete**   The commitment must be respected, which is why you may want to impose certain penalties if the conditions are not adhered to.

- **Visible**   The other party must be aware of the limits being imposed on you from outside. You should therefore make them clear at the outset of the negotiations, giving the other party time to get used to them.

- **Credible**   Restraints that are highly unlikely will do nothing to prevent the other party from trying to make you modify your position. Stick to the truth, or at least make it believable!

You can always establish an absolute bottom line, preferably a round figure. Or, you can refer to precedents set in other deals, saying that you refuse to set a new precedent which will be detrimental to future negotiations. Or you can refer to the reputation of your company as an exterior authority.

How to Move an Immovable Object

What if the other party uses the same strategy on you, saying they cannot budge on a certain issue because of a precedent or a commitment? What can you do?

- Do not accept the fact that the commitment is irrevocable: on the contrary, you're there to get the other party to change their mind!

- Find ways to help the other party modify their position without losing face, especially if they have made a commitment which seems firmly established right from the start. Try to get them to modify their initial position subtly, without making any obvious demands.

- Leave the door wide open, and never equate the other party's change of position with a victory or a gain.

- Look for extenuating circumstances like some new information, which would allow the other party to modify their position without appearing to concede anything. Make yours a 'special case', etc.

- If the other party's commitment is well known (a general company policy, for example) than assure them that any change in position will remain strictly confidential.

If You Have to Modify Your Position

If you decide to modify your position you must be able to break your commitment without appearing to contradict or demean yourself. If you do, you'll have trouble being taken seriously in future. You must never appear to be caving in under pressure. Instead:

- inform the other party that you've decided to change your position in the light of some new information

- use some change in the other party's position as a pretext to modify your own

- change the data you already have: say you've just been given some new information which sheds new light on the situation

- pretend that you misunderstood the other party's initial position to allow you to modify your own without losing face.

CHAPTER 24

Negotiating from a Weak Position

Would you like to be able to negotiate in a situation where the other party holds all the trump cards, yet you still come out ahead? Instead of being disgraced and losing your shirt, you will be able to prove once again that power is what you make it.

Obviously it is preferable to negotiate from a position of force. But this isn't always possible. No matter how large and powerful a company is, it will eventually have to convince superior interests, confront unfavourable circumstances and overcome unexpected and difficult situations. In short, it is very useful to know how to assume the role of David when confronted with a Goliath.

The important thing is not to come out looking a loser. And, in fact, you'll be surprised by the positive gains that you are able to obtain. To start, answer the following questions to test how much you already know.

Do You Know How to Increase Your Power?

Yes No

1. When I find myself in a comparatively weak position, I lay my cards on the table and rely on the honesty and integrity of the other party.

2. When negotiating from a weak position I make no attempt to influence the choice of location.

Yes No

3. I pay special attention to signs indicating the other party's personal status, and any other exterior influences that could improve my situation.

4. I make sure to appear very busy, as if I were occupied with deals that are much more important than the one in hand.

5. When my back is up against the wall, or when I'm being threatened, I respond aggressively to let the other party know that I'm ready for a fight.

6. When my position is weak I adopt a very relaxed attitude so that the discussions take on an informal character.

7. I bluff as much as possible.

8. I insist on stating and restating my objectives, at the risk of annoying the other party.

Now count up your points.

1. Yes=0 No=2	5. Yes=0 No=2	
2. Yes=0 No=2	6. Yes=2 No=0	
3. Yes=2 No=0	7. Yes=0 No=2	
4. Yes=0 No=2	8. Yes=2 No=0	

Results

Between 0 and 6 points: You seem not to be aware of your weaknesses. This is a courageous attitude which, however, lacks a measure of common sense.

Between 8 and 12 points: You understand the subtleties of the situation. But you can do a lot to improve your score (and your performance) in such negotiations. Study your weak points.

14 to 16 points: Excellent! You intuitively know what kind of tactics to use. Read the following explanations and see if you chose your responses for the right reasons.

Eight Tactics to Strengthen Your Position

The test you have just completed is based on eight strategic procedures which can either help you develop the power you have at your disposal or minimize the power of the other party.

When I find myself in a comparatively weak position, I lay my cards on the table and rely on the honesty and integrity of the other party

You should **never** do this. It's always possible to rely on the honesty and integrity of another party if their character seems to indicate a general attitude of goodwill. But that is not the point. You should never expose your position. Even if the other party suspects that you lack power, they should not be certain of it.

And you should never be the one to confirm the other party's suspicions. They should always be left to wonder if you may have other cards up your sleeve in the form of hidden alternatives and outside support.

When negotiating from a weak position I make no attempt to influence the choice of location

This would be a bad move. If you are given the choice, do everything you can to have the negotiations take place on your home territory where you'll be able to apply a greater number of tactics designed to impress and influence the other party.

In an unfavourable situation every ounce of influence you have will help tip the scales in your favour and should not be overlooked.

I pay special attention to signs indicating the other party's personal status, and any other exterior influences that could improve my situation

This is important. Every detail counts. Leave nothing to chance. Pay special attention to your appearance, to the quality of your presentation, to anything that can add to your personal prestige.

Image is extremely important these days, and even making a small effort to enhance it can do a lot to widen your margin of manœuvrability. Of course, image isn't the only thing you should be thinking about. An image with no foundation will be quickly exposed by people with any experience.

I make sure to appear very busy, as if I were occupied with deals that are much more important than the one at hand

This is not a good idea. First of all, if this kind of tactic is exposed, your image (which you've taken so much trouble to build up) will suffer a severe blow. Secondly, a company or a person who has any degree of organization will be sure to give their entire attention to the matter at hand, whatever its importance. You also risk antagonizing the other party, which is never a positive move. So don't pretend to be concerned with more important matters.

When my back is up against the wall, or when I'm being threatened, I respond aggressively and let the other party know that I'm ready for a fight

Never do this. Do everything you can to avoid an out-and-out conflict with someone who is stronger than you are. This is precisely the moment to apply tactics and strategies that will result in more co-operative negotiations.

When my position is weak I adopt a very relaxed attitude so that the discussions take on an informal character

Definitely a good idea. Try to create an atmosphere conducive to informal, friendly exchange. Emphasize the personal aspects of your relationship, or if there isn't a personal relationship already established, try to develop one. This will work to your advantage since people are less likely to crush someone they've taken a liking to.

I bluff as much as possible

In desperate situations, perhaps you could try it. But don't make it a habit. Every time you bluff you run the risk of being found out. If the other party calls your bluff and you're forced to lay your cards on the table, revealing just how weak your position really is, then you risk discrediting your reputation as a negotiator. People won't take you seriously any more, which will be a major handicap in future dealings.

I insist on stating and restating my objectives, at the risk of annoying the other party

If you do this you show that you're persistent. Don't give up anything without a fight. You must appear to be completely devoted to your cause.

Your objectives must be dear to your heart. Such an attitude can only serve to make you more respected.

Be friendly but firm. Restate your objectives as often as is necessary, and don't worry about tiring out the other party. His fatigue will work to your advantage.

To sum up

When you find yourself in a position of weakness:

- never reveal your position

- do all you can to negotiate on your home territory

- pay special attention to the quality of your presentation and to any tactics that enhance your image

- don't pretend to be preoccupied or disinterested

- avoid open conflict at all cost

- try to create an informal, friendly climate conducive to co-operation

- bluff with care

- be persevering and don't give anything away without a fight.

Strategic Steps to Enhance Your Power

Carefully prepare your strategy to suit your inferior position. When you find yourself at a disadvantage, preparation becomes all the more important and can make the difference between success and failure. Follow these rules when mapping your strategy:

- determine your objectives with care

- differentiate between your desires and your needs

- evaluate the other party's objectives, also separating their needs from their desires

- aim to satisfy your needs before your desires

- be prepared to make concessions as far as your desires are concerned

- be firm when negotiating your needs

- never give up one of your needs in return for one of the other party's desires.

If you've done all this, it's completely useless to waste time worrying. Tell yourself that these kinds of situations are the ones that teach you the most. This is where you really have to negotiate! Situations such as these are also the ones which can provide the most satisfaction!

CHAPTER 25

Closing the Deal

We will now take a look at how you should proceed when concluding a negotiating session. When you feel you are close to reaching an agreement, how can you make sure you succeed? There are a number of signs which can help you decide whether or not you're heading in the right direction.

The Five Indicators of Success

Two American negotiators, David Seltz and Alfred Modica, have identified five indicators which will tell you if a favourable agreement is imminent.

1. Counter-arguments fade out. They become less frequent and less intense. You get the feeling that the other party is just trying to make sure that they haven't forgotten anything, or that they are trying to dispel any remaining doubts.

2. The difference between your position and that of the other party grows smaller.

3. The other party starts asking about concrete details like delivery dates, modes of payment, samples, final budgets, etc. This means that the project is becoming a reality in their mind.

4. You are given a personal invitation (to dinner or to a party, etc). According to Seltz and Modica, this kind of invitation, which may or may not include your spouse, indicates that closing the deal is only a formality.

5. An offer is made to draw up a formal contract. This means that the decision to agree to a settlement has ripened sufficiently to warrant the investment of time and energy which will be necessary to draw up a formal contract.

If your performance has been convincing, don't detract from it by making an unnecessary effort to close the deal. You know that it would be useless to try to convince the other party any more than you have already – and doing so could even be counter-productive. You should now concentrate on speeding things up gradually. Don't push too hard, but don't let things drag on either.

The Last-minute Demand

Don't forget that negotiations continue right to the end. This means that you should be ready for a last-minute tactic or manœuvre. The other party can jeopardize everything just when a final agreement is about to be reached, counting on the fact that the energy and time you've already invested will incite you to accept their final demand without too much resistance.

But don't forget that the other party has also invested a lot of time and energy. It's a good idea to refuse such a last-minute demand politely, as if you were declining an invitation to dinner: *'No, really, I'm very sorry but it's impossible.'*

In some cases the pressure is intense. If you're tempted to concede to a demand that forces you to go beyond the limits you've set for yourself (your bottom line) then you should consider the following:

- Would conceding be the rational thing to do, or is it just that at this stage of the game you would prefer to reach an agreement – any kind of agreement – rather than run the risk of leaving the table empty-handed?

- Are you willing to accept because you're so close to your goal that you don't want to see everything go up in smoke?

Of course, you can also add one or two demands yourself at the last minute, especially if your position is strong. This is good strategy, but you should avoid antagonizing the other party over a couple of unimportant issues. Ask yourself if it's really worth the effort, and if you want to risk being taken for a rapacious cheat who only wants to get as much as they can out of the situation, without any regard for good faith or generosity. Is the damage this might cause to your reputation worth the reward?

How to Close Effectively

How do you lead the other party towards a final commitment? Making a decision is always a difficult process – do everything possible to tip the scales in your favour. Here are a few pointers to help you get through the final stages of negotiations more easily.

We will first assume that *you've* made the final offer. This is in keeping with your strategy of always trying to lead the discussions, of assuming the role of director.

- Review the points which have been settled and which point to an imminent agreement.

- When concluding negotiations, make sure you are not interrupted. The moment when the other party must make a decision is very delicate. Third parties who have not been involved in the discussions should not be included at this stage, since they might say or do something to incite further arguments and shows of strength.

- Keep a trump card in reserve. Always make sure to have some last little argument ready, in case the other party hesitates, when you would use it so that the decisive step will be taken. This tactic is based on good salesmanship, and supposes that you've had the patience and foresight to keep an argument hidden until the time comes to get the other party to make a final decision which is to your advantage.

- Only ask questions which imply positive responses.

  'Do you want a trouble-free car?'
  'Do you want a car that holds the road well?'
  'Do you want an easy conscience?'

- Ask questions which assume the other party's consent, and through which you can settle the final details:

  'Where would you like your order to be sent?'

- Formulate questions in the form of alternatives. This is a variation of the preceding technique:

  'Would you prefer drawing up a contract tonight, or do you want me to send a draft to your office tomorrow?'

- Ask the other party if they are ready to finalize an agreement, while avoiding questions which could illicit a negative response. Say something like:

  'What do you think about finalizing the agreement before we break for dinner?'

If there is something else they want to discuss, the other party may respond by saying something like, 'All right, but there's still one more detail . . .'. However, this is better than if you said, *'Are you ready to sign an agreement?'* which calls for a 'yes' or 'no' answer. If the answer is 'no', the whole negotiations may be at risk.

- Keep quiet. You've said everything you had to say, done everything you had to do, you have nothing more to add. In many cases, the silence will be broken by the other party's outright consent, or by a question about some detail. Your reassuring response will be enough to smooth out any remaining doubts.

- Stay calm – don't get excited. Be natural.

- A simple and direct way of getting the other party to make a commitment when you feel they are already won over is to present a contract or a letter of agreement, indicating where they have to sign. However, you should avoid using the word 'sign'. Use another expression like 'make your mark' or 'let's have your X'. Or just point to the dotted line with your finger. And try not to seem too eager about it.

- While the other party is signing, continue talking in a friendly way so as to avoid placing too much ceremonial importance on the act.

- Once you've reached an agreement, don't waste any time. Without appearing too hurried (which could worry the other party), move on to the final phase of giving a definitive form to your common decision. Get the agreement in writing. As we've already mentioned, it's in your interest to draw up the contract yourself.

Is everybody happy?

Heated exchanges sometimes occur during the course of negotiations which can sometimes be painful to swallow. Try to patch up any wounds, especially if you're the one who has been somewhat aggressive.

If you leave someone with the impression of having been mauled, it won't do much for your reputation. So, make sure that no one's ego has been trampled on or bruised.

The important thing is that all parties should leave the negotiating table in a positive frame of mind.

From rough draft to clean copy

There may still be some details that have to be ironed out, even after an agreement has been reached in principle. For example, both parties may have agreed on the substance of an accord. But the agreement still has to be put down in writing. Review all the important points verbally, and then prepare a clean copy which you can send to the other party to be checked the following day.

In many instances, especially in business, a verbal agreement is sufficient. Some deals would be too complex to handle if a verbal agreement could not be trusted. However, it's important in such cases to cover all the details (you might even have to make a list), to ensure that you've dealt with all the aspects of the question before completing the agreement. Always make notes when concluding verbal agreements. People's memories are notoriously unreliable!

Should You Wait Before Concluding?

When you reach the end of a negotiation, it's sometimes necessary to wait a while before making a final decision. This gives both parties time to think, digest the whole project, take a step back and gain some measure of objectivity.

However, you shouldn't step so far back that you lose sight of the issues! In some cases it could be risky to make the other party wait. Suppose a client makes you a counter-offer. The time you estimate you'd need to make a decision would vary according to the circumstances.

To judge whether it would be wise to postpone making a decision or not, ask yourself the following questions.

1. Are there any competitors who could step in while I'm thinking about the offer?

Is someone else after the account? Does your client possess a sought-after asset? Maybe you have no choice in the matter. Maybe you just have to take it or leave it, since the demand for the product is too great. Taking time to think without making any kind of commitment may result in you losing out completely.

2. Will the time I take to think soften the other party's position and bring it closer to my own objectives?

Time can be used as a negotiating tactic, so before closing, summarize the advantages of your proposal. Then say you want to think about it, knowing full well that the other party will do the same.

A week later you make a counter-proposal, and the uncertainty your hesitation has produced will induce the other party to accept a favourable agreement more readily.

3. Can I afford to risk losing the deal by asking for a postponement before making a final decision?

Examine the situation closely. In other words, before deciding to take time out to think – think fast!

4. Is the other party trying to pressure me into a decision?

One of the main pressure tactics used in sales is to cut down the time the buyer has to think before making a decision, without seeming to be in a hurry. You've surely heard sales talk that goes something like this:

'Don't wait too long, because there are other people interested in the deal. If they make me a decent offer, I won't wait.'
'The offer ends tomorrow.'

How do you know if the other party is really trying to inform you of the facts, or if they are just using a pressure tactic? This is where your preparation becomes indispensable. Do you know how this person usually operates? Have you spoken to anyone who's negotiated with them in the past? They may say this kind of thing to everyone. And are you familiar with the market? The person may well be acting in good faith and have other buyers waiting in the wings.

There are two overall possibilities. The first is that the terms of the agreement seem to be in order, but you still want to examine them at your leisure, and check all the angles. If this is the case, but you don't want the other party to cool down too much, you can:

- reassure them verbally and state your intentions clearly

- set a reasonable time limit, promising that you'll have a final answer by that date

- suggest drawing up a pro forma document which summarizes the main issues covered in the discussions and establishes a base upon which a final agreement can be made.

If, after the time limit is up, you decide to accept the proposal on condition that certain slight adjustments are made, you can conclude the agreement by letter or fax. In other words you don't have to go back to the negotiating table.

The second possibility is where you're planning to use the postponement to look for better conditions elsewhere. This is normal practice. It's up to you to evaluate the risks involved.

If you opt for the second choice you don't commit yourself to anything, but if you conclude on the spot:

- the other party is still under your influence
- your powers of persuasion are most effective
- both you and the other party save time.

The Moment of Closing

What is the aim of negotiating if it is not to arrive at an agreement which is as satisfying as possible? You should therefore be familiar with the means you can use to conclude an agreement and manage the final stages of negotiations.

Once an agreement is reached

Don't start bragging about the great deal you've just made. It's not a good idea to let the other party know that you would have accepted less from them. They will feel cheated, and if you ever have to negotiate with them again you can be sure they will be a lot tougher to deal with, knowing how well you play your cards.

This may be obvious, but be careful – you can sometimes let things slip during the informal conversations that usually follow the end of negotiations. The other party may say that it isn't easy to find a buyer at this particular time of year. If you agree too readily he may start wondering if the competition wasn't stronger than you made it out to be. To avoid these unnecessary errors, stick to generalities.

Reassure the other party

Once again, take time to summarize all the advantages the other party has achieved out of the deal. Doing this consolidates the positive results of the discussions and does a lot to prevent them from changing their mind after a night's sleep.

Insist that they have made a very good deal. Repeat the arguments which support this view, and add any new ones you can think of. This is where minor issuss can be used to advantage – they become even more effective when presented at this stage than during the negotiations themselves.

Keep it short and sweet

Some people seem to find it hard to stop talking after concluding an agreement. They go on and on about the weather and all kinds of banalities, they smile for no reason and tell bad jokes. Just get up, bid the other party a polite farewell and leave!

Not satisfied? Wait!

Negotiating is a game of give and take. You may get the impression that you've given more than you got. Obviously if the other party seems to be exultant and treats you like a poor sucker who has just been fleeced, you may have trouble avoiding a feeling of loss and defeat. However, don't let the other party read your feelings. It's better to keep them wondering. And who knows – an opportunity for revenge may not be far off.

Are you tempted to resume discussions after all seems to have been said and done? The manœuvre is not advisable. You'd have to start from scratch all over again, with the added burden of a lot of antagonism directed at you. This may be more costly than just accepting the agreement as it is.

You can't win all your battles. Some will inevitably leave a bitter taste. What counts is the combined results of all your negotiations. In some cases you'll realize that it's the other party who has reason to complain.

After Negotiations Are Over

Evaluate your performance. And, if you've negotiated as part of a team, you will undoubtedly analyse your group's performance after the fact.

Do the same if you've negotiated alone. List your strong and weak points, and don't overlook your faults if you want to improve next time around.

Use constructive criticism only

Don't single out one member of your team and place the blame on him or her, saying things like: 'We could have got such and such a concession if you hadn't opened your big mouth . . .'. This will only harm you in future negotiations. Just list the errors the team made and identify the gaps in your strategy, and keep your comments to yourself.

You should – in fact you must – list the faults and errors your team committed. But don't turn the evaluation session into a trial if things didn't work out the way you wanted. Obviously if one member of your group broke ranks and voiced support for one of the other party's proposals, or gave away some vital information, then you will have to take the proper steps to ensure that it doesn't happen again.

If you negotiated on your own, then don't blame yourself too much if you're dissatisfied for one reason or another. Learn what you can from the situation, and resolve to do better next time.

The follow up

Don't think that it's all over as soon as the papers have been signed. You have to ensure that the various clauses in the agreement are respected by the other party. If you've represented a large company, it's a good idea to call the other party and make sure everything's going well, especially if the implementation of the agreement is being handled by a department other than your own.

Positive memories

If negotiating is your business and you find yourself working in the same sector over a period of years, it can be very useful to create some positive memories which will influence future negotiations.

- Send a letter to the other party stating how enriching you found the experience of negotiating together, how you admire their honesty and skill, etc.

- Some negotiators even offer some kind of gift (preferably expensive) to create a positive reminder of themselves, when the negotiations turn out well.

Do use your discretion: these techniques can be useful at times, and superfluous or even harmful at others.

Conclusion

You now possess the main ingredients for carrying out successful negotiations. All that remains is for you to put what you've learned into practice.

Try to start with easy negotiations about relatively unimportant issues. Consider them as trial runs, and treat them as seriously as you would when negotiating an important deal. Be professional.

Before each negotiating session read through your notes and complete the checklists. In other words – prepare yourself.

After each negotiation, review the different phases and use the checklist in Chapter 14 to see what you omitted this time.

Whenever you meet a seasoned negotiator, talk about your technique, ask questions and learn from his or her experience.

You'll be perfecting the techniques you've learned here for the rest of your life, because the whole of life is one big negotiation. And you'll find that as you become more skilled at applying what you've learned, you'll become more and more successful as a negotiator, and will enjoy an ever greater sense of personal satisfaction. Good luck!

CHAPTER 26

Trumps for Success

You might be interested to look at how one of the best deal makers of the century, Donald Trump, approaches his negotiations. As you know, following the crisis in property in the United States Trump lost part of his fast-built fortune, but we can still learn from him. Please set aside any negative thoughts you may have about the man and discover the key to his numerous successful negotiations.

For Donald Trump, negotiating has always been an art form through which he expresses himself, just like a painter expresses himself on canvas, or a poet through words. Throughout his current business difficulties, Trump has negotiated for his own survival.

In a recent book, *The Art of the Deal*, Trump draws from his earlier experiences to reveal the elements essential for negotiating effectively, and explains how to put them into practice. In this chapter we include a general summary of these essential points so that you can compare them with your own methods.

Trump's Trumps: Eleven Keys to Successful Negotiations

1. Think big

Most people think in small terms because they're afraid of success. They're afraid of winning, and afraid to make decisions. Success, just like failure, requires making adjustments, efforts and adapting your point of view.

2. Give it your best shot

You must be able to concentrate and devote yourself entirely to the task at hand, almost to the point of obsession. What about enjoying life, you may well ask? Donald Trump will tell you that it is certainly not a recipe for happiness, but that it's the only way to attain your goals.

3. Be prepared for the worst – the best will take care of itself

Trump always makes sure he's ready to confront the worst possible scenario. If you can survive the worst, he says, if you protect yourself carefully, you'll be in an excellent position when things work out well.

4. Multiply your options

Always allow yourself as much flexibility as possible. 'I never get too attached to one strategy or one deal,' he says. If one option fails he always has a number of others in the wings. And by keeping a few deals in progress at any given moment, he always found room to manœuvre.

5. Know your market

Elementary! However, it should be noted that Trump had a special aversion for market studies. 'They're expensive, they're often inconclusive and anyway they usually arrive too late – the big deals have already been made.' Trump prefers to rely on his instinct.

Ask questions, always lots of questions. That's the secret. Before buying land or a building, Trump has always carried out his own investigation, interrogating as many people as possible, including taxi drivers, to gain an understanding of the area. Then he draws his own conclusions.

6. Use your power

'The worst thing you can do during negotiations', Trump says, 'is to appear to be desperate, to give the impression that you absolutely must make a deal. Power lies in possessing something that somebody else wants.'

It's even better to have something that someone else *needs*. Use any means you can to create an impression of power, including all the trappings and superficial embellishments.

7. Promote the value of your location

This applies especially to property projects, but in all kinds of deals the right location is important. You have to account for trends, fashions and business currents. 'Don't get sucked in to paying a lot for a trendy location. The important thing is to make the best possible deal – buying low and selling high.'

8. Promote your project

If nobody knows you have an extraordinary product for sale, you probably won't be able to sell it. Make the product known. Generate interest through the media and through any other interested persons or organizations you can.

For a promoter like Trump, this translated into spectacular property deals which the press were eager to report. This was worth millions of dollars to Trump in free advertising. Trump once calculated that a single article in a major newspaper which was in any way flattering was worth $40,000. He states that you just have to be a little different and dare to adopt controversial positions to attract attention.

9. Don't give in

Confrontations are undesirable but sometimes inevitable. Even if they prove costly it's best to let people know that you won't fold under pressure.

10. Deliver the goods

This simply means you should honour your commitments. Sooner or later your client has to get what you promised them. Fancy words and big projects aren't enough – you still have to produce. And there's nothing better than an excellent product to conclude a deal.

11. Have fun

Strange advice coming from a businessman? Perhaps so. But if making good deals is what you like doing best, money is only a way of measuring your skill in the game of negotiation.

Trump's success generated a lot of envy, and he has had his share of problems. Some people wonder whether a lack of ethics is the underlying reason. He has been sued countless times, usually, however, by people who were after a piece of the action. All we can say here is that the principles he espouses are solid and should be used as guidelines for planning your own negotiating strategies.

A Question of Ethics

Do saints get rich? The right attitude towards this is that moral values should be placed ahead of material ones. Of course, there are all kinds of marginal methods which are undeniably effective. But they cannot be recommended for a number of reasons.

So, why respect a code of ethics?

- You don't build a solid business by using unsavoury pressure tactics. Doing so undermines any confidence people may have in you, which is indispensable for long-term success.

- You don't have to use dishonest, illegal or immoral methods to succeed. You can take short cuts, yes, but you can also get sidetracked.

- A life founded on lies, cheating and violence will result in a tremendous amount of pressure on your conscience. You'd have to be totally insensitive to live with yourself. And you'd have to do without many of the joys life has to offer. Try to live without any joy, and you'll see just how terrible it is!

- What has any successful gangster always wanted? A legitimate business! They all want to be respectable and clean. But it's very hard to give up a life of crime and start all over again. You can launder money, but you can't launder a guilty conscience or a reputation. You see, there are other reasons for respecting a code of ethics – the psychological and financial implications are also extremely important.

Before resorting to force . . .

There are times when you have to know how to play rough, if only to force others to respect you, and prevent them from stealing the shirt off your back.

It's better to use prudence and a defensive attitude. Before making any highly aggressive moves ask yourself the following questions.

- *Is it worth it?* Are there any other ways you can get what you want? Look at the situation carefully.

- *Are you reacting out of pride?* In business people often feel the need to exchange blow for blow when their pride is wounded. It's like the feeling you get when someone cuts you up on the motorway. It's much better to learn to let things pass in most cases. Wait until you're confronted with a case of flagrant abuse before using force to resolve the conflict. This will only give you more power when the time comes to act.

- *Did you perceive the situation correctly?* We often imagine things. We think we may be dealing with the devil himself only to find out later on that he's just an ordinary bloke like you or I. He may simply have a different point of view.

- *If your tactic were made public or got around by word of mouth, how would you feel?* Could you hold your head high, or would you have to leave town?

- *If the people you love and respect were to find out about what you plan to do, would they approve or would they consider you dishonest?* Ultimately the choice is yours. You're the one who has to deal with the situation and no one else.

The aim of this book throughout has been to provide you with the maximum number of means to enter into negotiations and successfully bring them to term within a general code of ethical behaviour, so that you may enjoy the benefits of success while keeping your reputation and your conscience clean – two things which can neither be bought nor negotiated!

PART IV

USEFUL NEGOTIATING TECHNIQUES

CHAPTER 27

Communication Techniques

If you only concern yourself with your desires, objectives and results in negotiating and ignore the other party when planning your strategy, you'll be forgetting one essential point: it takes two to negotiate. And that implies at least a minimum of communication.

Are you sufficiently aware of how important it is to provide the other party with accurate feedback about his or her proposals and arguments?

Respect the Other Party's Arguments

If you're negotiating with a serious person, then his or her argument merits serious attention. To start, you should rephrase the other party's argument in your own words, being careful not to distort its essential meaning.

There is a tendency to debase or twist an argument if it is in conflict with your own position. This only leads to misunderstandings, and the dialogue will become more and more difficult as long as you refuse to admit you have made a mistake in interpreting the original argument.

It's important to understand the other party's position. This may seem insignificant at first, but you'll soon learn that it has considerable impact on how the negotiations turn out.

The Importance of Feedback

Trying to provide accurate feedback implies a certain degree of objectivity, even if you're directly involved. Rephrasing the other party's argument requires an ability to remain detached, and sends a positive signal to the other party: they understand that you're ready to talk things over.

It is useful to take some time to see things from the other party's point of view – what their position and arguments mean to them. And remember that they are likely to be emotionally attached to these proposals since they think they're going to provide them with something they want. Otherwise they wouldn't be talking to you in the first place.

This is another reason why you may antagonize the other party if you treat their arguments frivolously or ignore them completely.

By accurately paraphrasing the other party's arguments, you let them know that you're aware of their position and that you respect it. It is surprising how many negotiations turn sour simply because one party considers the other's arguments to be ridiculous or stupid.

A refusal to accept the other party's proposals as they are can have two causes.

- For many people admitting they've made a mistake is a sign of weakness.

- They think that by distorting an argument they weaken the other party's position. They refuse to respond to an argument because they have no valid answers. And that is exactly what the term 'acting in bad faith' means.

You won't get anywhere by trying to change the subject or ridiculing the other party's proposals. When you distort the other party's proposal:

- you undermine your own credibility as a negotiator

- you jeopardize the confidence the other party has in you, and confidence is indispensable for profitable negotiations

- you turn the other party into an enemy who only wants to harm you

- feelings of frustration and aggression will soon appear

- you do nothing to reinforce your own position. In fact you weaken it by showing your fear.

It's always better to restate the other party's arguments in a way that makes it easy for them to intervene, using words like, '*If I understand you correctly . . .*'. And if you want to make changes, state them clearly. In other words, you may restate the spirit of the other party's argument, but you don't necessarily have to use the same terminology.

Feedback is essential for effective negotiations

You should always provide accurate feedback if:

● you consider yourself a serious negotiator

● you want to instil confidence in others by demonstrating a willingness to discuss issues

● you want to express your self-confidence

● you understand that arguments which have been openly and successfully refuted are dead and gone, while those which are ignored or distorted keep coming back

● you wish to save both parties considerable time and energy.

Different types of feedback

To provide accurate feedback:

● think about what the other party said while you're speaking

● quote the other party

● rephrase what the other party said in your own words

● summarize the important points of what the other party said.

The importance of feedback rests on the fact that it allows both parties to adjust their communication as time goes on. It helps eliminate grey areas and misunderstandings. In other words, all those kinds of negative phenomena which seem to develop naturally in human communications and only serve to impede the effectiveness of negotiations.

Obviously, it's also just as important to summarize your own position with clarity and precision. That goes without saying.

At this point it will be useful to list the four conditions necessary for effective discussion as outlined by John Belanger in *Techniques and Practice of Argumentation* (Dunod, 1971):

1. the ability, at least at the outset, to study the problem as objectively as possible, without allowing yourself to be influenced by the other party

2. holding as your principal objective the attainment of some degree of intellectual development

3. knowing how to respond with intellectual honesty

4. knowing how to communicate.

Conditons 1 and 3 are very similar, and reinforce the importance of making a concerted effort to be objective.

Of course, there is a risk that the other party may try to take advantage of your objectivity and gain more than they would ordinarily. But objectivity works both ways: it's up to you to get the other party to reciprocate your efforts to be objective.

Being objective and offering feedback both require at least one thing: that you listen to the other person. We will look at the importance of effective listening next.

Are You Always Receptive?

A good negotiator must exhibit a keen ability to listen. If not, he or she isn't a true professional. And the same goes for a sales rep, a mediator or a manager. The advantages of being able to listen should encourage you to make an effort to develop the skill.

Why should you listen?

When you negotiate wouldn't you prefer to be dealing with someone who listens attentively, who considers your arguments and objections seriously? A person who is reasonable, and who doesn't ignore an objection you've repeated over and over again? Who, on the contrary, tries to understand your point of view and seek a solution? A person who seems to want to save time instead of waste it, who seems to be able to smooth the way towards a settlement, a person you know you can agree with in a lot less time than it usually takes?

You can be that person!

All you have to do is learn how to listen.

You make think that you always listen to what people tell you. It's the other people who don't listen to me. That may be true. But someone has to break the vicious circle of negative communication based on bad listening.

Listening means being listened to

That's the way it works. If you are able to listen to another person attentively and completely (which isn't always easy or pleasant), then you'll have less trouble communicating what *you* want to say later on.

By listening effectively you set up a special kind of interaction. Some people may even find it disconcerting. They see negotiating as a fight, a contest and include words in their struggle for power. By giving such persons free rein to vent their aggression, you show that you have other goals. You'll automatically find it easier to get your points across later on, because silence always arouses curiosity. The other party is eventually going to want to know what you have to say.

It isn't easy to listen effectively

The average period of adult concentration varies from *one to about eight seconds*! That's why we so easily get distracted when someone is talking to us. So, why do people have such short attention spans?

Usually, our attention span is short because of too much input, not because of a lack of input.

The brain requires constant stimulation. Judge for yourself: you think at an average speed of between 400 and 700 words per minute. But someone talking to you can only use about 120 words per minute (a good salesman can go as high as 150).

Result?

Your brain is lacking input to the tune of some 300 words per minute. What does it do? It looks elsewhere for stimulation. You lose interest. Your mind wanders while the other person finishes their sentence. Once you've heard the first few words you already know pretty well what they are going to say. And the chances are that you've heard it all before!

You'll start thinking about other things. Your mind will wander for a fraction of a second, and never come back, whereas a disciplined mind may wander for an instant, but it always gets back in time.

What happens when your mind wanders as the other party is speaking?

Silence. The other party finishes speaking and looks at you expectantly, waiting for an answer. You say, hurriedly, 'That sounds interesting. Could you leave the file with me and call me on Monday morning? I'll see what I can do.'

There you go – you've just lost at least 10 minutes of valuable time. Now you have to dig out the information yourself, try to discern if there are any hidden aspects to the deal, etc. You could have found all this out by listening to the other party. You could have asked yourself various pertinent questions right away, and possibly even have made a decision on the spot. Now you have to wait, and make the other party wait as well, doubling the time you need to conclude the deal.

Don't only think about what you have to say

People often don't listen because they're preoccupied with talking themselves. They are so busy talking that they cannot listen to another person for more than a couple of seconds. This prevents them from communicating with people, so they end up with very little to say that's new or interesting, and probably begin to repeat themselves without being aware of it.

Why is this?

Because the major part of your concentration is devoted to yourself. It would be much better to spend one hour a day thinking of nothing but yourself than to be preoccupied all day long!

The advantages of better listening

- Listening saves time. Having a clear understanding of what has been said is vital to your evaluation of the situation.

- You show respect for the other party who knows very well if you're listening or not.

- Listening allows you to seek out pertinent information on the spot. Repetition, subtle nuances in the way an argument is presented, hesitations – they all have meaning. The issues which are avoided by the other party are often as important as the ones they cover. Listening attentively will enable you to discern the other party's objectives, strategies and tactics more quickly.

- Does your own position incite interest, indifference or rejection? When you know how to listen you can feel someone's reaction even before you finish speaking.

- The other party will be able to sense that you're listening attentively: this is very important, especially at the start of negotiations.

- The other party doesn't have to repeat themselves to make sure you've understood. Again, this saves everyone a lot of time.

- When grievances are aired, listening provides a kind of immediate, soothing effect.

- Listening gives you the opportunity to detect errors in the other party's reasoning.

- Listening is absolutely essential when negotiating from a position of weakness.

- Last but not least: listening results in being listened to.

Now answer the following questions to see how well you listen. Think about your last important meeting, preferably one to one, which took place either in your office or in some other place where you felt comfortable. Choose an instance where you had to speak for at least 10 minutes.

Do You Know How to Listen?

Yes No

1. Do you remember the colour of the person's eyes?

2. Do you remember what kind of lips he or she had?

3. Can you honestly say that you observed the person during the entire discussion (more or less) instead of letting your gaze wander around the room?

4. Did you look the other person in the eyes (almost) the whole time?

5. Did you answer the phone during the meeting?

6. Did you doodle or play with some other object during the conversation?

7. Did you interrupt the conversation to talk to anyone else?

8. Did you rephrase what the other person told you to make sure you understood correctly?

9. Did you express your interest by nodding your head or making other signs during the conversation?

10. Did you start cracking your knuckles or fidgeting while the other person was talking (think hard – these things are sometimes so automatic you don't even notice them)?

11. Can you sum up what the person told you in a few words?

12. When you try to recall what the person said, are there some parts which remain foggy and difficult to remember?

13. Can you recall three things you thought about during the meeting which had nothing to do with the discussion?

Yes No

14. Can you recall encouraging the other person to continue talking at least once?

15. Can you recall at least three different gestures, poses or attitudes used by the other person during the discussion?

16. Do you recall trying to discern the underlying reasons for what the other person was saying?

17. Were you disturbed by any noises during the meeting?

18. Can you recall at least one instance where both of you were silent?

19. Did you complete one or a number of the other person's sentences before he or she had a chance to finish speaking?

20. Do you recall making any judgements about what the person was saying at the time he or she was speaking?

21. Do you recall trying to analyse what was being said as it was being said?

22. Did you ask the other person to clarify or develop any points in particular during the discussion?

23. Did you interrupt the other person, even once?

24. Finally, when it was your turn to speak did you get the impression the other person was listening or just waiting for you to finish so he or she could continue talking?

Count up your scores and give yourself one point for each time you answered 'Yes'. Now take away a point for each 'Yes' answer to Questions 12, 20, 21 and 23.

Results

Between 0 and 10 points: You tend to form ideas quickly and base your approach on them without worrying too much about the other person's reactions and any new information he or she might be able to provide. In other words, you don't listen. In negotiations that can be a serious handicap. Take this as a warning!

Between 11 and 18 points: Your attention is average. For everyday situations that may be enough. But in a negotiating situation you may suffer because of it. Read the questions over again and try to be more attentive in future.

Between 19 and 24 points: Excellent! You're a great listener, and that's an important advantage when you're involved in a negotiating situation, unless of course *all* you do is listen!

Read the test over once more. Questions to which you responded with a 'No' indicate your weak points, excepting Questions 12, 20, 21 and 23 where a 'No' answer is the correct one.

The Process of Effective Communication

If you found the preceding questionnaire somewhat exhaustive, remind yourself that it represents only a fraction of what your brain stores up during a half-hour conversation in someone's office.

But what is listening, really? Is it a passive activity?

This is how the process of transmitting messages is summed up in communication theory. The diagram below was developed by the Bell laboratories to explain how telephone communication works. But it can, in fact, be applied to all types of communication.

Intention _____ *Feedback* _____ *Comprehension*

1. Sender   2. Code   3. Transmission   4. Decode   5. Receiver

1. A **Sender** has a relatively clear idea that he or she wishes to communicate.

2. The **Sender** converts the idea into a message using a **Code** of words and/or symbols.

3. The **Code** is **transmitted** directly or by telephone, radio, newspaper, fax, letter, telegram, etc.

4. The **Receiver decodes** the message: if the **Sender** speaks a foreign language that you don't understand you won't receive anything, even if the message is **transmitted** with faultless clarity. Therefore the **Receiver** must possess the same **Code** as the **Sender**.

5. The **Receiver** returns the message to indicate that he has understood. This is **Feedback**.

Three principles of effective listening

There are three important concepts which must be applied in order to listen better. Practise them for even a few moments, and you'll understand the benefits of what is termed 'active listening'. The positive results of really attentive listening go way beyond improving your performance at the negotiating table. Attentive listening has a great impact whenever you communicate, whether with friends, children, your spouse or your colleagues. Here are the three concepts.

1. **Concentrate**   Does this seem obvious? Well, what is concentration exactly? Some people can stare straight at the person they're talking to and still be thinking about something else.

2. **Summarize**   This gives your brain something to do while the other person is talking. Periodically summarize in your mind what the other person has said, noting the important points of their argument.

3. **Verify**   From time to time interrupt the other person and say something like: *'If I understand correctly, you mean that . . .'* or *'To sum up what you've just said, would you agree that . . .'*. This ensures that you're both on the same wavelength, and lets the other party know that you're following his or her train of thought and that he or she won't have to repeat anything. Providing feedback enables you to clarify what the other party is saying and at the same time confirms that you're listening attentively.

The eighteen rules for active listening

Below, we outline 18 rules that will help you to be a good listener. A good negotiator absolutely must know how to listen in order to anticipate the other party's reactions. As soon as the other party opens their mouth they become your major source of information simply because they know what they are going to do. Here are the rules.

1. **Do not interrupt**   The principle is elementary, but it isn't always easy to put into practice. Wait for your turn. It's more polite, and you'll learn a lot more.

2. **Don't carry on an interior argument**   There's a right time for everything. For the moment consider yourself a sponge. Absorb. Assimilate. If you spend your time preparing arguments and looking

for answers, you'll miss half of what the other party is saying. Also, a response that has been thought out in advance doesn't always cover all the issues involved.

3. **Be aware of your posture** Sit straight and look the other person in the eyes. Leaning forward from time to time shows that you're interested.

4. **Avoid thinking about other things** As we've already said, you have to concentrate.

5. **Don't let yourself get distracted** It can happen very easily. You lose track of things, your mind wanders and it takes twice as long to cover a few minor issues, so that when the important issues roll around you are hurried and you can't give them the attention they merit.

6. **Don't complete the other person's sentences** You risk giving away your own thoughts on the subject, as well as never finding out what the other person *really* wanted to say. So you may ruin an opportunity to learn something important. You will also show that you're impatient.

7. **When the other party stops talking, wait a moment** Don't jump right in and start talking as soon as the other party stops or pauses to take a breath.

8. **Use silence** Silence can be a valuable ally, but you have to know how to use it. Not everyone can. Get used to letting silences last for a while. Listen to the ambient sounds in the room.

9. **Don't jump to conclusions** Make sure the other party has finished talking before forming your conclusions. When we form an opinion we tend to stick to it, rejecting information which doesn't coincide with our views. So make sure you have all the information beforehand.

10. **Observe the other party** Non-verbal communication, which includes gestures, looks, expressions, etc, can be extremely revealing.

11. **Don't allow yourself to be overly influenced by the physical appearance of the other party** Be observant, but exercise a certain detachment. Concentrate on the other party's body language, but be sure you don't lose track of what is being said by concentrating on appearances.

12. **Don't get too absorbed in your notes** Or you won't see the forest

for the trees, as the saying goes. Note down the main ideas only. If you want to summarize what the other party is saying, use little diagrams instead of sentences. And work on your notes during pauses in the discussion. This is a way of telling the other party that you're interested.

Doing this also accomplishes something else: if you wait for the other party to continue he or she may have to play another of his or her cards. And if the other party has just played one of his or her important cards, the fact that you are calm and seem to expect more can be disconcerting.

13. **Cultivate patience**   If you get bored quickly when concentrating on a single subject, you may not be cut out for negotiating. This is a major obstacle which you must learn to overcome.

14. **Don't listen selectively**   Listen to everything, not only what you find flattering or want to hear. Learn to see both sides of the coin.

15. **Practise empathy**   Empathy means being able to see things from someone else's point of view. Think something like: *'If I were in their shoes, how would I appear?'*. Of course, this doesn't mean that you should start to defend the other party's interests!

Just because you understand something doesn't mean you agree with it. On the other hand, you'll be in a better position to evaluate the other party's position.

16. **Ask questions**   As we've already seen, asking questions is an excellent way of making sure you haven't missed anything.

17. **Sum up the main points of the other party's argument**   Synthesize. Forget about anecdotes, digressions and secondary issues. Concentrate on what is essential. If you can't find it, it may not be there!

18. **Be open-minded**   This is the most difficult thing to do. Don't judge what the other person is saying. You'll only get loaded down with all kinds of objections and petty arguments, and you won't be able to concentrate. Make sure you understand before analysing the situation. And wait until the end before drawing your conclusions.

What if the Other Person Doesn't Listen?

There's nothing more frustrating than to feel you're wasting your breath, especially if you've taken the trouble to be attentive when the other person was talking.

This is one occasion where interrupting is a positive move. Wait for the other person to pause for breath and then politely interrupt them. The more attentively you've been listening, the easier it will be to this. Interruptions are like mustard in a sandwich – they can help if they are used with restraint.

During your interruption, summarize what the other person has said. Then turn to another person present (assuming there are others present) and ask if he or she understood the same things you did. If the arguments have been repeated a number of times, you're likely to get a positive response. Then turn back to the other party and say something like:

'I think we've all grasped this point. Maybe we can move on to something else now'.

And you then ask them to continue.

There are some occasions when diplomacy is not called for. If, instead of the polite statement above, you say: *'I think we've all understood what you're trying to say . . .'*, you make your statement a lot stronger, which tells the other party that you're a little fed up and would like to move on to another issue. This must be done with care – there's a fine line between stimulating and antagonizing someone.

When the Speaker Lacks Clarity

Some people speak very quickly and are difficult to follow. Others slur their words or speak too quietly. Obviously you don't want to offend anyone. But you must make sure you understand what's being said.

If you are faced with such a person, interrupt from time to time and politely ask if you've understood correctly: summarize what has been said in your own words. In this way you avoid suggesting that the person has a problem or a speech impediment. Your wish to clarify a statement cannot be taken as a personal reproach.

Unnecessary Digressions

There's nothing more tiring than having to sit through lengthy and unnecessary digressions, especially if you have a full agenda of issues to cover. Once again you can influence the course of the discussions in a gentle way.

You don't have to come right out and say: 'I think you're getting off the track . . .' or 'Let's get back to the issues, shall we?'. Unless, of course, you want to be a bit aggressive.

A good way to proceed consists of interrupting the other party while he or she is digressing, add something to the digression itself and then steer the conversation back to the issue at hand. You could say something like:

'I'm happy you were able to handle that situation so well. And while we're on the subject, I don't think we've discussed the question of price in your proposal . . .'.

There doesn't even have to be a connection between the digression and the issue you want to cover! The important thing is first to say something which continues what the other party has been talking about. You still cut short the meandering, but you don't make the other party feel that you're not interested. So they will be more likely to accept the new tack.

CHAPTER 28

Negative and Positive Thinking

A study has shown that 80 per cent of the thoughts of an average adult were negative. Imagine that! Eighty per cent!

When you consider this, it's surprising that we ever manage to do anything or win any argument or negotiation.

Negative thoughts are what Forest Patton, author of many books on persuasion, auto-suggestion and selling, called *poisonous* thoughts, and their devastating effect should be recognized. It has repercussions in all areas of our existence, starting with our health. In fact, there is an important connection between our thoughts and our physical state, and the current flows in both directions! These poisonous thoughts end up by creating a constant current which undermines our hopes and beliefs.

Practise Positive Thinking

If you want to improve your self-image and your communication skills, it is worth taking the time to concentrate the mind and allow the right (positive) messages to go straight to your subconscious. Indeed, the ability to relax really deeply is a very useful asset for everyone who works in today's fast-moving and stressful world.

As we have already seen elsewhere (in Chapter 15), one of the best times to practise deep relaxation is in the morning when you are just awake. This is the time when you are most receptive to messages to your subconscious.

Start by breathing deeply and evenly. Some people like to count backwards, slowly. Let your thoughts go, without stopping them or concentrating on them. If one thought dominates, try to put it to one side, promising yourself that you will come back to it at the end of the meditation session. Avoid thinking about this one question. If you find yourself in this trap, free yourself gently by letting another thought take over. You will find that you have plenty of them.

Once you have got used to this, and you feel relaxed and in touch with your subconscious, you can start to be positive about yourself. Most authors suggest that you start with an affirmation, or assertive statement, which could be like the following:

'I can develop the discipline necessary to achieve what I want. I have the discipline necessary to spend 10 minutes a day in deep meditation. I am getting better and better at it. This is now programmed.'

This is a key assertion, with the following advantage: from the beginning you programme your mind to programme itself. Your conscientiousness in your daily session will be your first tangible achievement, and don't forget that success is bred on achievements.

You will also see that with a little practice you are able to 'let your thoughts go' more and more easily, and that your state of mind is clearly affected. Tell yourself:

'I am going to programme my mind, my body and my life. I am capable of achieving my objectives, I can take control of my existence. This daily session is the most important thing I do today. This is now programmed.'

According to Forest Patton, it's a good idea to add something like this: 'Today I will help at least one person to have a better image of himself. I will find something positive to say about him. This is now programmed.'

Then, you can follow it up with a sentence which is more directly connected with your present situation:

'I am an excellent negotiator. I manage to win over my opponents and when the moment comes to close the deal I am in a good position. I manage to look after my own interests and also allow the other party to be in a situation that is advantageous for him. This is now programmed.'

You can also add more general affirmations, which concern your state of mind and your life conditions:

'I'm in great health and full of energy.' 'This year I'm going to earn £xx.' 'I'm going to be less aggressive in the car. I'm going to control myself and stay calm in all situations.' 'I'm making a living doing exactly what I like doing.' 'I get on well with other people and every day I derive pleasure from doing what I'm doing.'

Tailor-made affirmations

If you think that you have some expensive gaps when it comes to negotiations skill, each gap can be filled by an assertion which makes you feel more positive. Here are some examples:

'I am confident and people don't intimidate me any more.' 'I am well organized and I am always ready when the negotiations start.' 'I get on well with people and I have lots of charisma.' 'I am always well organized and I turn up to negotiations well prepared.' 'In a negotiating situation, I manage to find common ground and to convince the other party that it is in his interest to close a deal with me.' 'I find it very easy to communicate with others and I grasp easily what others are seeking in a negotiation.' 'I concentrate exceptionally well in a negotiating situation.' 'I know how to get the best out of a situation.'

The ability to reason is an extremely important factor in all negotiations, and a distracted person who cannot follow reasoning will always have difficulties in this sort of situation.

'Cosmic' affirmations

Certain assertions are by nature more general and can have an influence upon all the areas of your life – health, work, personal relationships, and so on. Try saying to yourself:

'A real fountain of joy is constantly bubbling away inside me. Each day is an adventure to which I look forward with renewed pleasure.' 'I am in contact with the universal qualities of energy, intelligence and love. They empower me, inspire me, guide me and stimulate me every day of my life.'

Coming back to earth

Once your affirmations have been made, you will come back to full alertness.

'Now I'm going to come back to full alertness. On the count of 20, I will open my eyes and I will be refreshed, ready for the day's tasks which await me. Ten, I'm coming back, 11, 12, I'm coming back, 13, 14, 15, I'm coming back, 16 . . ., 17, 18, 19, 20.'

The whole session will have taken about 15 minutes. Of course, you can stay longer in this not unpleasant state, but it is not necessary. Spending your day meditating will not produce any more results from a practical point of view.

Do you have any questions so far? Probably. We will try to answer them in the following section.

Program Yourself Effectively

Here are some 'technical' points which will help you to benefit as much as possible from your relaxation sessions.

First, remember that consistency pays dividends. It is important to practise regularly, conscientiously, almost religiously. This very simple mental technique demands only 15 minutes' concentration a day from you. It is really your attentiveness which will produce results.

Once the enthusiasm of the first weeks or months has waned, however, you might find yourself getting bored! However, you should persist. And the greater the challenges you have to overcome, the harder you must work.

You should not expect results straight away. In fact, do not expect anything. Proceed with a certain detachment. Vary the formulations you tell yourself, so that your mind is constantly interested in them. This demands a little effort, but you will quickly get used to it.

In order to reinforce your affirmations and positive statements see yourself in the situation that you desire. Visualize yourself carrying out the activity which interests you, or living the long-awaited moment. This strengthens the feeling of reality and helps to influence your subconscious.

Do not forget that this process is helping you to get out of a rut, and to get rid of negative mental habits acquired over a long time. These things are deeply rooted. It takes more than a day for these habits to be shaken off and replaced by new, improved behaviour. Two ingredients at least are indispensable.

- Repeat the affirmation several times *every day* for one or two months. Out loud if possible.
- Choose something that you want *very badly*. You must really want the change.

Your emotions must be interested in this project: they represent the energy that is absolutely essential for the transformation.

Know how to make positive statements

1. It is important that your affirmations are formulated in a positive way, today.

Your subconscious is very literal and it will believe that the assertions are a situation that has actually been lived and is actually happening. It has to interpret them as experience, not simple statement. So it generates situations which are favourable to the realization of your desire. As a result, it will modify the image you have of yourself. This allows you to release your deep energies, which have been imprisoned by your old conditioning and beliefs.

2. Your affirmations must also be accompanied by images, which gives them a realistic character, that of experience.

3. State your affirmations in different ways.

4. Always finish your affirmations by saying: 'This is now programmed', or 'So be it'.

CHAPTER 29

The Secrets of Body Language

It has been said that the words we use only express 7 per cent of our emotions: 38 per cent of what we feel is expressed through our tone of voice and inflexion. The remaining 55 per cent is expressed through facial expression (eyes, lips, etc) and gestures.

Wouldn't it be useful to gain access to this 93 per cent slice of information about what other people are feeling, especially in negotiating situations?

How can this be done? Reading body language isn't something you learn at school.

First, you should tell yourself that you're already receiving all the information, whether you are aware of it or not. The problem is for you to filter it out and improve your perception of non-verbal language. You may not find out 100 per cent of what the other person is feeling, but improving what you already perceive by 20 per cent or 30 per cent would still give you an enormous advantage.

Extra-Sensory Perception

When you walk into a room, you immediately know if you like it or not, if you feel comfortable, whether you could live in it for a week, a month or for the rest of your life. You haven't analysed its contents, yet you know after a fraction of a second if you like it or not. In some cases you may be put off by a certain style of wallpaper, or the way the room is divided. In others, you rely on a general impression that seems to come to you as soon as you enter. Where do these impressions come from?

In fact, they occur because it only takes your senses a fraction of a second to register all the details of the room. Your brain then adds them all up and compares the results to your tastes and preferences. Colours, shapes, proportions – everything is examined with a fine-tooth comb in less time than it takes to read this sentence.

Observe yourself

The same process occurs when you meet people or even pass them in the street. Observe yourself: you'll soon become aware that you are constantly making judgements about everyone you encounter.

The same thing happens when you're negotiating. We always form an opinion of the other party based on the clues we have at our disposal. It's quite normal to want to try and discern what kind of person you're dealing with before a relationship has had time to develop. But a person is not a room.

The opinions we form in the first few minutes after meeting someone tend to stick and influence the way we perceive that person. And, of course, the process works both ways – you are also being appraised and categorized. So, we'll start by taking a look at your own non-verbal communication. Your appearance plays an important role in the social dance we call negotiation.

Your Personal Appearance

Studies confirm that clothes do a lot to modify the way others perceive you. Dressing informally indicates an inferior rank in the corporate hierarchy. That's why high-ranking executives almost always dress in a style that reinforces the impression of power they wish to create.

The power of stereotypes

We all tend to base our ideas on stereotypes (the ideal secretary dresses in a certain way, the dynamic executive wears his three-piece suit, etc). In a study on job interviews, the American scientist E. C. Webster has shown just how fully we base our judgements on preconceived ideas. His results can be simply summarized as follows and are just as applicable to people about to undertake negotiating sessions.

- Interviewers create an image – a stereotype of the ideal candidate – and compare all applicants to that image.

- Impressions are formed very rapidly, and are followed just as rapidly by a decision.

- Unfavourable impressions have more impact than favourable ones.

This last observation merits particular consideration. Say you're a talented designer, and you wear jeans and a cowboy shirt to make an important presentation. You'll have to work extra hard to counterbalance the negative impact of your clothes in order to create a favourable impression, even though you may have designed a palace or two!

Play your role

The idea someone forms of what a designer should look like acts as a filter: everything about a candidate which resembles that image will illicit approval, and everything that doesn't will result in criticism. In other words, you'll be making things easier for yourself if you actually *look* like the person who should have the job.

Does this sound superficial? Shouldn't people be more concerned with substance rather than form? Maybe. But don't forget, *you* also do exactly the same thing!

Everyone has an image of what a particular type of person should look like, be they designer or sales manager.

And, based on that image, every negative element you present counts for double. The negative element is only relative, of course: all it does is detract from the artificial image the other party has formed. But, unfortunately, it's what counts.

So it's important to take these things into account. You're not judged only on the content of what you say, but also on how you say it, how you look and how you behave. And these so-called secondary messages come across so strongly you might as well be shouting them at the top of your voice!

The five important factors of non-verbal language

Research on interview behaviour has isolated five non-verbal factors which seem to have the strongest positive influence on interviewers (and negotiators too):

1. **Style** Everything related to spoken language (except information content) such as ease of expression, voice quality and intonation, rhythm, etc.

2. **Posture**   Appearing relaxed, leaning back slightly.

3. **Gaze**   Candidates should look interviewers in the eyes (without staring).

4. **Appearance**   Candidates should wear appropriate clothing and accessories.

5. **Facial expression**   A lot of smiling and nodding of the head.

And, of the five factors listed above, the two most important are appearance and looking the interviewer in the eyes.

Before the interview starts appearance, punctuality and a firm handshake are the most important factors. During the interview, facial expression and appearance continue to play an important role, but interviewers claim that eye contact influences them the most.

Of course, this research was based on job interviews, but one thing remains clear: **A positive initial impression is essential**.

In the case of negotiations, you want to do everything you can to create a favourable first impression. You should then try to reinforce this initially favourable impression through signs and subtle forms of behaviour so that the other party ends up wanting to reach an agreement with you.

Why?

Because they liked you from the moment they met you. Why do anything to change their mind?

Reading Gestures

A large part of non-verbal communication is expressed through body language. We will now look at how you can learn to decipher the other party's non-verbal language. First, you have to become extremely attentive in the way you observe other people. Then you must learn to improve your concentration and increase your attention span.

Certain expressions and gestures can be translated into states of mind and attitudes. They can provide valuable information about a situation and indicate how to proceed by shedding new light on proposals that previously seemed obscure. In any case, it's always a good idea to observe the other party.

The quality of your observation depends on two factors:

- your ability to concentrate, and
- your skill at interpreting the signs you observe.

But first we should issue a word of warning. Unlike verbal communication, non-verbal language has no rigid code of grammar and syntax. This means that you can't entirely depend on the interpretations you pick up from books or other sources.

To develop your capacity to analyse non-verbal communication, practise observing people wherever you go – in public places, during informal conversations and impromptu meetings. Make use of any face-to-face encounters, where the person you're talking to is improvising what they are saying and not delivering a prepared text (where gestures can be as carefully planned as the speech itself!). You will find that your ability to read the signs of non-verbal communication will improve the more you practise.

Follow these three rules to help you avoid errors.

- **Group the signs**   An attitude can be deduced from a *group* of gestures. So, it's not a good idea to base your interpretation on a single gesture. Wait until you've observed a number of examples of the same or a similar gesture before forming an opinion.

   When there are enough signs to form a pattern, you have a much better chance of interpreting them correctly. Below you'll find an exercise which helps illustrate this point.

- **Compare non-verbal signs with language**   Observation of non-verbal communication is accompanied by a simultaneous interpretation of verbal language. Try to compare the two, noting parallels and contradictions.

   What you're interested in is the relationship between the two forms of communication, not simply non-verbal signs. Together they can tell you something. Ask yourself if the two types of communication coincide, or whether they contradict each other.

   Can any of the feelings and attitudes you've observed in the other party's non-verbal communication be used to explain one or another of their proposals? Say, for example, that according to your observations the other party's non-verbal communication reveals a degree of indifference towards your position, even though what they say seems to express interest. In such a case you shouldn't be surprised if you cannot reach an agreement. And you can justifiably ask yourself if the other party is lying or perhaps has some ulterior motive.

- Don't base your decisions on non-verbal communication alone. Don't make hasty judgements. Remember that body language can lie just as much as verbal communication.

Beware of rehearsed gestures

There are a number of reasons you should be wary of rehearsed gestures.

- You can't entirely rely on the accuracy of your interpretation. Don't be fooled: human feelings and behaviours are extremely complex. Even the most practised observer can make mistakes.

  If you can interpret non-verbal communication correctly 75 per cent of the time then you're doing very well, and your services as a negotiator will be very valuable. But there's still the other 25 per cent to worry about.

- Non-verbal signs can often be interpreted in a number of ways. Different schools of thought accord signs different meanings.

- Awareness of body language has grown considerably over the last few years, so signs that may seem spontaneous could actually be well rehearsed and actually calculated to produce the desired effect.

  The first few times a sign is observed it may really be spontaneous. But once a gesture or an attitude has been seen to produce a certain result, there's nothing to prevent someone from using it again intentionally, as a bluffing tactic, or to confuse you by emitting contradictory signs.

  In short, a skilled negotiator may find it amusing to fool you by simulating certain non-verbal signs.

  And people whose job it is to create images tell their clients how to act in certain situations, what attitudes they should adopt, what gestures to use, etc. They can teach a person to exude confidence, superiority, calm, and so on, as the occasion requires.

  They can also show their clients how to control their gestures in order to reveal the least amount of doubt, anxiety or fear, which is especially useful when you're trying to bluff someone.

  So, before jumping to conclusions you should make sure that the non-verbal signs you are observing are spontaneous.

  How? Well, as you'll eventually discover, people always give themselves away sooner or later. This is why we've suggested all along that it's better to work on your own preparation, strategies and attitudes, rather than trying to manipulate the other party through carefully rehearsed non-verbal communication.

Test Your Ability to Observe

Here are two exercises designed to help you recognize certain types of identifiable behaviour. They will help you to develop your ability to visualize the signs described and then form them into groups.

Exercise 1

Select which of the list of attitudes below matches with which group of signs, numbered 1 to 5.

In other words, if you observed one or more of the following body signals during a discussion, which of the attitudes would you assign to that person?

Two of the characteristics listed are completely unrelated to any of the signs. Place the number of the corresponding group of signs beside the correct attitudes. Fill in a zero if you think there's no connection.

Rejection =Sign group [ ]   Confusion=Sign group [ ]

Indifference=Sign group [ ]   Interest =Sign group [ ]

Cheating =Sign group [ ]   Candour =Sign group [ ]

Suspicion =Sign group [ ]

Group 1

- a slightly scowling expression
- pursed lips
- an occasional puzzled look

Group 2

- when talking the person touches their face or chin
- the person shifts around in their chair, or if standing shifts their weight from one foot to the other
- the person doesn't look you in the eyes
- they blink a lot

Group 3

- facial muscles seem to collapse

Test continues ▶

- the person looks haggard
- occasional tapping on the table
- shifting in their chair or leaning back and folding their hands behind their head
- the person stands up and refuses to come closer
- very short answers to your questions

Group 4

- the person nods their head when you speak
- their eyes sparkle
- the person leans back from time to time
- the person then leans forward towards you
- their voice is lively and animated

Group 5

- the person sits with arms crossed and clenches their fists from time to time, or touches their nose
- their shoulders are at right angles to the way you're sitting
- they frequently look away
- their voice is sombre
- their responses are laconic

(Adapted from Forest Patton,
The Force of Persuasion)

The correct answers are:

Group 1=Confusion   *Group 4*=Interest
Group 2=Cheating   *Group 5*=Rejection
Group 3=Indifference

So, how did you do? If you scored well, don't be fooled. When patterns are grouped in this way it's not too difficult to identify what they mean.

The hardest thing is to recognize them when they occur in real-life situations where they aren't always easy to decipher. You may only be able to identify two or three at a session, which is hardly enough to form a pattern. And you must also remember that the meanings we've assigned aren't carved in stone. The interpretations provided here are only guidelines to help you decipher your own observations.

You must learn to combine precision with a measure of concentration and intuition. As we have already said, a good way to develop your skills at reading non-verbal communication is to sit in some public place, like a restaurant or a waiting room, and observe the way people around you interact for a few minutes.

Exercise 2

In this exercise try to identify what feeling is being expressed when the other party exhibits the following signs.

Example 1

- the person hesitates
- they exhibit impatience
- sudden nervousness
- sudden aggression
- the person leans back suddenly with arms crossed
- systematic avoidance of certain subjects
- sudden flare-ups during the discussions
- the person looks away suddenly

Indicate what type of attitude, situation or emotion corresponds to this kind of behaviour:

Example 2

- the person clears their throat frequently
- they spread their arms and grip the edge of the table
- they often cover their mouth when speaking
- they let a cigarette burn in the ashtray without smoking it
- they whistle softly
- they often change position, shifting around in their chair

Indicate what type of attitude, situation or emotion corresponds to this kind of behaviour:

Example 3

- the person leans forward
- they look you in the eyes most of the time
- their posture is relaxed
- if standing, they move closer
- when talking the person sometimes touches your arm

Indicate what type of attitude, situation or emotion corresponds to this kind of behaviour:

Example 4

- the person leans back
- they avoid looking you in the eyes
- their posture seems tense
- if standing they keep their distance
- the person never touches you

Indicate what type of attitude, situation or emotion corresponds to this kind of behaviour:

Answers

Example 1 This example includes a number of signals which generally point to a breakdown in communication. In other words, they indicate that a serious disagreement is imminent.

When observing such behaviour you could, for example, reiterate the point you think is the cause of the problem.

If the signs of dissatisfaction persist, you will have to deal with the problem sooner or later before continuing negotiations.

If you decide to put the problem aside for the moment, you are at least aware that there is an obstacle which will eventually have to be overcome.

Example 2   This kind of behaviour obviously indicates a state of nervousness (which you should equally recognize in yourself as well as in others). Depending on the circumstances, it might be appropriate to do something out of the ordinary in order to relax the other party like going out for lunch or taking a walk. You may also want to try and find out what the cause of his or her nervousness is.

Example 3   These signs are generally interpreted as indicating a positive attitude. They signify that the other party is relaxed and feels good in the negotiating situation.

Example 4   Since they are opposite to the signs in Example 3, these obviously indicate a negative attitude. The person isn't comfortable in the situation. It's up to you to find out why. Some people are always uncomfortable, but generally you should look for any special circumstances in the negotiating situation that might be the cause.

Not all signs are signs

You should again remember that observing these kinds of behaviour should only put you on the alert: they are not unequivocal and unerring indications of certain states of mind.

For example, the act of scratching your nose doesn't necessarily mean that you're lying. After all, a nose can get itchy, and people do touch their noses occasionally for no no special reason. But *in some situations*, scratching the nose can be a sign of dishonesty.

You can try to review the negotiations in your mind as if you were watching a silent film – no more sound. All you see are the gestures and behaviour patterns. Talleyrand once said, 'Words were invented to confuse our thinking.' By eliminating the words you avoid any false impressions they may have been intended to create. Then ask yourself how you feel about the meeting? What effect did it have on you? Did the other party seem sincere or devious? Listen to your intuition!

To recapitulate, and to provide you with some added information before the end of this book, see if you can separate the grass from the weeds in the following statements.

Test Your Understanding

1. In face-to-face discussions non-verbal communication plays as important a role as verbal communication.

   true ☐   false ☐

2. Non-verbal communication varies according to culture, personality, age, sex and race.

   true ☐   false ☐

3. Women are more receptive to non-verbal language, and are more precise senders of it than men.

   true ☐   false ☐

4. When verbal and non-verbal communications are contradictory, most adults generally hold that the non-verbal message is true.

   true ☐   false ☐

5. Social occasions allow you to determine the quality of relationships through observation of non-verbal communication.

   true ☐   false ☐

6. You must interpret and apply non-verbal language differently during various stages of a relationship.

   true ☐   false ☐

7. In the context of a working situation, you should be aware of the non-verbal signs you are sending because they indicate your degree of power, credibility and self-confidence, and prove that you are conscious of the effect you have on others.

   true ☐   false ☐

Test continues ▶

8. We generally assume that non-verbal communication is sincere and spontaneous, but we should remember that it can be manipulated to produce a specific effect.

true ☐   false ☐

The answer is that all the above statements are true!

Bibliography

Brooks, Carl, and Odiorne, George, *Managing by Negotiations*, Van Nostrand Reinhold, US, 1984

Brownell, Judi, *Building Active Listening Skills*, Prentice–Hall, US, 1986

Cohen, Herb, *You Can Negotiate Anything*, Citadel Publishers, US, 1988

Fisher, Roger, and Ury, William, *Getting to Yes*, Penguin Books, US, 1983

Funkhouser, Ray, *The Power of Persuasion*, Times Books, US, 1986

Gould, Joe Sutherland, *The Negotiator's Problem Solver*, John Wiley and Sons, US, 1986

Harris, Charles Edison, *Business Negotiating Power: Optimising Your Side of The Deal*, Van Nostrand Reinhold, US, 1983

Hawver, Denis, *How to Improve Your Negotiation Skills*, Modern Business Reports, Maywood, US, 1982

Hickson and Stocks, *Nonverbal Communication*, WC Brown Publishers, US, 1989

Ilich, John, *Power Negotiating*, Addison Wesley Publishing, 1980

Jandt, Fred E., *Win-Win Negotiating*, John Wiley and Sons, US, 1987

Karrass, Gary, *Negotiate to Close*, Fontana, 1987.

Kennedy, Gavin, et al, *Managing Negotiations*, Hutchinson Business, 1987

Kuhn, Robert L., *Dealmaker*, John Wiley and Sons, US, 1990

Lax, David A. and Sebenius, James K., *The Manager as Negotiator: Bargaining for Cooperation and Competitive Results*, The Free Press, US, 1986

Leritz, Len, *No-Fault Negotiating*, Thorsons, 1991

Lewis, David. V., *Power Negotiating Tactics and Techniques*, Prentice–Hall, 1981

Maddux, Robert, *Successful Negotiation*, Kogan Page, 1988

Morrison, William F., *The Prenegotiation Planning Book*, John Wiley, US, 1985

Nierenberg, *The Art of Negotiating*, Cornerstone Library, US, 1968

Nierenberg, *The Complete Negotiator*, Souvenir Publishers, 1987

Patton, Forrest, *Force of Persuasion*, Prentice–Hall, US, 1986

Raiffa, Howard, *The Art and Science of Negotiation*, Harvard University Press, US, 1985

Schatzki, *Negotiation, The Art of Getting What You Want*, New American Library, US, 1986

Seltz, David D. and Modica, Alfred D., *Negotiate Your Way to Success*, New American Library, US, 1980

Smith, H. B., *Selling Through Negotiation*, Amacom, US, 1988

Sparks, Donald B., *The Dynamics of Effective Negotiation*, Gulf Publishing Company, US, 1982

Winkler, John, *Bargaining for Results*, Institute of Marketing, 1981, Heinemann Professional, 1989

Index

Piatkus Business Books

Piatkus Business Books have been created for people like you, busy executives and managers who need expert knowledge readily available in a clear and easy-to-follow format. All the books are written by specialists in their field. They will help you improve your skills quickly and effortlessly in the workplace and on a personal level. Titles include:

General Management Skills

Be Your Own PR Expert: The Complete Guide to Publicity and Public Relations Bill Penn

Brain Power: The 12-Week Mental Training Programme Marilyn vos Savant and Leonore Fleischer

The Complete Time Management System Christian H. Godefroy and John Clark

Confident Decision Making J. Edward Russo and Paul J. H. Schoemaker

Dealing with Difficult People Roberta Cava

The Energy Factor: How to Motivate Your Workforce Art McNeil

Firing On All Cylinders: Tried and Tested Techniques to Improve the Performance of Your Organisation Jim Clemmer with Barry Sheehy

How to Develop and Profit from Your Creative Powers Michael LeBoeuf

The Influential Manager: How to Use Company Politics Constructively Lee Bryce

Leadership Skills for Every Manager Jim Clemmer and Art McNeil

Lure the Tiger Out of the Mountains: How to Apply the 36 Strategems of Ancient China to the Modern World Gao Yuan

Managing Your Team John Spencer and Adrian Pruss

Psychological Testing for Managers Dr Stephanie Jones

Sales and Customer Services

The Art of the Hard Sell Robert L. Shook

How to Close Every Sale Joe Girard

How to Succeed in Network Marketing Leonard Hawkins

How to Win Customers and Keep Them for Life Michael LeBoeuf

Sales Power: The Silva Mind Method for Sales Professionals José Silva and Ed Bernd Jr

Selling by Direct Mail John W. Graham and Susan K. Jones

Telephone Selling Techniques that Really Work Bill Good

Presentation and Communication

Better Business Writing   Maryann V. Piotrowski

The Complete Book of Business Etiquette   Lynne Brennan and David Block

Confident Conversation: How to Talk in any Business or Social Situation   Dr Lillian Glass

Powerspeak: The Complete Guide to Public Speaking and Presentation   Dorothy Leeds

The PowerTalk System: How to Communicate Effectively   Christian H. Godefroy and Stephanie Barrat

Personal Power: How to Achieve Influence and Success in Your Professional Life   Philippa Davies

Say What You Mean and Get What You Want   George R. Walther

Your Total Image: How to Communicate Success   Philippa Davies

Careers

The Influential Woman: How to Achieve Success Without Losing Your Femininity   Lee Bryce

Marketing Yourself: How to Sell Yourself and Get the Jobs You've Always Wanted   Dorothy Leeds

Networking and Mentoring: A Woman's Guide   Dr Lily Segerman-Peck

Which Way Now? How to plan and develop a successful career   Bridget Wright

The Perfect CV: How to Get the Job You Really Want   Tom Jackson

Ten Steps to the Top   Marie Jennings

Small Business

The Best Person for the Job: Where to Find Them and How to Keep Them   Malcolm Bird

How to Collect the Money You Are Owed   Malcolm Bird

Making Profits: A Six-Month Plan for the Small Business   Malcolm Bird

Organize Yourself   Ronni Eisenberg and Kate Kelly

For a free brochure with further information on our complete range of business titles, please write to:

Piatkus Books
Freepost 7 (WD 4505)
London W1E 4EZ

PIATKUS